Fly Fishing the Louisiana Coast

*A variety of fish (here, the cobia), large and small,
await the saltwater fly fisherman in Louisiana waters.*

Fly Fishing the Louisiana Coast

A Complete Guide to
Tactics & Techniques,
from Lake Charles to the
Mississippi River Delta

Pete Cooper, Jr.

The Countryman Press
Woodstock, Vermont

Library of Congress Cataloging-in-Publication Data

Cooper, Pete
   Fly fishing the Louisiana coast: a complete guide to tactics & techniques, from Lake Charles to the Mississippi River Delta / Pete Cooper, Jr.-- 1st ed.
   p. cm.
   ISBN 0-88150-665-6
   1. Saltwater fly fishing--Louisiana--Gulf Coast. I. Title

SH501.C66 2004
799.1'6'09763--dc22
                                                              2004053668

Maps by Paul Woodward © The Countryman Press
Book design by Faith Hague
Composition by Chelsea Cloeter
Front cover photograph © Russell A. Graves
Interior photographs by the author
Fish illustrations courtesy of the Florida Fish and Wildlife
Conservation Commission, artist Diane Peebles

Published by The Countryman Press, P.O. Box 748, Woodstock, Vermont 05091

Distributed by W. W. Norton & Company, Inc., 500 Fifth Avenue,
New York, NY 10110

Printed in the United States of America

10 9 8 7 6 5 4 3 2 1

To my beloved grandfather, the late Clifford Herbert Zirkel of San Antonio, Texas. It all began with, and because of, him.

Contents

Acknowledgments

These short lines came close to taking as long to create as any chapter in this book, having to determine who to include and who not to include without hurting anyone's feelings in the process. I finally decided that since I was the hero of this book, I would only specify those who did the most to help me become so. For sure, without them—their love, their friendship, and their assistance—the world of saltwater fly fishing in Louisiana would still contain a lot of wilderness!

So here's to Barbara—my life-mate, who tolerated my excesses and showed just the proper amount of interest in my quests and enthusiasm for my discoveries.

To the Ballay family—Dave, Debbie, Brandon, and Brent—who tolerated my unconventional ways, invited me on many trips, some of which resulted in momentous experiences and all of which were much enjoyed, and who actually grew to discover that saltwater fly fishing was both fun and productive.

To Capt. Bubby Rodriguez, who tolerated my crude ways, showed me how to refine them a bit to a much better end, accompanied me on many glorious discoveries, and helped a lot in the picture-taking of it all.

To Mr. Art Scheck, once an editor who tolerated some rather radical article ideas, whose advice was always beneficial, and whose time that I shared over the phone was priceless.

To the Orvis Company for their help in keeping me supplied with the equipment necessary for undertaking such exploratory adventures.

To the now-defunct OMC Fishing Boat Group, who furnished me with a "memo-boat" for many years, without which many paths would not have been discovered.

And finally to the Good Lord who allowed me both the time and the health to do it.

To them I say "Thank you," for it could have never been done without them.

Prologue

The Sportsman's Paradise" has been emblazoned upon many of Louisiana's license plates of certain vehicles for many years. The phrase is also displayed boldly on advertising handouts in order to attract the attention of tourists with hunting and fishing interests. It is a very appropriate moniker for Louisiana. Many residents who know the state's real worth in that role have kept a pretty tight lip about it, though, and others—like advertisers—often promote it in such a fashion that it sounds almost too good to be true. Could there actually still be a place, in these days of over-population and overexploited resources that offers such a diversity of excellent sporting opportunities?

You'd better believe it! And one of the best of those opportunities is also one of the most recently "discovered": fly fishing in salt water.

I myself was once one of those tight-lipped types, having frequently and ardently fished with flies for many varieties of Louisiana's briny beasts since 1971. During much of that time, if there was someone else around who was practicing the exercise, they sure weren't admitting to it! It wasn't that I was being clandestine about it all; it was simply that virtually no one else cared about it—or was radical enough to stray from the conventional mind-set to try it. Most Louisiana residents are pretty conservative.

Anyway, some time back I became a full-time purveyor of general fishing information through articles and photographs in outdoor magazines, and the fly-fishing part just sort of naturally evolved. And I still occasionally have a problem convincing a New England editor that a piece I just sent him is not science fiction but the God's honest truth!

The opportunities for saltwater fly fishermen along the coast of the Sportsman's Paradise are indeed frequently hard to believe. I have had the great fortune of helping to develop some of them, and friends and I have almost singularly developed others. It was a grand experience—not unlike that of a pioneer. Permit me to tell you about it.

Introduction

Texas Beginnings

My grandfather on Mother's side—the late Clifford Herbert Zirkel—came from stout German stock and lived his entire life in San Antonio. His formal education ended at the eighth grade, but he had great business sense, and upon retiring after some 30 years of running his family's successful monument works, he was named chairman of the board of a big savings and loan company, a position he held for some years after a surgical operation left him legally blind.

Because of his business acumen, he was fairly well off, which allowed him to pursue the outdoor activities he enjoyed so much—deer and turkey hunting and fishing, and toward the end of the Great Depression he bought a ranch way back in the wilds of the Hill Country of central Texas. There, he and my father were to teach me the wiles of the fisherman and the lore of the hunter.

He and his family also had a second retreat: Rockport, Texas—then a small, obscure fishing village on the central coast. Even then it was much more civilized than the ranch, with electricity, telephones, and even refrigerators, and the locals were nice folks. Still, he never did buy a house there, choosing instead to rent an apartment or cottage for their stays, and by the time I entered the world, summer trips to Rockport had become a ritual.

For the first 10 years of life I was relegated to the care of the womenfolk while the men fished. Most of my time was spent swimming in the bay, doing boyish things, and tagging along when the ladies went browsing through the few local curio shops. Toward my tenth birthday I began to fish, catching mostly sea catfish on dead shrimp from the piers where I remained secure under watchful eyes.

The piers. Almost every waterfront home or apartment building that fronted on Aransas Bay had its own pier back then. Who knows what kind of wood these piers were made of, but they were created upon two parallel rows of pilings that were driven into the bay's hard, sandy bottom, and they extended across the broad expanse of nearshore flats to a point just beyond that where the water began to rapidly deepen, some 200 yards, sometimes farther, from the bank. There, a "tee" was constructed at the end of the pier to provide room for several fishermen. Many of these creations were works of art; most, however, were a test of one's coordination—and nerves—as he made his way across the loose and askew planks to reach the tee. None were very wide, and I cannot recall one with handrails, but all were strung with an electric wire, and a half-dozen or so bright lights were attached to up-rights toward the ends of the piers and along their tees. The purpose of those lights was for attracting baitfish after dark, and for the hope that spotted sea trout—"specks," the fish of choice along the Texas coast—would soon follow.

As a child I never did catch much from the piers, as most specks usually arrived at night, long after I had gone to bed. As a teenager I fared somewhat better, catching a few from the piers, and once, while wade-fishing near one that had been beaten into near-oblivion by a recent storm, I hooked a great something that took my lure and a lot of line with it as it surged away. But early on, I spent most of my time on the piers on my stomach, peering into the water beneath that bright blue Texas sky—or beneath the lights—just to see what might be there.

At age 10 I began to fish with the men.

By then, due in great part to a lot of loving patience from my grandfa-ther and the blessing of a beautiful creek that ran through the ranch, I had become fairly adept with a casting rod. At about the same time, I discovered an ancient bamboo fly rod with a rusting automatic reel and a silk line in the rafters of an outbuilding there. (In later years Granddaddy would tell me that I caught a bass with it that summer on a ratty Grey Ghost streamer. I do not remember, but I do know that I began fly fishing about that time, and within a year or so I was as comfortable with the fly rod as I was with the casting outfit—on the creek, anyway, and on the lakes near home.) But since the world of saltwater fishing was just beginning for me, I gave no thought to entering it with a fly rod in hand—a practice unheard of at the time.

Granddaddy bought a boat the year I turned 12—the year my youngest sister was born. Mom sent me away with him for a couple of weeks after she got back from the hospital, and I passed them in youthful bliss with him aboard his boat on Aransas Bay. And, in the mornings before that eternal southeasterly gale began to build, we caught specks, and I met the ladyfish and the sail-catfish—pests to the old ones, wonders to the young. In the afternoons I began to wade the flats around the piers, and in the evenings I'd fish from them. Sometimes I'd catch some specks; always I'd look a lot. From daylight to well after dark, saltwater and all that was within it saturated me, and I loved it.

I loved the creek at the ranch, too, and by the following summer the casting rod was usually left inside the house during my afternoon hours on it. I passed many spring, summer, and autumn evenings probing the creek's deep, sycamore-shaded pools and long, rocky runs with poppers and streamers. And I caught some nice bass—and always felt a little more satisfied than when I caught one on the casting rod. At home—and at school—I daydreamed endlessly of fly fishing on the creek and catching specks at Rockport. For a gift that year, my parents gave me my own fly rod.

It was a Shakespeare Wonderod—8-foot for an 8-weight line and bright yellow, and, in retrospect, it was quite heavy for my purposes. But it was mine; I doted on it, and I saved my meager allowance to buy flies for it. One of those was a long, thin, green popper in a size that was really too big for the creek and the panfish and bass I usually caught in the lakes near home. But when I saw it, I simply had to have it.

Late the following spring my parents told me the saddest news I had ever received: My grandfather had decided to sell the ranch. That summer my family all gathered there for one last retreat, then my parents and sisters drove home, leaving me with him for a final week there together—the week of my fourteenth birthday. And after the packing and cleaning chores were done in the afternoons, I would take my fly rod down to the creek and cry as I fished with it.

He felt as badly about it all as anyone, but it was something that had to be done. In an effort to ease the pain of it—his own, I'm sure, as much as mine—he suggested that after we finished up at the ranch, we should spend a week in Rockport. That was in July 1958.

By then a handful of motels had been constructed between the cottages and apartments along the waterfront. We stayed in one of those that had sufficed in recent years when our favorite cottage wasn't available—and when he and I were alone there together. It was located right at the mouth of the boat basin, and its pier extended almost to the basin's channel, pointing toward the foot of the basin's jetty. It was a familiar, time-honored place, a place that would host us in future—and happier—times. And at the turn of the millennium, the motel was still there.

Too many years have passed for me to be able to recall the particulars of that week. It's likely they are repressed by the events that took place during our last days at the ranch—and by the pain of the loss of my beloved creek. But I do remember that one night, after supper, while my grandparents were sitting on the porch, I walked out onto the pier—just to look.

It was not the usual summer night for that part of the Texas coast. The afternoon gale did not build that day, and the water beneath the lights was as clear as I'd ever seen it. Specks and ladyfish were plainly visible, chasing small brown shrimp across the water's placid surface. The regulars—farther out on the tee—were having fine luck, and as I watched the fish and the shrimp, a thought arose of the long, thin, green popper: Perhaps—just perhaps—those fish might strike it.

I returned to the motel room, rigged up the fly rod—which I had not taken from the car after our return from the ranch—and tied on the popper. And I'll never forget Granddaddy's expression as he looked up from pondering the smoke of his after-supper cigar and saw it. But he said only "Good luck," and soon I was back beside my light.

And for a while, anyway, the pain of my recent loss was soothed as the ladyfish slashed at the popper, hooking themselves, cavorting wildly across the lighted water, and then, usually, throwing the hook. But I caught three before the mangled fly was engulfed by a big speck and the badly frayed leader parted. And that was it for the night.

More than four decades have passed since I caught those first saltwater fish on a fly. That rod, and almost all of the old ones, are now gone. Rockport has become a major venue for Texas fly fishermen, and the ranch—well, who knows. But they all came together on that one night to conceive in me a love of saltwater fly fishing that would last a lifetime—a love that would not have blossomed had it not been for dear people and dear places. I have been a very fortunate person.

Six years would pass after the night of the ladyfish before I caught my first redfish. During that time the sights in the bins of Rockport's fish-houses and the tales told by the regulars fanned a strong desire in me to catch one, and with Granddaddy's blessing and assistance, I did. And the fact that I caught it on a surface lure created for largemouth bass would eventually lead to an almost stoic refusal to use any flies other than poppers for these fish—for a while, anyway.

Two years after capturing that first red, by then having fly fished extensively on the lakes, rivers, and bayous across much of Louisiana, I again carried the long rod to Rockport and caught my first red on a fly. The following September I married, and a year later my wife and I moved to Buras in the Mississippi River Delta where I continued to fly fish for bass and conventionally fish for specks and reds. And one fine June morning three years later, while bass fishing from a pirogue in a canal near Venice, a red weighing almost 15 pounds struck my popper. The door to the world of saltwater fly fishing now stood fully ajar.

Confessions of a Louisiana Fly-Tyer

I'm not really certain what stimulated my initial interest in tying flies. Back then my home was in Shreveport, Louisiana, where (A) almost everyone fished with either cane poles and "bait" or casting rods and "plugs"; (B) creating one's own lures was as dark a practice as Cajun voodoo; and (C) none of the local sporting goods stores carried fly-tying equipment anyway. I remember only that prior to my 12th birthday I had tied small shreds of Mother's sewing yarn to some perch hooks and caught bluegills with them.

None of those fish were noteworthy, and most were too small even for skillet material. Nevertheless, my folks apparently felt that my fly-fishing and fly-tying activities were harmless enough and were keeping me out of bad company. So, as a present that year I received a mail-order fly-tying kit complete with vise, bobbin, hackle pliers, and enough feathers, hair, and other stuff to tie at least six of every trout-fly imaginable. Of course, there is a marked paucity of trout in Louisiana.

However, the kit also contained a dozen or so preshaped and slotted-cork popper bodies of various sizes, along with some hump-shank hooks for them. The accompanying instruction booklet, though, was apparently designed for tyers with a much greater engineering capacity—and a much larger vocabulary, especially in physiological terminology and Latin—than a 12-year-old possesses (this one, anyway), so it ended up forthwith in the trash basket. I then proceeded—without any form of instruction whatsoever, as literally no one I knew of was tying flies at the time—to create the poppers.

They were fashioned along the lines of the few available at the five-and-dime store that was about a 10-minute bike ride from my home, and I recall they turned out quite well in the eyes of an untutored 12-year-old. I never could figure out how to get all the rubber legs into them, though, and the hackles—slightly overwrapped and mashed during the tying process—often came unwound after a fish or two, but they did catch fish. The bluegills came in skillet-size much more often than when I fished with my yarn-flies, and occasionally a respectable largemouth would accompany them. My folks seemed happy to see me enjoying such a "wholesome" activity, and I was happy to be catching fish on my own creations—whether my buddies implied it was a dark practice or not.

There was also a distinct economic factor involved with those poppers. Twelve-year-old Coopers received sparse allowances that prohibited purchasing the dime-store versions with any regularity. Now, when one of my creations would become mangled from bass and bluegill encounters, I could simply retie or repaint it. That beat the heck out of doing extra household chores to earn the quarters necessary to purchase a new one. Life was wonderful.

Some of those poppers lasted until I reached high school. By that time, though, all the grizzly hackles, turkey quills, dubbing, and associated trout-fly stuff had been relegated to the trash and the supply of popper feathers used up. My allowance had increased a bit and was being supplemented with income from part-time jobs, and while most of that was usually spent entertaining young ladies, there was often enough left over to buy one or two of the dime-store models. School, girls, and fishing left little time for anything else; tying ceased, and once I left for college all the associated odds and ends vanished as a younger sister took over my room.

I doubt I would have ever tied flies again had I not moved into the Mississippi River Delta and found almost limitless saltwater fly-fishing opportunities within minutes of my house—and absolutely no flies of any type within 60 miles! And since all this took place long before the sport became fashionable enough for the mail-order companies to include appropriate accoutrements in their catalogs, my flies—"poppers" marketed as freshwater bass bugs—had to be purchased in New Orleans.

Those worked well, and it didn't seem to matter a bit that their hooks weren't stainless steel, since the redfish, especially, would chew them apart long before corrosion had a chance to set in. But there were occasions when I'd run a little short, and a 60-mile trip to town to renew my supply was distinctly dissimilar to the 10-minute bike-ride to the five-and-dime store in Shreveport. Then there were the times—infrequent, but still there—when the fish did not respond well to the poppers and thoughts of sinking flies arose.

So it came to pass that I placed an order to a mail-order house for a large box-full of feathers, bucktails, vise, bobbin, and all the other associated odds and ends whose likenesses had once been discarded. And once again I began to tie flies—though now they were saltwater flies.

Think about that for a moment. Back then, fly fishing in Louisiana, even for bass and bluegills, was a rare enough exercise, and the practice of tying one's own flies for it was comparable somewhat to Creole necromancy. I, now, was performing the act upon saltwater and conjuring hair-and-feather concoctions (not entirely unlike voodoo dolls) to ply therein. Needless to say, I had few close friends and was shunned by the local society for many years.

Nevertheless, I caught fish—lots of fish—mostly redfish taken while spot-casting to them in the shallow marshes. And it didn't take long for me to discover that when a red refused a popper, he would often refuse a sinking fly, too. But I'm getting ahead of myself.

Having no idea of what a sinking saltwater fly should look like, and still possessing the limited engineering capability I had shown so well as a 12-year-old, I decided to replicate my poppers in sinking versions. So I tied two types. The first was created by simply tying an orange saddle hackle about 3 inches long to each side of a size 1/0 hook, then tying a pair of yellow saddle hackle over them. The second was a bucktail, green over yellow. Both worked, but I could never shake the thought that when they did, the fish would have probably hit the popper. And by that time I had become totally addicted to that form of rambunctious entertainment!

So I reverted entirely to poppers. And since I again had tying apparatus, I began to make my own. That presented one very distinct problem: bodies.

On rare occasions—like once in a small general store way out in South Texas Comanche Country—I would find some preshaped assortments; who knows what their purposes were. But even then most of them were too small for my redfish poppers. So I cut, chopped, whittled, sanded, and ground wine-bottle corks and shrimp-trawl floats until my fingers cramped. They came out like snowflakes—none were ever quite the same—but they caught fish when dressed with green-over-yellow bucktail and painted similarly with model-airplane enamel. And if the paint chipped from excessive contact with redfish teeth, no problem; there was much more paint around than bodies. Life was again wonderful, and I couldn't care less about not being invited to the community "socials."

But nothing ever stays the same, and I'm not sure whether it all began with a precipitous influx of out-of-state fly fishermen or whether a bunch of local guys got bored with slaying vast numbers of reds on shrimp, or read a book about bonefishing with flies and then put it all together. Whatever, someone discovered I'd been doing it for some time, and suddenly my dark practice became an "expertise" and that was in great demand.

Of course, that expertise included the types of flies I was using, and while those were satisfactory, to me and quite acceptable to the fish, they may have lacked a certain degree of "refinement" to tyers of talent. So, for the clinics, seminars, and such that I began to give, I had to construct some "presentation models"—and eventually I began fishing with them.

By that time I had also begun fly fishing for reds during winter in slightly deeper water and for specks in the nearby bays and along the surf. In those settings I discovered that Clouser Minnows were quite effective and well within my limited engineering capabilities. And not long thereafter I began the pursuit of offshore beasts—with tarpon flies, which I could also tie.

My tying desk is now much more cluttered than it once was. I even bought a hair-stacker a while back, though apparently it's either too small for a clump of size 1 Clouser-bucktail (or I just don't know how to use it correctly—that's always a possibility). Still, the flies I tie are much more "socially acceptable" than they once were, albeit I limit myself to the four or five patterns I'm capable of creating. I also find myself tying them more often now for pleasure than out of need, and though I'm still viewed with great suspect by the non-fly-fishing members of my community, I believe it's more of a curiosity than a fear of one who practices dark deeds. I even have a couple of close friends.

And I continue to catch fish on my flies. Life is indeed wonderful!

PART I

Popular Saltwater Sport Fishes of Louisiana

CHAPTER 1

Redfish

The Marsh Reds

Much of the Louisiana Coast is rimmed with marsh estuaries of the numerous rivers that flow through the area. In many places the salinity of the water gradually decreases the farther away they are from the Gulf. Marshes change with changes in salinity; types of spartina grass are common in outer, saltier marsh, while three-corner grass, common bull rush, and bull tongue, as well as various submergent grasses, make up those of fresher values. Others maintain only salt grass to the point where they meet land. Each marsh serves as a valuable nursery for the young of many species covering the entire food chain. A large part of that life is made up of red drum—"poisson rouge" as Louisiana Cajuns call them.

With a few exceptions they are juvenile fish; by age four and some 10–12 pounds, most of them have moved offshore to join the massive schools of adults—the spawning stock. But the numbers of fish in the 4–8-pound class present in this inshore "nursery" is tremendous—more than enough for any fly fisherman. And they love flies!

Living in an area literally surrounded by them—the lower Mississippi River Delta—and being possessed with a fly-fishing temperament for nearly a lifetime, I was one of the first to cast flies at these fish in this area. It began in 1971, and I must confess it was initiated by an accident of sorts, which is a tale worth telling.

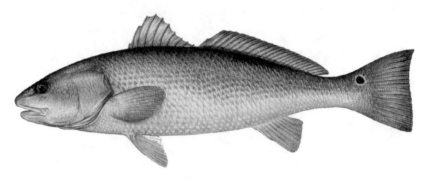

red drum (redfish) (Scianops ocellatus)

Besides all the saltwater opportunities coastal Louisiana offers, there is also some bass fishing which can be so good at times that I'll target them in lieu of the local briny beasties. Early that year I had located a section of a long pipeline canal that had been isolated by wooden bulkheads in order to prevent saltwater intrusion, and those enclosed waters were loaded with largemouths! To catch them, I had to ferry along a "pirogue" (the low-slung and rather tipsy Cajun "canoe") in my bass-boat, which I would secure near a bulkhead, then drag the pirogue across the bank and into the enclosed section of the canal.

That particular June morning was handmade for fly fishing—sultry, and flat, calm, and the bass were obliging, crawling all over a short-tailed size 4 chartreuse-and-black popper with rubber legs. I was working it along the edges of the grass overhanging the canal's shorelines—with absolutely no thoughts of redfish on my mind—when a red suddenly stuck its tail out of the water a short distance away. I then made a very casual cast at it, feeling the fish would probably show no interest in such a small offering, but it rose to the popper like a broaching porpoise, crashed it like an alligator grabbing a muskrat, and then began the closest thing to a Nantucket sleigh-ride I have ever experienced! But after towing me up and down the canal for 20 minutes or so, I netted it and managed to get it aboard without capsizing. That fish—which I have previously mentioned weighed just under 15 pounds—remains the largest inshore red I have ever taken. Incidentally, I caught it on the 7½-foot, 6-weight outfit I had bought for smallmouth bass near my wife's home in Missouri. Mercy!

It wasn't long thereafter when I discovered a practical reason for fly fishing for reds: shallow, grass-choked water where every other lure would either foul or its impact would spook nearby fish. Poppers (with a much more suitable 8-weight outfit) floated above it, and their entry was much softer than that of a conventional surface lure. Many years, and many fish, later I began fly fishing for them in areas where there was no reason for doing so except that it was fun. And it produced a lot of fish—and year-round, except for the most extreme cold of winter.

Early March through November is considered the best fly-fishing time hereabouts, with both ends being prime. That does not mean that they cannot be caught on flies during the depths of winter; they certainly can (it will be discussed in later pages). But back to warmer months. Throughout this time the varying weather and water conditions you will encounter will either allow excellent sight-fishing or demand prospecting with blind casts.

The brackish marshes—those that are not quite "fresh"—consistently offer the clearest water and therefore the best potential for sight-fishing. But those same submergent grasses that create this clarity will mask a redfish; spotting them even here is much more difficult than it is over a shell or sandy bottom. Polarized sunglasses are a must; bright sunshine is almost equally as important, and a slow, methodic search-pattern will generate the most opportunities for a cast.

Often when they are actively feeding, reds will announce their presence by tailing, finning, or "pushing"—creating a large wake as they move through the shallows. Occasionally they will enter water so thin that their backs become exposed; these are referred to as "crawlers," and when you see one, it's a sight guaranteed to raise your pulse-rate! Reading about it all might conjure thoughts of wading after these fish, but alas, the marsh bottoms across much of the area are too soft for wading.

Those "indicators" of fish not only occur in the clear waters of the interior but also in the often slightly less clear water nearer the coastline. Here, there is little submergent vegetation to act as a filtering agent, but here, too, are great numbers of redfish. The opportunity to sight-fish for them, though, requires the attention to a few more details than it does in the clear-water areas.

The first is the tide. I have taken more reds during the last half of the falling tide than all the other stages combined. Besides the fact that it drains the shallow ponds and nooks and crannies within the marsh—an act that draws shrimp and various minnows into slightly deeper adjacent waters, such as bays, tidal cuts, and canals, and thereby triggers feeding activity—those areas themselves now become shallow. That makes it easier to spot fish movement than when the tide is up.

Wind is another consideration, and not just because it makes casting difficult. While light breezes don't necessarily have too great an effect on sight-fishing in the clear, rather protected waters of the interior, the ripples they generate in the dingy marshes can make it tough to spot a fish. Therefore, the windward shorelines should be scouted, since the grass creates a small area of flat water just downwind of it. And here, bright sunlight is even more important than it is in the interior.

Unfortunately, you cannot always fashion a trip around light winds, sunshine, and the falling tide. Nevertheless, you can still catch a lot of reds by blind-casting. While this technique is not often required in the interior, it can be the only alternative when rather stiff southerlies flood the outer marshes—as well as during the cooler months. Still, two "particulars" make it a lot easier than you might imagine.

The first is the oyster beds. While there are a few wild reefs in these waters, many oysters are cultivated on bedding grounds—sections of bay-bottoms that are leased from the state, which permits it. The oysters are dredged from the public seed-grounds, transported to the private, more fertile leases, and "bedded" until they reach marketable size. Those leases are usually plainly marked with long willow branches or lengths of PVC pipe stuck into the bay's bottom. Find an accumulation of these pipes, move into water within them that is 3 feet deep or a bit less, and fan-cast the area.

The second is junk: run-down petroleum facilities, derelict fishing camps, sunken boats, and such. It may not be too pretty to look at, but where there's an accumulation of it, it can draw redfish like a magnet. Anything trashy-looking and well weathered should be thoroughly prospected; the largest fish in the marsh are often found around such junk. That makes it no place to be fishing "fine" with light gear.

Along that line most of the redfish I've taken, from both the interior and the outer marshes, have been on an 8-weight outfit. But living right next door to them allows me the luxury of picking my days. Since a visitor is not so fortunate, I recommend a 9-weight outfit for better coping with the breeze.

In interior areas the bigger rod will also give you a better chance to turn a fish before it plows into thick patches of various submergent grasses. Here, a 9-foot knotless leader tapered to 16 pounds offers the dual advantage of strength to supplement the rod and no staging knots for grass to foul on. A shocker is not needed.

The same outfit will suffice when fishing the oyster beds and junk in the

The state coastal marshes offer fly fishermen an opportunity with redfish that is second to none.

outer marshes. In these places a 7-foot leader—knotted or otherwise—tapered to the same rating and with a foot of 30-pound for a fray-resisting shocker is appropriate. But should you manage to time your trip into this area when everything is just right for sight-fishing—and it does happen—you can step down a long way. Like to 4-pound class on a 4-weight!

I've caught a dozen or so good fish like that, but a 5-weight with an 8-pound tippet is preferable for the light work, as it helps cast the required flies a lot better, those being size 6 pink or chartreuse Charlies and green-over-white poppers. If you have the means to carry a 5- or 6-weight outfit along with the 9-weight into this area, then do it. It could really make your trip!

One of the most popular flies now being used in the clear-water interior is a local version of Jon Cave's Wobbler fly in size 1/0 and in gold, black-and-gold, and all black. It is tied with a mono weed guard, sinks very slowly, is easily castable with a 9-weight rod, and the fish can't resist it. Being a staunch traditionalist I think it is pure fly-fishing heresy and refuse to tie one to my tippet, opting for poppers and bend-backs in size 1 for daily use. They work just fine in both areas while sight-fishing, as do similar-sized Clouser Minnows tied in chartreuse-over-white and with plastic necklace-beads instead of weighted eyes.

When reds are active they are not usually hesitant about striking; the trick is for the fly to gain their attention. Most of the time, reds won't move any great distance to intercept it, and when they have their noses in the grass, waving their tails at you, they become highly "focused." Cast the fly only a couple of feet or so in front of them, and immediately begin short, moderately paced strips (or long, slow "pulls" with a Wobble Fly, if you're a bit more "liberal" than I am). As in every other saltwater setting, strive to prevent the fly from approaching the fish; should the infrequent event occur of a fish that follows but is reluctant to strike, a continuation of the pace is usually better than changing it—usually.

You can't tell how a fish is responding to your retrieve when you are blind-casting. Most often, fairly slow, steady, 6-inch strips with the fly near bottom are good enough. On that note, and no matter whether you're sight-fishing or blind-casting in either the interior or outer areas of Louisiana's marshes, full-floating lines are best, since almost year-round, the best water is usually less than 3 feet deep. In the blind-casting mode simply count the fly down to the point where you begin your retrieve, and if it ticks a shell or piece of junk, don't count so far next time.

In the outer marshes the fly's color should be chosen dependant on the water's clarity. Early and late in the season, when the water is at its clearest, the chartreuse-over-white Clouser Minnow—now with weighted eyes—is my favorite pattern. During warm, dingy months, dark-green-over-chartreuse is preferred, but at all times I carry along some in purple, just in case. Simply put, you don't need a lot of gear—or a lot of flies—to catch redfish in Louisiana.

The Winter Reds

I had been here/done that countless times, even in much colder weather, and if the wind had allowed me to cast the big Clouser Minnow 40 feet or so, I usually caught fish. But as I sat in Capt. Bubby Rodriguez's boat (see listings in Destinations chapter)—my hat's ear-flaps down and my insulated coveralls' collar up—gritting my teeth against the sting of speed as we raced down the meandering little bayou, the thought arose as it always has: "I gotta be out of my ever-loving mind!"

Actually, at daybreak it was only 48 degrees: the "warming spell," which occurs between the last cold front's blow-down and the arrival of the next—that being forecast to rip across the coast that evening. On the previous morning, frost had covered my front yard, and though the thermometer had almost reached 50 that afternoon, the north wind built throughout the day. But last night it again had laid; the zephyr, or light breeze, that barely ruffled the water's surface at the launch at Myrtle Grove, just southeast of New Orleans, was now set in the east. If someone wishes to fly fish for red drum in winter, this was a fine time to do so.

There was no water in the marsh and not much in the little bayou—the result of three days of stiff offshore winds combined with our day's normal low tide. That was good; less water means fewer places the fish can be. Assuredly they had retreated to the bay—our destination—with the falling tide. There they must wait until the water again begins to rise, allowing them to scatter into the flooding marsh. I had little doubt we would find them, and when we did, we should find them in bunches.

The bay was almost clear—remarkable, considering the blow of the past three days, but a blanket of low, thin clouds had arrived with the easterly breeze: there would be no sight-fishing today. Soon, Bubby killed the outboard, took up the push-pole, and mounted the stern platform as I ascended the bow with my 9-weight. We worked two spots, blind fan-casting with my trusty chartreuse-and-white Clouser, without a sign of a red, and I soon recalled the sage words an old bayou-boy once told me: "You can't catch 'em where they ain't."

A suggestion was then made to try to "push" some—an effective tactic now but one that will spook 'em onto dry land during warmer months. Soon we were moving along the shoreline—following its contours some 15 to 20 feet distant—at a little faster than idle speed, but we covered more than a quarter of a mile without moving a single fish. In winter that can be expected, but I knew they had to be here somewhere.

Eventually we flushed a small school in the back of a pocket, swung away from them, and invested a few minutes looking for others in order for those to settle down. That wouldn't take long, and they should not move very far— a world of behavioral difference from summer.

There were no others nearby, and we soon returned to the pocket where I quickly connected with one—a 6-pounder that tried to fight but didn't seem to be firing on all cylinders. As I unhooked and released him, I felt his body's chill, and it occurred to me that I, too, might not be up to peak performance if I lived in water that cold.

Cold. Winter is an anathema for those who fish with flies in saltwater. It's the time when many of their favorite species have either migrated to

Reds are remarkably tolerant to low temperatures. During winter the tide and the wind govern the fishing more than the thermometer.

warmer climes or moved into the depths where fly fishing for them becomes difficult at best—or so they have been conditioned to think. It is a time of brutal cold and gale-force winds—a time when most thoughts of fly fishing are of Floridian or Bahamian flats—or of somewhere in the tropics. It's the time for tying flies, cleaning gear, and attending tackle shows and seminars. And it is a time for fishing friends to gather in the evenings and reflect on past good days—and dream aloud of those they hope will come—over tall glasses of warming amber liquids. But for some of us across the Louisiana Coast, winter is still fly-fishing time for redfish.

We don't have any real secrets about it—except maybe that reds will be found in some pretty shallow water in all but the coldest weather. Their metabolism slows down a bit in winter, and they are subject to a freeze-induced coma when they're caught in the shallows on a rare visit by the Arctic Express; the "Christmas freezes" of 1983 and 1989 killed a lot of them. But they are remarkably resistant to typical winter weather, and they do have to eat. Being creatures of the shallows, that is where they feed, even now.

And at this time fly fishing for them is not that complicated—once you've found them. The problem most folks have is the willingness to try it, and it's so simple: You fish with flies just like you would with hardware, casting to a likely spot—shoreline irregularities, oyster beds, and "pushed" or visible fish—and retrieving the fly with short, slow strips. There really is nothing to it if the wind allows it.

That's the real bugaboo for fly fishing for reds down here during winter, not the cold. But often it's not as bad as you may imagine—provided you dress for it. A 15-knot wind is no real deterrent to fly casting, but if it's combined with high humidity and temperatures below 50 degrees, it will cut through insulated coveralls like a filleting knife! But the wind, and one a bit stronger, will not prevent casting 40 feet or so, and that's usually all it takes to get the job done. Reds don't spook as easily at this time as they do during warmer times, and with a minimum of boat noise, they can be approached quite closely.

They also tend to bunch up on specific spots on the bay bottom, such as accumulations of oysters or shells, subtle humps and depressions, and along the edges of small, shallow channels; and when they do they will stay there—provided you don't spook them—until the tide returns. If you find such a spot with fish on it, you can safely assume they'll be there again after the next front has pushed through, this winter, next winter, and the following winter.

I have a secret little honey-hole like that: some scattered shells near the mouth of a small tidal cut through the marsh and in about 3 feet of water at mean sea level. When a "norther" drains the marsh through the cut, the reds gang up on top of those shells, and it's nothing to catch 8 or 10 on Clousers. But let the wind turn to the south and begin to drive the tide back in, and you can't pull a strike there on a dare; the fish have followed the rising water back into the marsh. That pattern has been consistent for 11 straight winters, and need I say the spot is closely guarded!

The bay where Bubby and I were fishing is not; it's a popular place and time-proven for producing post–cold front redfish in great numbers. With the exception of the fish in the little pocket, they just hadn't been where they were supposed to be. We'll find 'em—or so I try to convince myself.

The sun makes a brief appearance, then ducks back behind the clouds; so much for any "radiational warming" of the water. I've read a lot about that, but I have never jumped into it during changes of sunlight intensity to verify any differences in its temperature. Don't intend to, either. Still, reds do seem to bite better in winter when the sun is brightly shining. Maybe it wakes 'em up. Now, with the almost solid overcast, they are all probably in one big gang, asleep with their bellies on the bottom out in the middle of the bay. Yeah....

We burn fuel, trying to flush another school. With little more than half an hour remaining before we must head in, we cruise the bay's eastern shoreline, looking hard. The tide is now slack and dead low; soon it will begin to rise—prime time is almost over.

Bubby is watching forward as a hint of motion near the bank seizes all of my attention. Then a big V-wave surges across the shallows, followed by another and then many more. "There they are, Bubby!" He smiles and nods: Got 'em!

He makes a long, wide turn around them, idles back, and approaches the spot from upwind. At 100 yards he kills the motor, takes up the push-pole, and eases us to within casting range. At 60 feet I take a shot, and the Clouser is struck almost instantly.

After releasing the fish, several casts are required to locate the concentration. Then Bubby spuds down the push-pole, ties it off, and joins in the festivities. The fish are ganged up at the mouth of a small cut, apparently waiting for the tide to begin to rise so they can gain the marsh, and they are hungry. We count coup with five more very nice fish—and prematurely release a couple of others—within the 20 minutes before our time runs out. It has been a good day—not a great one or even a very good one, but one to remedy a bad case of cabin fever, and I'll take one like it every time.

No, it wasn't the "classic stuff"—spot-casting to visible fish, but it sure beat staying home and tying flies, or cleaning reels, or going to seminars, or daydreaming of warmer times. Too much of that, and I would be out of my ever-loving mind for sure!

Blind-casting Clouser Minnows across 2–3-foot depths is far from being the only way to catch Louisiana's redfish during winter. As I stated earlier, these fish are highly temperature-tolerant and can be found in surprisingly shallow water in all but the coldest weather. The key is *bright* sunlight!

Shallow flats with light, shell-covered bottoms are prime spots to find these fish on chilly, sunny days. During periods of light winds the water can become as clear as it ever gets, and sight-fishing is quite feasible. Size 1 bend-backs and weedless SeaDucers in both purple and chartreuse-over-white are effective, but poppers can provide some outstanding action (even if you're having to wear insulated coveralls to stay warm)!

So the next time you read in the outdoor page of your Sunday newspaper that all the redfish have gone deep, just smile knowingly. Then, if the sun is bright and the breeze is light, stow the 9-weight and the fly box in the boat, grab your jacket, and head for the coast. Once there, locate water about a foot deep—preferably with scattered shells on bottom, and start drifting, either looking or blind-casting. And you really should try a popper if you've been suffering from withdrawal symptoms caused by the lack of recent surface action. You'll find 'em, and thanks to the outdoor editor of your newspaper, you won't have a bit of competition!

The Bulls

The psychological progression most fishing folks go through as they practice their sport over a period of time has been well established in print. First, they desire to catch large numbers of their target species, then they seek the largest of that species, and finally they pursue the best overall experience. Thus, it's somewhat strange that the great majority of the fly fishermen who have become enraptured with red drum seem to have skipped phase two. Have you? Numbers and aesthetics aside, haven't you ever daydreamed of a chance to test yourself against a big, broad-shouldered bull?

Well, there are plenty of them in the waters along the Louisiana Coast, and they can be very fly fishable!

The abundance of reds in these waters—a true fisheries management success story—is the result of coordinated programs between the federal and state governments. By the late 1980s commercial purse-seining had led to a drastic decline in the numbers of the breeding stock—the "bulls"—which inhabit the Gulf. The National Marine Fisheries Service then suspended both commercial and recreational fishing for the species in federal waters, and possession of these fish is still prohibited there—the waters being designated by NMFS as the Exclusive Economic Zone (EEZ). That means you cannot have any redfish aboard your boat while you are in the EEZ, even if you caught it in state waters!

The federal government's action eventually stabilized the offshore population. New state regulations allowed many more fish to reach breeding age and "escape" the inland waters to join the offshore stocks. More breeders made more babies, and more babies have now grown into breeders. Bulls are again plentiful, and everyone but the commercial fishery is quite happy about it all.

Most reds "escape" inland waters at around age 4 or 5 and a weight of roughly 10–15 pounds. There are some notable exceptions, most coming from large bays or sounds. However, the fact remains that inshore fishermen of any persuasion have only a slight chance of catching a bull in this area—lots of numbers and often in some very pleasing settings, but no really big fish. Those inhabit the Gulf, and for our purposes here, the Gulf comes in three forms: the open offshore waters, the surf, and the water adjacent to jetties protecting ship-channels and such. Each offers excellent potential in season, but each requires entirely different tactics.

Offshore, it's "run and gun": Burn fuel and look for them on the surface. The normally calm time of summer is when this procedure is most effective, and the commotion a school of bulls may kick up can be seen from quite a distance.

Occasionally the white water will be created almost entirely by reds as they trample through schools of silversides, Spanish sardines, or menhaden. If that's the case, it is usually best to idle the boat to within 50 to 60 feet of them, drop a size 3/0 green-and-white Deceiver or chartreuse-and-yellow tarpon fly into their midst, and give it one short strip. That's about all it takes!

Bulls also join forces with crevalle jacks to herd schools of baitfish to the surface, so if what appears to be only a jack attack is discovered, don't leave until you are certain no bulls are in attendance. Of course, you could stay and entertain yourself quite nicely with the "damnjacks," but if you want a bull, move on. However, if you see some along with the jacks, put the fly right on one's nose or you are destined to hook one of the fork-tailed beasts!

Another source of white water you may encounter here is the little tunny. Upon ascertaining those speedsters are the cause of it all, it's best to continue the search, since reds are seldom found associating with tunny—they simply aren't fast enough to keep up with them. However, reds will readily join a pack of blue runners, or "hardtails," in a surface melee.

*The best spots for a fly fisherman to catch bull reds
include jetties and barrier islands.*

Runners tend to corral baitfish rather than chase them down like the tunny do, and gulls and terns frequently dive and wheel over the white water. When a ruckus like that is come across, idle the boat to within casting distance of it, and if any reds are present, they will be plainly seen. Pick one, cast just ahead of it, and retrieve the fly with short, moderately fast strips. For all these offshore opportunities, an 11- or 12-weight outfit with a floating line, a 20-pound-class leader, and at least a 50-pound mono shocker is advisable. This is not because of the size of the fish, which averages between 20 and 30 pounds, but because at any moment, while you are pursuing offshore reds, a school of tarpon or an outsized cobia—among others—might appear. And the bigger stick will beat a bull quickly so that you can get it revived and back in the water faster than you could if you were using a lighter outfit.

And at this point it is necessary to make a special note on the big stick and casting big flies. Casting a size 3/0 Deceiver or 4/0 Clouser Minnow with a fast-action 12-weight is much different than casting a size 1/0 Clouser with a 9-weight. There are a lot of great 12-weight opportunities along the Louisiana Coast. If you decide to take advantage of a few of them, it is highly recommended to practice, practice, practice before your trip—or take a 12-

weight casting lesson—to get the feel of how it works. It will be time and money well spent!

Bulls reds are also commonly found in the surf of the state's barrier islands and infrequent sandy mainland shores. While a chance encounter with them is a year-round possibility, they are most plentiful in this setting during late summer through winter, with the highest numbers usually present at both ends of the time frame. That, of course, is based on my own experiences.

Tactics and suitable gear for fly fishing these areas include 9- or 10-weight outfits with reels with decent disc drags and holding a clear sinking-tip line and at least 150 yards of 30-pound Dacron backing. Leaders 7 to 9 feet long that are tapered to a 16-pound-class tippet, and finished with a foot of 40-pound fluorocarbon shocker, are adequate. Clouser-types in sizes 1/0 and 2/0 are effective; in most places the largest you can cast (safely!) will work the best. Long casts, 5- to 10-second countdowns, moderately paced 6- to 12-inch strips, and a hearty strip-strike or two is the pattern. Fish the dark water of the troughs and pockets in the surf by blind-casting, but always keep an eye out for fish on the surface or on top of any shallow bars.

Generally speaking, clear water, a reasonably gentle surf, and the top half of the rising tide are optimum conditions. Some of these areas may be quite popular spots, and they can become quite crowded during late spring and summer, but once the school season begins—especially during weekdays—there is much more "untroubled" water for you to fish. And that goes for anywhere you will find suitable surf.

The onset of the new school year also signals a very productive time for pursuing bulls along the beaches of Grand Isle, Fourchon, the Chandeleurs, and Constance Beach to the west near Johnson's Bayou. This is during the time these fish move shoreward for spawning and in doing so move into the range of shore-bound anglers. It is also the time of the striped mullet's spawning aggregations, and when gangs of these favored baitfish move along the surface of the Gulf just outside of the surf line's first bar, they draw big reds like magnets! Here you will have no problem determining their presence: If they are not blowing huge holes in the schools of mullet passing before you, then they can often be plainly visible in the clear water as they swim about in search of one.

If neither bait nor bulls is offering any visible indication of their presence, and if conditions for them to be around and active are favorable, blind-casting the points at the ends of the barrier islands can lead to action. Fact is, that's exactly the way I captured a state-record fly-caught red: no sign of either bait or bulls, but in clear, rising water at the south point of Grand Gosier in the Chandeleurs. Incidentally, that occurred in late winter, and that's a wonderful time to go fishing—if you can catch a decent day—for reds along a barrier island!

That record didn't stand for very long. I myself broke it with a fish of 36 pounds, thank you very much, that I caught off a jetty one drop-dead gorgeous early-November morning three years later. In my opinion—humble, as always—I think Louisiana's offshore jetties offer the fly fisherman his best chance at a brawny bull red. On decent days throughout the year, the potential is there, and one of these rocky red-attractors just might rate as the undeniable redfish capitol of the Gulf Coast (if not the entire world)!

That in itself presents a problem in catching the biggest of the beasts: Often, there are so many "regular reds" and "baby bulls" around these jetties— namely, at Cameron, Belle Pass, and the Mississippi River's South and Southwest Passes—that getting the fly in the face of a brute before a smaller fish can grab it will require a lot of luck. I certainly had plenty of that the day I caught my big one, and I'll take it any time it is offered! Still, I doubt many fly fishermen will complain too much about catching only baby bulls.

The bulls that attend jetties during autumn occasionally ravage schools of mullet on the surface and can be taken by fishing fairly shallow. However, even then—and during the remainder of the year—much more consistent action comes by working them deep.

An intermediate sinking line usually requires a countdownof between 20 and 30 to reach the depth that is normally most productive and lies from roughly 10 to 20 feet outside of the jetty's visible rocks. Here, a 12-weight outfit is again preferred, mainly because of the potential for encountering king mackerel and wayward crevalle jacks, which need to be persuaded to come to Papa quickly so that he can shuck 'em as fast as possible and get back to business with the reds. Size 3/0 and 4/0 Clouser-types are favored here; slow-strip them, and after five or six strips, allow the fly to sink back into the strike zone. And always be ready to pick it up for a quick shot at a school of fish passing nearby on the surface!

So if you want a bull redfish on fly, those techniques, times, and general places are your best bets. But if I simply had to catch one and the time was only close to being right, I'd head to the east jetty of the Mississippi River's Southwest Pass. From March through much of December it could be the best spot in the world for these fish—and flies work there very nicely!

CHAPTER 2

Specks

The Summer Specks

Specks (spotted or speckled sea trout) are, without doubt, the most popular fish along the entire Gulf Coast—with conventional fishermen. Fly fishermen seem to prefer redfish, which typically fight harder, grow larger, and can be caught while sight-fishing. However, specks can provide very fast action, and when they've gained some length and some meat on their ribs, they're able to put up a very respectable resistance to capture.

And they taste just fine, thank you very much!

The fly-fishing techniques for catching them change with the seasons and with the locations where they are most commonly found. During spring and fall—those times that are usually considered best for these fish—two factors can arise that can adversely affect this fishery. The first is the fact that large flies are usually most effective. In spring—normally the best time for really big fish—they are the surest way to tempt a trophy, although typically of the species, most of them will have a long time growing before they reach that prestigious size. And during autumn big flies more closely match the size of the various prey species that specks then pursue.

The second factor is the wind—the often-persistent 12- to 15-knot breeze is still fly-fishable but demands an 8- or even 9-weight stick to cast those large flies. So here's the rub: In the inland waters across the northern

spotted seatrout (speck) (Cynoscion nebulosus)

Gulf Coast, a 9-weight outfit is simply far too heavy to provide any real sport with most of the specks that you'll encountered during the "prime times." However, if you fly fish for the specks of summer, you can often use gear that allows them to really strut their stuff.

In coastal Louisiana that is a result of the normally light winds and relatively small prey of the time. Now, a 6-weight outfit can be just fine. Imagine yourself catching two dozen very respectable, if not large, specks on a 6-weight outfit on one afternoon's tide—and on poppers! Then too, what about the hundred or so others that could be classed as "shorts" but still hit the popper with very entertaining enthusiasm! Incidentally, I've had several 100-plus summer speck days using a 6 weight. Need I say I had much fun!

While a smorgasbord of appetizing morsels awaits the specks during summer, in Louisiana one of the primary sources of protein is small white shrimp. However, in the typically dingy waters of the season, an exact match is not necessary, and size 4 Clouser Minnows and poppers in chartreuse-over-white or green-over-chartreuse suffice as "near-nuff" imitations of the shrimp as well as small menhaden and bay anchovies, which are also on the specks' menus. Tie them a tad on the bulky side, tie 'em tough, and bring along a bunch—if you find fish, as I have a few times, you'll need 'em! And remember to flatten your hooks' barbs; you may lose some fish when they surface and perform their familiar head-sloshing routine, but you will injure far fewer of those you intend to release.

The outfit I normally use could be deemed more appropriate for river-dwelling smallmouth bass than for saltwater applications, but it has proven ideal for summer specks. The rod is a very fast 9-footer and is equipped with a fighting butt—which might seem a bit out of place on a 6-weight stick, but it

Specks are the most popular saltwater species across the Louisiana Coast and will readily take a variety of flies.

doesn't seem to hurt anything. The reel is a beefed-up and corrosion-resistant trout model holding 100 yards of 20-pound Dacron backing and a floating braided monocore line.

The leader is around 8 feet long, tapered to 12-pound class, and finished with a foot of 20-pound fluorocarbon for resistance to fraying by the specks' raspy teeth. As it is, the outfit is light enough to prevent undue fatigue from several hours of nonstop casting (and sometimes nonstop "catching") in the broiling heat, it casts the aforementioned flies with ease, and it allows the fish to show their spunk while still being capable of handling a decent-sized redfish should one of them make an appearance—a fairly common event in many areas. And on that note, you may recall me telling you that the largest inshore redfish I have ever taken, which weighed almost 15 pounds, was captured on a 6-weight outfit, so fear not an encounter with a red while using one!

There are two tried-and-true ways to enjoy the spectacular light-tackle action that Louisiana's summer specks offer: Either hire a guide (see listings in Destinations chapters) or time your own trip to coincide with moving water. In the larger bays and sounds, that is frequently best when it is rising; in more interior areas the falling tide is often best. Frequently, some of the best fishing takes place during the hottest part of the day, so carry a lot of water and sunscreen along with your "bunch of flies"; you will need them all!

On the other hand, the heat doesn't seem to bother the specks too much, provided there is current present—the factor that generates the "bite." Here's how it works.

As the tide falls, it drains the shallow ponds and cuts in the marshes surrounding the bays. The shrimp and various minnows that inhabit these havens during the periods of the high tide are thus drawn into deeper waters where they become affected by the current. Since none of these prey species is a particularly strong swimmer, they are carried along with the flow in a very vulnerable state. Find a place that tends to bottleneck that flow and thereby concentrates the bait, and you've found a prime feeding spot for the specks. Notably, the best of these are often found closer to the seashore than the hot spots of spring and fall.

One of my favorite spots—but only on a falling tide with a range of a foot or more—is the point where a moderately sized and fairly deep tidal cut enters a shallow bay. Here, the bottleneck is the water's depth: The bait is constricted within the water column as the bottom of the cut rapidly rises to meet the bay bottom. Finding such a spot is an easy task if you pay attention to what your depth recorder is telling you—or if you get lucky like I did and have it given away by a flock of squawking gulls diving onto shrimp being driven to the surface by the specks!

Current—either from a rising or falling tide—passing around a grassy point along a bay's shoreline creates another good feeding opportunity for specks, since bait becomes concentrated as it is swept around the point. Also, clamshell dams and wooden bulkheads, which once isolated canals but over time have become washed out at their ends by the current, are great schooling spots for bait and specks alike. Find any of these, and you won't need to be told where to cast! The falling tide is best here, too, since it pulls prey from inside the canal into the waters on your side of the dam or bulkhead.

One last bit of local inshore structure, which was mentioned in the chapter on redfish, is an accumulation of shells—clams, natural reefs, bedded oysters, and such. Those that occur in water roughly 3–5 feet deep are prime spots for fly fishing for specks, spring, summer, and fall. Once one is located—either by depth recorder, by probing bottom with a push-pole, visually, or by markers of willow branches or lengths of PVC pipe—fan-casting the area is the proven tactic. Here, too, the falling tide is often best during summer, and since the water will probably be a little dingy as it flows across the bed; the darker Clouser Minnow is the best choice. Of course, here as in anywhere else, if the fish are active on the surface, then try the popper; even a 15-inch speck will strike one of those with so much gusto that you surely wouldn't want to miss out on it! A moderately paced retrieve consisting of continuous soft pops is recommended. Don't try to set the hook until you actually feel the weight of the fish; often they will miss their mark a time or two, and you don't want to snatch the fly away from them—something quite easy to do in the excitement of it all! Keep it coming—they'll eventually zero in on it.

On days when poppers are effective—and that's most of them during the summer—this opportunity becomes even sweeter. Imagine this: more than 100 specks in one afternoon, all of them smashing, gulping, and jumping all over poppers, often three or four times on a single cast! Talk about a riot! Then, when they finally manage to get themselves stuck, you have them on a 6-weight outfit. Believe me, that's hard to beat. Get yourself some of Louisiana's summer specks and you'll see why!

The Surf Specks

Surf fishing along the northern Gulf Coast is a long-established tradition for many and offers a saltwater fly fisherman excellent potential. Across coastal Louisiana there are a few places you can even drive to and park your car within mere yards of the beach. Specks are the most popular target in these waters, though during much of the year the surf can provide good to great action. Indeed, not long ago both the largest speck and the largest redfish I had taken on flies came from surf fishing! And if you pick the right spots—or properly time your trips to the others, you may find some really appealing scenery.

First, though, let's take a quick look at some of the surf's best seasonal opportunities.

During winter, redfish—and bull redfish—are common targets. By April, specks, pompano, and big crevalle jacks have become more predominant. The latter half of May through the first half of June is typically the best time for a wall-hanger speck. Summer and early autumn offer school-sized specks, Spanish macks, and ladyfish, and, as autumn progresses, pompano can reappear and redfish numbers increase dramatically. And, at any time, a surprising and delightful exception can come along to prove that rule!

No matter the season, whatever fish are present at the time will usually be found in roughly the same places. Generally speaking, wadable surf along

*During the warm months Louisiana's barrier islands offer a fine
fly-fishing opportunity for specks.*

the Louisiana Coast can be divided into two categories: natural and altered.
Both types can be equally productive, but fish-holding structure in one is
quite different from that in the other.

The natural surf is the way God made it. In many areas across the coast,
this begins with a trough against the beach, then a bar, another slightly
deeper trough, a deeper bar, and then bottom's gradual offshore descent. At
times—like at first light or at the top of a spring tide—the first trough may
hold specks and reds, especially during the cooler months. At other times—
like from midmorning through suppertime during spring break and
throughout summer vacation-time—it is often overrun with beach bunnies.
Time your fishing days—and hours—accordingly!

To be sure, there are places along the Louisiana Coast where, during late
fall through winter, you can actually stand on dry land and catch reds from
the crystalline water that the season creates in the first trough until you are
beat to the bone. However, more consistently good action—and the largest
fish—usually come from the second trough.

Here, even in that wonderfully clear water found here in winter, you won't see the fish like you can in the first trough. Blind-casting at an angle across the trough is the best technique; covering water until you find fish is the key. With the proper flies—that will be discussed shortly—Pete's First Rule of Surf Fishing is one that should be followed devoutly: "No strikes, no fish; change spots, not flies!"

While fish of many types can be found virtually anywhere along the troughs, some feature that might concentrate them should be sought out. Generally, those are detected by a change in the water's hue. For instance, a small, submerged point extending seaward through the troughs will appear as a light-colored discontinuation of the darker water of the troughs, and will serve as a blocking element for predators herding prey. I found a gang of reds one late-winter morning at the point where a trough "pinched out" (an oil-field term used for a type of discontinuation of a geologic stratum) and had some excellent sight-fishing for them.

Another anomaly found in the natural surf is a tidal cut through the beach. These are not actual "passes"—which themselves are also good spots, especially on a falling tide, but which require very cautious wading practices—but are more like drains from interior areas. As they can be found on the mainland, they appear to be more common on barrier islands.

While the series of troughs and bars—and any discontinuation of them—is usually best when worked on the rising tide, tidal cuts emptying into the surf shine best when it's falling. So do simple washouts through the first bar: avenues for both prey and predator between the first and second troughs.

Look for color changes in the water, understand their significance, and use them to your benefit. Again, dark is deep, light is shallow.

Many people would not consider altered surf to be as pleasing to look at as natural surf. One probable reason for that is they have never experienced the action it can produce! One of the finest examples of alteration, though, is recalled quite fondly every time I look at the painting of it that hangs in a sacred spot on a wall of Sandy Herrington's houseboat in the Venice Marina (see accommodations on p. 207).

The picture is of a shrimp trawler that washed ashore and wrecked on Breton Island—the southernmost of the Chandeleur chain—during a storm many years ago. Over time the island shifted as the type is prone to do; eventually it receded from the boat, and the waters around it became a favorite spot for Sandy's late husband and my dear friend, Capt. Bill. Before Hurricane Georges in 1998 created shoal waters around the boat, some fine specks had fallen to my flies and those of friends there. Now it is almost unrecognizable, and a winter storm—or something worse—is destined to soon send it to oblivion. But in its time it was surely a fine alteration—and one strangely appealing to look at—in the Breton Island surf.

Still, there is a lot more to this area than Breton Island, and there are man-made alterations much more common than wrecked boats. One is a seawall made of boulders and positioned parallel to the beach and a short distance offshore of it. Its purpose is to prevent beach erosion, and in a few instances the structures have even resulted in rebuilding badly eroded shorelines. Some of the older ones may have water that is too shallow on their shoreward sides for most species, but there is usually ample water located just offshore from these.

Rock jetties are another fairly common alteration of the surf. Some protect the channel of major shipping routes through the seashore; others are created as another form of beach stabilization. While channel-protecting jetties usually hold the largest fish, the smaller types found along beaches are most easily worked, and a reasonable double-haul can often cover their entire length.

The various "rock piles" are highly popular with predators because prey species use these for protection in the otherwise rather featureless surf. Piers don't offer that degree of protection, but virtually any form of solid structure found in the surf can hold fish. Find something that fits this category, and fish it.

Appropriate flies for the surf, in most cases, are pretty basic. Size 1/0 Clouser Minnows in chartreuse and white—and in size 2/0 when big jacks and bull reds are about—are time proven. Same-sized Deceivers in green and white or green and yellow are good choices for calm surf. (And if you have any clue as to what type of fly a pompano will strike, I'd sure like to know about it!) During late winter and spring, and again in late summer and fall—the time of beasts as well as specks—a 9- or 10-weight outfit is advisable; during summer scaling down to an 8-weight is a reasonably safe practice, though it's only necessary for getting a little more action out of the fish.

The normal setting when fly fishing the Louisiana surf is quite unlike the image of it some folks might have, erroneously based on pictures of it being done on some storm-ravaged northeastern coast. Here, the calmer the weather the better, an intermediate sink-tip line on your 9-weight outfit is just fine, and you'll only need a slicker or waders during the cool months—and a stripping basket is much more of a hindrance than a help! (However, you will need plenty of SPF 30 sunscreen, a hat that shields your eyes and protects the top of your ears, polarized sunglasses, and either tennis shoes or "flats boots.") Still, it's just as exciting—and at least as rewarding—especially when the fish you encounter are either prime table fare or are better measured in feet than inches! And in the calm, promising half-light of daybreak, with the beach bunnies still fast asleep in their concrete warrens and the ocean wrapping itself around you, you will discover a lot more appeal to fishing here than just the catching part.

And you can take that to the bank!

The Trophies

Most of Louisiana's fly-catchable specks will run on the smallish side—generally 6-weight material. Trophies of 6 pounds or more are relatively rare, though their numbers are increasing due to the cessation of commercial gill-netting and the creation of some tight recreational restrictions, especially in southwestern Louisiana. Trophy specks are often found over oysters or clams in large bays and sounds, alongside jetties, and in the surf. The best time for them is typically May through mid-June, though occasional brutes can be found near the seashore throughout summer.

Big specks present angling problems that few other inshore species do. If you want one for the wall, you must follow some well-established rules—and be more than a little lucky.

Primarily, if a big speck even suspects your presence, you won't catch it. If your anchor or trolling motor's prop clicks against an oyster shell or if a soft-drink can falls from the console onto the deck or if your long, early-morning shadow passes across the area that is holding a big one, you still might catch some decent fish, but there will be no trophy from that spot. They are wary to the max, so stealth is paramount.

Big specks eat big prey, so they don't feed as often as the smaller ones do. Finding one of these relatively rare fish when it's hungry—and, in the process, not inadvertently spooking it—is no mean accomplishment and demands a healthy dose of good luck. Then, should you be fortunate enough to come across such a fish without alerting it, you must be prospecting for it with a fly large enough to tweak its interest, a practice few would-be trophy-hunters follow. Finally, the fish has a very fragile mouth, so a big speck—which resists capture much more violently than the smaller ones do—has a considerably greater chance of slipping the hook than something like a redfish.

Most of Louisiana's best trophy spots have a characteristic that tends to concentrate the fish—the more of them there are in a limited area, the more likely the fly will be seen by a hungry speck.

The surf is the first "best spot" for a trophy. Here, the biggest biggest specks are usually found in areas of maximum local depth. Many of the troughs found here can hold a lot of filleting-sized fish during the prime months of spring, but the larger specks tend to prefer the security of the deepest water around, even though that may not be more than 4 feet or so and over a relatively small area. These deeper pockets are characterized by the darkest-hued water. The pockets are normally most productive on the rising tide, and they are almost always most likely to give up a trophy speck during periods of low light—as during the very early morning. Still, that is entirely dependent on how secure the big momma feels, and she won't feel at all secure if she senses abnormal disturbances in the water.

The second rule you must follow to catch a big speck from the surf is to practice strict antisocial behavior. Pete's Second Law of Southern Surf Fishing is "The amount of racket in the water increases exponentially with the number of its occupants." This rule was created on the foundation of my never having caught a big speck, nor have I seen a big speck caught by anyone else—on fly or conventionally—with another angler within 50 yards. Fish alone—way alone! As with redfish, usually the best time for fishing for trophy specks in the surf is on the rising tide. Notably, all four of my largest fly-caught specks were taken from barrier-island surf.

Another prime spot for a trophy speck is a jetty or seawall. These, like the small, deep pockets in the surf, also serve to concentrate the fish, and they are much easier to read. Generally, they are best worked from a boat with a bow-mounted trolling motor. Maintain the boat at about 40 feet from the jetty, cast the fly at an angle to the edge of the seawall, then combine various count-downs with various retrieve rates until you get a strike. Class III or IV sinking-tip lines are best here. Combine one with a big and heavy Clouser-type fly, and you'd best be using a 9- or 10-weight outfit—same song, same dance.

While trophy specks never come easily, several places along the Louisiana Coast offer a fly fisherman a very good chance at one of these prizes.

That might seem like an awfully abbreviated description of one of the best ways there is to catch a trophy speck on a fly, but it is a pretty basic technique. The best tide is usually incoming, the best water depth seems to be around 10 feet—and that can occur at any given point along any given jetty, so you must seek it out with a depth recorder. But all that isn't nearly as important as being able to fish the thing in the first place! A big heaving groundswell—or a steep chop driven by a stiff onshore wind—makes fly fishing a jetty virtually impossible. Fish them when conditions allow you to. (A friend got a 7¼-pounder off the South Pass seawall one fine May morning a while back—on my rod, my fly, my time, my tide, my wind . . . well, anytime anyone gets a speck that big on a fly, he deserves the credit.)

The last "best place" for a fly fisherman to catch a trophy speck is Louisiana's Calcasieu Lake, south of the city of Lake Charles. Unlike the two places I mentioned, it is not characterized as being or containing a concentrating element; it's included here because it has historically produced so many big specks for conventional anglers. It has also produced several fly-caught trophies for my good friend, Capt. Jeff Poe (see his contact info on p. 149), which includes the fly-caught state-record 9.31 pounder! And that is a grand trophy!

Normally, the best techniques here are working small, fresh slicks caused by feeding fish, chasing birds diving on bait which has been driven to the surface by feeding fish, and blind-casting over reefs. Sinking-tip lines are again best for the large Clouser- and Deceiver-types, which are as productive here as anyplace else. Also, in appropriate conditions poppers can be a great bet for a trophy, as conventional surface lures account for large numbers of the lake's big specks every year. A floating braided monocore line is best for working poppers, with those in size 1/0 and 4 to 5 inches long being just about right to tempt a big one. Some of the favored spots in the lake are Turner's Bay, Nine-Mile Cut, the Washout, the reefs around the "Engine," the old Cameron jetty, and Commissary Point (see the chapter on the Lake Charles area).

There are a lot of guides working Calcasieu Lake. They, in combination with the sport fishermen who also fish it, can cause the lake to be become pretty crowded, especially on weekends. If you want a trophy, do as you would in the surf and avoid the crowds. Fish on weekdays during the prime times of spring and fall, and stay away from other boats.

Also, Calcasieu Lake's salinity and clarity is directly affected by runoff from the Calcasieu River. Typically those conditions are most likely to become adverse during late winter and early spring—a time when the fishing can be excellent provided the water is reasonably clear and salty. Also, a tropical system may dump a lot of rain onto the river's drainage during summer and early autumn, and that runoff can shoot down the action for several days. If you decide to make a trip to the lake and one of those events occurs shortly before your visit, contact your guide or Hebert's Marina (see the contact information in the section on Lake Charles in Destinations), and if conditions are indeed marginal or expected to become so, try to reschedule your trip. Trophy specks don't like muddy, fresh water!

What they do like—anywhere they are found—are big flies! Since big specks usually hold near bottom over shells (where those are present), size 2/0 Clouser Minnows around 4 inches long and heavily dressed in either chartreuse-over-white or dark-green-over-chartreuse-over-white make good choices, riding hook-point up and imitating mullet and menhaden, which are primary protein for the specks. Those flies have accounted for several 6-pound-plus fish. Besides the snag-resistance of the fly's inverted hook, its large profile offers good visibility in the often rather turbid water found across much of the Louisiana Coast. And the Clouser-type, even with its weighted eyes and its large and heavily dressed configuration, is more easily cast than similar-sized Whistlers and SeaDucers (at least it is for me). Still, with the size 2/0 Deceiver types in green-and-white or olive-with-red flash material, which can work well when the fish are not hugging oysters, it will take a big stick—9- or 10-weight—to cast them. With these flies a floating line with a clear intermediate-sinking tip is again a good choice. A leader with a total length of 8 feet is adequate in all but the clearest times; the butt section should be tapered with 3 feet of 40-pound and 2 feet of 30-pound mono, then about 1½ feet of 16-pound-class tippet, and finally a foot of 30-pound for a shocker. In that last position, fluorocarbon can be a definite advantage in clear conditions but if you make a habit of using it in all occasions, you'll never get caught short!

One last thing about trophy specks. Remember their tender mouths as they thrash the surface, jump about, or go tearing off toward the horizon. Fight them with a firm but gentle hand and with no jerky motions (or jerky drag from your reel!). If you're fishing the surf, do not attempt to grab the fish when the fight is over—beach it! Anywhere else, net it—headfirst, if you please. Then, if you do not intend to have it mounted, take a couple of quick pictures and slide it back into the water. The pictures of the event, set in a nice frame and hanging from a wall in your den, will remind you that you accomplished one of the—if not "the"—most difficult inshore fly-fishing tasks along the entire northern Gulf Coast.

And that's something yours truly has yet to accomplish.

CHAPTER 3

Flounder

Of the numerous types of flatfishes inhabiting Louisiana waters, only one is important to recreational fishermen: the southern flounder *(Paralichthys lethostigma)*. Inshore they can be found in water of virtually all depths, with 5 feet or less being appropriate for fly fishermen and shallower almost always being better. As creatures of the shallows, it might seem weird that, unlike specks and redfish—which spawn in late spring, summer, and early autumn quite near the coastline—flounder do their thing in late autumn and early winter in the deep waters of the open Gulf.

Interestingly, a recent and rather in-depth biological, sociological, and economic study has revealed that while most folks love to eat them, only about 3 percent of all recreational fishermen actually target flounder. Most of these fish—as they have been in my case—are taken as incidentals, and incidentally, a good portion of the 3 percent who make directed efforts toward them do so with gigs.

I learned that—plus a whole lot more—during the two years I served as the recreational fishing representative on a task force of the Gulf States Marine Fisheries Commission, whose purpose was to establish an interjurisdictional management plan for these fish. Some of that information won't do anybody a whit of good in helping them catch these fish, whether they try intentionally or catch them incidentally while fishing for other types. But some of it—along with my experiences with flounder—will help, and let me tell you this: if you like fried flounder fillets with creamed white beans and rice as much as I do, you will be thankful for every one of them that you catch!

Oh yes, you can catch them on flies intentionally if you work the right water at the right time. And since southern flounder are common, grow fairly large, and occur in many places, the following information is intended for use in fishing for them.

Southern flounder are quite tolerant of salinities ranging from 0 ppt (that's freshwater) to 35 ppt (Gulf of Mexico water) and even inhabit the hypersaline waters of the upper Laguna Madre in south Texas. In being so adaptive they can be found in some pretty diverse settings throughout most of the year—coastal rivers, fresh marshes, brackish bays, and high-salinity sounds, for instance. While they can be quite fly-fishable in several of those settings (as proven by my accidental catches of them in the past), they are usually scattered. However, during early autumn they begin to stage toward the seashore in preparation for their offshore spawning migration. Throughout the first half of the season their numbers increase rapidly in this area; that, in turn, increases the chances for a fly fisherman to catch them.

Flounder are highly predatory creatures and will feed actively as well as from self-concealed ambush—the method most people associate with them. While feeding can readily take place in water of some depth where fly fishing is a chore at best, there are two "patterns," if you will, that bring them into easy reach of fly fishermen: shallows and current. Combine the two and you have a prime area.

There are two specific types of location where that combination commonly occurs. The first is in shallow tidal cuts—either through outer salt marshes or through the seashore itself—on the falling tide. The second is in deltaic areas where a river's discharge through small, deep passes flows out across a shallow washout in a pass's shoreline and into a nearby bay, sound, or the Gulf.

Actually, the first scenario can be productive during much of the year, though more fish will usually be found there in autumn. If the cut is through marsh grass, it is often best to anchor your boat just off one of the points defining the cut's mouth. Make your casts "up and across" the current—which should be flowing toward you—and work your fly with moderate-paced short strips. On that note, do not think your fly must slowly bump bottom in order to attract these fish; if they can see it as it passes above them—whether they are half-buried on bottom in ambush or actively swimming about in search of prey—they will strike it. The shallow water in these

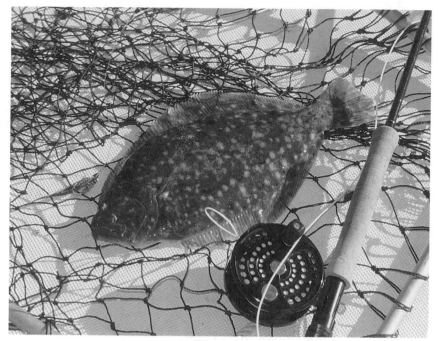

southern flounder (Paralichthys lethostigma)

settings—and through a marshy backside of a barrier island—makes it easy for them to do just that.

In working a shallow cut through the seashore, it is often best to beach your boat nearby and either wade or walk to it. Do not enter the deeper water of the cut—say, knee-deep or a bit more—or you will end up stepping on the fish instead of catching them, and need I say flounder don't especially like being stepped on. Neither do stingrays, which also feed in the current-swept shallows! Always slide your feet rather than take regular steps when wading this type of water.

Seashore "washouts"—which is a more accurate description as they can be quite wide, though still very shallow—need not be exclusively worked "up and across" the current. Simply cover the deepest water (it will be in narrow "guts" and appear slightly darker than that alongside it), and always be alert for any fish striking minnows or shrimp on the surface or even flipping completely out of the water. After either of those instances occurs, the fish will often hold in the same spot, so a quick cast to it is a very good bet.

The washouts through the shorelines of small deltaic passes are my favorites for autumn flounder. Locating them is as simple as noticing current

Southern flounder are seldom targeted in Louisiana waters, but in the right settings they provide a good opportunity for fly fishermen.

flowing from the pass through a break in its shoreline, then determining that the water in the break is shallow by its hue, which will be lighter than that in the pass.

Anchor your boat on one side of the washout, setting the anchor in the deep water of the pass and allowing the boat to swing back with the current until the outboard hits the edge—or "lip"—of the shallows. That will prevent your boat from becoming stuck on bottom during a falling tide of good range; it will also prevent the boat from swinging into the shallows and spooking any nearby fish.

Here, because of the boat's positioning, your casts must be made either cross-current or directly down-current. Except during the strongest falling tides, that is no problem, as the water is shallow enough for the fish to see the fly without it having to sink very deeply. However, even though flounder use the current to feed, they are not creatures of flowing water like, say, striped bass—and specks to a lesser extent—are, and hard-falling tides in spots like this are a hindrance rather than a help to them. If possible, when you fish deltaic passes try to time your trip to coincide with the rising tide. That will slow the river's current somewhat, allowing the fish to feed more efficiently.

There are a couple of things you should know about presenting to a flounder in these settings, even though it will be done in a "blind" fashion. First of all, strikes seldom occur while simply allowing the fly to swing down-current across the shallows; most will come as it is being retrieved. Second, missed strikes can be successfully followed up by allowing the fish a few moments to settle down, then retrieving the fly over the exact spot where the miss occurred. Also, I recall a fish I once lost near the boat, which apparently laid up at the point where it had slipped the hook, soon forgot something rather unusual had just happened to it, and a few minutes later slammed the fly again. And it did so at exactly the same point where I had lost it! Take heed!

Flounder can, and will, eat comparatively large prey; a 3-pounder I once caught had a 6-inch mullet in its throat. Nevertheless, during autumn killi-fish can make up a large part of their diets in many areas. That favored little baitfish can be matched closely enough with size 1/0 Clouser Minnows (also see One *Ugly* Fly! on page 231). They need not be heavily weighted, since even in the current, shallow water, which offers the best fly fishing, does not require they sink very deeply. Chartreuse-and-white versions, as well as those in solid purple, are autumn favorites.

A floating line is all you should need, and a 9-foot leader with a 12- or 16-pound class tippet and a foot of 30-pound mono or fluorocarbon for resistance to fraying by a flounder's raspy teeth is recommended. Finally, I suggest using an 8- or 9-weight outfit. Flounder taste a lot better than they fight, but redfish like shallow water with current, too, and autumn is a fine time for incidentally sticking a big one while intentionally fishing for flounder.

Give it a try. Most likely, it will probably be something different, and fun, for you—working a fly across current-swept shallows, and if you follow the patterns it should lead to some mighty fine eating.

CHAPTER 4

Sheepshead

There aren't too many really "testy" types of fish—like permit—to be found along the northern Gulf Coast. Redfish can be easily spooked on occasion, and every now and then one will actually rush a fly only to refuse it. Frequently, though, reds seem to be eaten up with an acute case of the stupids and will fall all over themselves in an attempt to strike a variety of patterns. And that's not really all that bad, considering "fly-catching" is much more fun than just fly-fishing.

Specks, too, will usually strike, as will cobia (who are usually fearless as well as mentally impaired), and I guarantee that if you let a flounder see a purple Clouser Minnow, he will eat it. Tripletail can be somewhat of an exception when they're in one of their tentative moods, but, when you get right down to it, usually the hardest part of catching fish hereabouts is finding them—well, that's if you leave sheepshead out of the equation.

Now I've never laid an eye on a permit, but I've read a lot about them, and they seem to be quite similar to sheepshead in one specific aspect: If you leave the bait bucket at home, you can have fits enticing either of them to strike! There's one big difference between them, actually there are quite a few, but one that's most important is that sheepshead are much more plentiful throughout their range than permit are in theirs.

And sheepshead do have their advocates. The fish is a popular target in some areas along the northern Gulf coast, as its fillets are firm, white, and quite tasty (though converting a whole fish into fillets has been the ruination

sheepshead (Archosargus probatocepahlus)

of many a good knife!). They are tough to clean! They are also tough on the end of a fishing line, resisting capture about like you'd imagine a 5-pound bluegill might.

Besides those admirable characteristics, sheepshead can also be found in a wide variety of settings. Rock jetties, oyster reefs, bridge and pier pilings, and sunken boats are all prime locations as they provide the fish with one of its primary sources of sustenance: barnacles.

I've never been able to create a fly that adequately depicted a barnacle on a piling, so I've never intentionally fly fished for sheepshead around those types of structure. However, sheepshead also love the shallows, be they soft marsh or firm barrier island sandbars, where they feed on small shrimp, crabs, clams, and the like, often in the shallowest water that will float them. It is there that they present themselves as a fly-fishing target of the first order— no, let me rephrase that: a fly-casting target of opportunity . . . sort of like a permit. . . .

I'd give some pretty good odds that within the established parameters of the sport of sight-fishing with flies, there have been more permit caught than sheepshead. Of course, one reason for that may be that most anglers who have tried to catch the jailhouse fish (a common name due to the fish's black stripes) in this way were smart enough to quit early and move on to more re-alistic goals—like yellowfin tuna. Whatever the case, while practicing the sight-fishing exercise I've caught exactly three. And, by the way, broken two perfectly good fly rods in the process.

That's probably not particularly relevant here, though I feel I must say both of them had accounted for redfish exceeding 14 pounds. What may be interesting is the fact that all three fish—each in the 2- to 3-pound class—were tailing nicely on shallow, grassy flats, all three were misinterpreted as being reds, and all three hit poppers like there would be no tomorrow!

Unfortunately (besides the broken rods), all that took place very early in my northern-Gulf fly-fishing career and it left me thinking that sheepshead would occasionally take a fly—sort of like a permit. And on the occasions when I specifically sought them out, I discovered they were also spooky and finicky, especially in clear, shallow water—sort of like a permit. In fact, it reached the point where they became pretty aggravating, and since I knew from my experiences with the three that they would destroy the popper (and possibly my new rod, too) should they ever choose to eat one again, I began making a conscientious effort to avoid them.

Many years later it came to pass that I would began writing about my fishing experiences, and it wasn't too long thereafter that my editors began to complain about my lack of variety—I guess some people actually do get tired of reading articles about fly fishing for reds. Anyway, one day it occurred to me that the ever-present and intentionally ignored sheepshead would make a fine topic—if I could catch some and do it in an exciting and challenging way. Hmm . . . I thought, how about sight-fishing for them on the flats with a 4-weight outfit, 4-pound class tippet, and bonefish flies. . . .

There have been times I would have sold my soul to the bad guy to have had the conditions I met on the first morning of my quest: slick calm, bright sunlight, and low, clear water. The flat I had in mind had been loaded with them on a recent redfishing trip, and I was sure the #6 pink Crazy Charlie—delivered with the precision and delicacy the light outfit provided—would adequately ring their chimes.

It didn't—even with a 10-foot leader and the 4-pound point! And no shocker! Of the possibly two dozen fish to which I showed the fly, most immediately spooked, a few never acknowledged the fly's presence, and a couple followed it a short distance only to turn away. Then I got sidetracked by some reds and had a very nice day, taking five to just over 6 pounds on the sheepshead-rejected fly.

Stuff like that tends to mess with my mind, especially after the second glass of after-supper sour mash. Sheepshead shouldn't be that difficult to catch on flies, I thought. When I am out on a meat-run with my casting rod, they're always thumping my trusty chartreuse spinnerbait. Chartreuse? Hmm . . .

Here, I must offer an explanation. For some incomprehensible reason, that particular color is extremely appealing along the Gulf Coast. Freshwater and saltwater species alike (as well as some Cajun women I've known) simply cannot resist the color. And I did have some chartreuse Crazy Charlies I had purchased long ago for some forgotten reason. Two days later I was back on the same flat. Conditions were again near ideal, and again the water was thick with sheepshead. Okay, those of you who are enamored with the wiles of the permit, take note.

I maintain a very low profile, casting while sitting on the bow's swivel-seat. Distances range from 40 to 50 feet—the fish are unaware of my presence. I place the fly 4 feet ahead of one—and it spooks; 4 feet in front of another, and it couldn't care less. One is tailing, its nose in the roots of a clump of grass. I put the fly right on him, he quickly turns toward it, then loses interest—in chartreuse!

I swap the Charlie for a Horror—and could have saved myself the effort. Four-weight line-shadow spooks them; the impact of skimpily dressed size 6 flies spooks them—or it doesn't, and when they decide to take a look, their attention span proves to be very short.

I cast to fish that are tailing, fish that are swimming along with apparent purpose, and fish that seem to be just sitting there doing nothing—all to no avail. Finally, at a total loss, I gave up and sought out the reds, taking six of them to 7 pounds and again on the flies the sheepshead had scorned—or panicked from!

Later that evening I felt an urge to experience one of those rowdy surface strikes that reds are somewhat infamous for and speculated a small popper. In some slightly deeper water I misinterpreted a shadow, made a decent cast at it, and would you believe one of those spooky, snooty, striped, snaggle-toothed sons of bitches of tried to obliterate the popper!

I didn't get my story. The fish managed to slip the hook—a very uncharacteristic maneuver that left me without the pictures necessary to accompany the prose. The editors require that. But at least I didn't break the rod. . . .

Anyway, in case you are looking for something "testy" to try your skills on and can't afford too many trips to Belize to try for permit, I highly recommend you give sheepshead a try. For sure, all across the northern Gulf Coast you will get a lot more shots at them than at their counterparts in a more exotic locale. But I sure wouldn't cast bonefish flies at them.

Bream bugs!

Even as popular as sheepshead are in some local circles, there really isn't much more to say about fly-fishing for them. Since my "quest" I have taken a few others, all while blind-casting for specks with Clouser Minnows. Some friends have taken a few others in the same fashion, and I wouldn't be surprised if some enterprising guide somewhere along the Gulf Coast has invested enough time and effort to come up with a technique (or a fly?) that is more consistently effective than what has been tried in the past.

If you simply must catch a 'head on a fly, then make a run offshore in April, find a petroleum platform in 20 to 40 feet or so of water, and drop a size 1/0 Clouser Minnow—color shouldn't matter—down alongside one of its legs. Use a 12-weight outfit with a sinking line, a 20-pound-class tippet, and an 80-pound fluorocarbon shocker. Once you hook one you will know why you need the heavy stuff. Sheepshead don't hold tightly to those pilings for nothing; they may be out there at this time to spawn, but they still need to eat—barnacles! Get him coming quickly or he will cut you off! Figure one fish per fly, so bring along plenty. And though as I mentioned they are excellent table fare, they are mortal hell to clean, as they come equipped with lots of sharp edges and spines, so handle them with care.

CHAPTER 5

Tripletail

I t would be hard to imagine someone who is an ardent saltwater fisher but who doesn't have his or her own particular "thing."

Most of us take advantage of seasonal opportunities and the different creatures that are involved. Indeed, I know of no one who fishes for a single species or does not fish at all. Still, most of us do have our favorites and our favorite techniques for catching them, and some of us have gotten pretty good at it—our "thing." My thing is fly fishing for tripletail, and after many years of practicing the exercise at every available opportunity, I have gotten pretty fair at it. The reason why I am not pretty *good* at it is the same reason why I enjoy it so much: it is the temperament of the fish.

If you show any given tripletail a fresh 36/40-count shrimp impaled on a jig-head that is suspended a foot or so beneath a weighted popping cork, he *will* eat it—even if he tries to eat the cork first! But if you show the same tripletail a fly, there's no telling how he will respond to it. That makes him much different from most other popular fly-fishing targets found along the northern Gulf Coast—which normally do their utmost to quickly ingest any decently presented fly, and it is the trait that so endears him to me.

Besides being so entertaining in their appraisals of your offerings—and yes, the best method for taking them is sight-fishing—they pull very nicely, occasionally jump, and simply can't be beat when filleted, skinned, cut into small chunks, coated in a beer batter, and fast-fried! They seem to have no average size; most you will come across will range between 2 and 15 pounds. However, fish much larger are by no means rare; the top tripletail in several states bordering the Gulf are in the 40-pound class. They are commonly found in large bays and sounds and in depths of 6 feet or more out past the rim of the Continental Shelf. And although size and possession limits on them are almost nonexistent throughout their range in our waters, and though they are by no means rare, catching enough of them to get a decent stink out of a skillet can be a real problem. Indeed and obviously suffering from the same affliction that plagues most other saltwater anglers, I both worked and fished in waters inhabited by them for almost 25 years before I caught my first one. The reason? I simply wasn't looking for them.

These fish have an affinity for literally anything at the water's surface. While they can be found around petroleum platforms and channel-marking piling clusters, better potential lies around flotsam, both random and that which has been collected along a current line. And while they do inhabit large bays and sounds, the nearshore and offshore waters of the Gulf are usually the best choice.

For sure, tripletail are often found holding to random flotsam, and a big log or patch of various types of grasses can provide for some great action, as they are found in groups (Not schools!) almost as often as they are found alone. However, normally the most fish will be found scattered along a current line. In any case the fish will look like giant crappie. When they are upright in the water they appear mottled brownish; when they are lying on their sides they seem starkly white, and I have no clue as to why or how that works!

Most folks who venture offshore will likely cut a current line on their ways out and back. Some of those may be quite obvious; others may be vague with little current, little associated trash, and with little if any change in the water's color across them, but all can hold tripletail.

Upon encountering a current line, begin moving along it on the side and in the direction that offers the best subsurface visibility and at a distance that does not impair that visibility but will prevent the boat from spooking the fish. On that note, if hull-slap noises are excessive in that manner, then reverse your direction, even though that might make it more difficult to see the fish. Also, should you come upon a relatively large piece of flotsam—and this goes for the random stuff as well as that on a current line, if fish are not immediately apparent, take a few moments to allow one that was not initially visible to move into sight along the flotsam's edge.

tripletail (Lobotes surinamensis)

When you locate one and make your cast at it, you can expect one of these responses.

On a solo trip offshore I came upon a garbage sack with a school of small baitfish holding tightly beneath it. A very nice 'tail was patrolling the perimeter of the sack, and it immediately ate the fly on the first cast to it. That's the response you'd prefer.

A friend and I were working a lovely grass-packed current-line when we came upon a good one. Just as I was making my cast to it, the fish left the line and began swimming away at a good clip just beneath the surface across open water. In hot pursuit, I made three casts to it—all quite long and amazingly accurate—without generating any response whatsoever. The fourth cast, made with very little hope but again with uncharacteristic precision, was immediately taken. That response does not occur very often!

A mediocre specimen we once found sniffing the bottom of a cardboard Coca-Cola carton refused to even look at three time-proven patterns presented to it on a total of at least two dozen casts! That response occurs all too often!

The "competition factor" often results in strikes—but not always. A pair, initially lying on their sides beneath a lost life-jacket, followed the fly for 40-odd feet before turning away at boatside. Both then returned to the life jacket and would not respond to subsequent casts. That's another typical response.

Tripletail provide a real fly-fishing challenge, and there are plenty of them in Louisiana's nearshore waters to check out your abilities!

On the other hand, when a pair of real beauties was suddenly discovered emerging from beneath a thick patch of grass no more than 15 feet distant, the fly—the very same fly—was taken instantly! Go figure!

Instances like those characterize the reactions a tripletail will usually have toward a fly. The aggressive fish need no discussion at this point; however, the finicky ones and those that show no interest in the fly do.

First of all, whenever a tripletail is encountered around flotsam, it is best to assume it will be a finicky one; if it's aggressive, you will know it right away—likewise if it's one of the "couldn't care less" types. Since these fish are not overly spooky, the fly should be placed just beyond and just ahead of it and the retrieve begun immediately. That will prevent the fish from getting an initial good look at the fly and will often result in a quick "reflex strike." Generally speaking, the longer the fish follows the fly, the less likely a strike becomes.

Let's assume either a particular fish is one of the finicky types or your cast was slightly off-target, and the fish is now following the fly. Your initial retrieve consisted of short, moderately paced strips; now, knowing that the odds of a strike decrease proportionately with time, you must do something different quickly!

In witnessing the fish's response to the changes you make in your retrieve, you will see firsthand what not to do next time, what has no effect on the fish at all, and what just might inspire it to strike. Take heed, though, that each technique can have a different effect on different fish. It's all a little complex, isn't it? That's why I get such a boot out of catching the rascals!

The first variation is to begin to barely "tick" the fly. In other words, impart only the slightest twitches on it. When this is done properly, all you will notice is the fly remaining basically in the same plane of the water column; you will not be able to see movement in it, but there will be just enough for the fish to detect and maybe tweak its interest. Maybe . . .

If it doesn't, try stopping the retrieve entirely. If the fish maintains some interest and follows the fly as it slowly sinks, you may lose sight of it before it decides to strike. Therefore, when you stop the retrieve you should remove any slack line hanging between the rod's tip and the water by dropping the tip to the waterline and gently taking in the slack. That will allow you to feel the subtle thump when the fish takes the fly, and sometimes the technique actually works, though it should be considered a last-ditch effort because once you stop and you resume the retrieve, you most likely will send the fish scurrying away. In any case, do not increase the speed of the initial retrieve.

If somewhere in the middle of all this the fish loses interest and begins to retire back to its floating cover, do not make a quick follow-up cast at it. Instead, allow it a few moments to forget what just happened while you regain your composure. Here, you might consider changing flies to a smaller version of the same pattern—that has worked on several occasions after an initial refusal, but do not speculate an entirely different pattern.

Actually, there is an exception to that rule. On calm days a popper makes a very good follow-up fly. It is also effective on first casts, and friends, watching—and hearing—a tripletail strike one is lifetime guaranteed to ring your chimes! Just ask Jose Wejebe, who caught his first 'tail on a popper during a trip with me a few years back. Retrieve it moderately slowly with soft pops—again, as close to the front end of the fish as possible—and you'll see!

Gear that might seem a bit heavy for most of the tripletail you'll encounter is recommended, with 9- or 10-weight outfits being preferred. There is one really good reason for that: The chance for a big cobia to suddenly appear, especially on a grass-laden current line. When one does, there is normally not enough time to swap a lighter outfit for a heavier one before the fish disappears.

Because of the cobia potential in many areas where tripletail are found, an appropriate reel should have a quality drag system and hold at least 150 yards of 30-pound backing, plus a floating tarpon-taper mono-core line. That type aids in loading the rod for the quick and fairly short casts that are the norm and that must be made accurately. A 9-foot leader tapered to 16-pound class and with a foot of 30-pound for fray resistance is sufficient; fluorocarbon in the shocker position just might convert a finicky fish into an aggressive one.

Tripletail eat a variety of prey, and small crabs are a favorite. In fact, the first one I ever caught was taken on a piece of cracked crab. So when I began fly fishing for them I bought a bunch of crab patterns. Those resulted in only a complete waste of perfectly good dollars. I have heard that those patterns are effective; perhaps I simply didn't know how to present them. Whatever, stick with flies until someone shows you differently.

Since the fish's diet is so diverse, attractor patterns are recommended. Deceivers and SeaDucers—both with the tail-feathers trimmed a bit—and bend-backs in sizes 2/0, 1/0, and 1 are good choices. Color combinations of green and chartreuse, green and white, and green and yellow work well. They should not be weighted in any fashion, and they—and a couple of size 1/0 poppers—should be tied with a mono weed-guard encircling the hook. That is imperative, since frequently you must cast across a piece of flotsam in order to gain the interest of a fish that refuses to respond to a fly worked alongside it.

Along the Gulf Coast tripletail offer a very viable fly-fishing opportunity from roughly mid-May through September. Just remember that in order to catch them that way, you have to be looking for them! They are indeed a challenge to a fly fisherman, and if you don't let them rattle you, they are great fun. Give them a try; who knows, fly fishing for them just might become your thing, too.

CHAPTER 6

King Mackerel

T alk about an attitude adjustment! Up until a few years back king mackerel rated well down on the list of my favorite saltwater fishing targets. I had caught quite a few over the years—drift-fishing with dead cutlassfish, live-lining white trout and blue runners, and trolling Magnum Rapalas and Russellures—and I had a fairly respectable specimen to my credit. But fishing for them in those fashions never really rang my chimes, and I've never cared for eating them.

Still don't, but since I began fly fishing for them, their esteem has increased tremendously, and when the opportunity to catch them on flies arises, I'll head out after them in a New York minute! Here's why.

Most often the strike is unlike any experienced with other fish. There is no solid thump, no sudden weight. One moment I am wrapped in total concentration on the retrieve of the fly, the next moment all the loose shooting line has shot into the Gulf, and in half a heartbeat I stand in shocked amazement at how quickly my backing is disappearing!

The fish's first run could be compared to that of a bonefish, but I am not fishing with bonefish gear. The outfit is a 12-weight, and its reel's drag is set at fully five pounds. And still the fish tears away—"Smoker" is indeed an appropriate nickname for these fish, not because that's the best way to cook them but because it's what they can make a less than suitable reel do during that first run! Finally—though actually only scant seconds from the time I first felt him—he slows, then stops 100 yards distant. Then the work begins.

Two shorter runs—almost as fast as the first—break up the hump-and-pump routine, and then he is at the boat. In reach now, my companion quickly grabs the fish's handle at the base of its tail, and after a pair of vigorous kicks it is slid aboard for unhooking, a couple of quick pictures, and a safe release. It is only a fair one—20 pounds or so, but kings like that are a whale of a lot of fun on a fly rod. And it is quite possible that in a couple of specific spots along the Louisiana Coast, the very next cast could account for one half again as big—or bigger! Super stuff!

In some areas, notably in South Florida, fly fishing for king mackerel has been a fairly popular sport for some time. Invariably it is centered around chumming or chunking, and it is not very "species specific." There's no telling what you might hook, though that might have appeal to some folks. Whatever, it is a productive technique; my friend, Ben Bergeron of Houston, whose 55-pounder presently holds the top spot in the 20-pound-tippet category of the I.G.F.A. fly-fishing records, caught that fish while on a chunking trip out of the Keys.

Some friends and I have tried it in more northern waters without much success, and I wasn't too impressed with the technique. Of course, that could have arisen because we didn't know what we were doing—a common affliction during my "pioneering days." Anyway, there's another way kings can be effectively taken on flies, which, to some of us anyway, is a bit more lively than chunking, and if it is not as productive, then we who've done it could care less! Three or four 20- to 30-pounders in one morning are more than enough for this ol' boy!

The opportunity is created around the combination of a jetty extending seaward into depths of roughly 20 feet or more and the autumn spawning run of the striped mullet. That is not to say kings cannot be taken around jetties on flies during other times of the year; one of my most memorable times with them occurred in July. Nevertheless, autumn is the time of the most fish, the largest fish, and the most consistent action.

The proximity of the fish to the jetty is what governs their fly fishability. Here, the jetty serves not in its usual role as a microcosm of local prey and predators but as a blocking element for the predators. As such, it concentrates both the mullet and the kings in a relatively narrow band of water, thereby making it easier for the fly to be detected than if it had to be cast into more open water. Any fish skyrocketing more than around 50 yards from the jetty only serve as an indication of their general presence in the area. Working them—in my experiences, anyway—is a complete waste of time.

king mackerel (Scomberomorus cavalla)

However, should you notice a few of them raising merry hell within 30 yards or so of the jetty, then you are quite likely to experience the signature of the king mackerel—that first screaming run—very shortly!

Working them with flies requires good teamwork between the angler and the man at the helm. While I have been able to both fly fish and maintain the boat's position with a bow-mounted trolling motor on very infrequent gut-slick days with little current, that practice is really asking for trouble during more normal conditions. It is best to keep the outboard running—at idle if possible—at all times, holding position and slowly moving from one indication of fish to another, then in neutral while casts are being made, and finally moving the boat into open—safer—water after a hook-up. Constantly running the outboard is also safer, allowing for a rapid retreat from the jetty if a rogue swell or the wake of a passing ship demands it, and the kings don't seem to mind it a bit. On most days my outboard is shut down only for lunch and then well offshore of the jetty.

Jetties, seawalls, and breakwaters, which fall within the parameters mentioned earlier, often have two things in common; they are made up of large boulders—frequently granite, and a cross-section of their lateral axis would reveal the shape of a pyramid with its base on the seabed. As a pack of marauding kings drives a school of mullet toward the jetty, the baitfish will be forced upward by the slope of the boulders. Once near the surface, they are trapped by both the rocks and the abrupt cessation of their natural habitat, i.e. water.

Therefore even though your boat may be in 25 to 30 feet of water, your flies can be worked fairly shallow. I prefer to cast mine at between a 30- and 45-degree angle to the rocks—placing it about 6 feet from them, then let the intermediate sinking line settle for about 10 seconds, and then begin the retrieve.

On that note, you cannot take a fly away from a king mackerel—and they like it moving fast! Nevertheless, I will not advocate placing the rod between your upper arm and body to allow you to strip with both hands, as that is an open invitation to have it suddenly transferred from armpit to ocean by the king's strike! Of course, if you need an excuse to buy a new outfit . . .

The strike, which I related earlier, is usually very fast. It can be so fast that within the time from its detection to the point where all your loose fly line is in the water, your rod's tip is near the water, and your reel begins to scream, you discover you neglected to set the hook. (And yes, I have honestly heard a reel—possibly in need of some strategically-placed lubricant, emit sounds like real, honest-to-God screams!) Well buddy, it's too late now!

That happens all too often, and it is the reason why your hooks should be as sharp as you can make them. Still, with hooks that are sharp enough to cut your eye by simply looking at them (well, almost), I am frequently unable to get a good hook-set and have lost roughly half of my fish, usually at the end of their first run. Since my friends seem to suffer from the same affliction, apparently that is simply a part of the exercise.

During that first run—assuming you remembered to lay a wet towel across the trolling motor and any other potential line-grabbers and successfully got the fish on the reel, the rod should be held low and pointed at the fish with very little bend in it. Then, when the work begins, pump him back with short upward strokes of the rod; the big rod bend you see in calendar shots and the like works much more on you than it does on the fish! Keep it low, and keep the heat on him.

The release should be done quickly. While you can slip a small hand-gaff through the fish's lower jaw and then pull it alongside to revive it after it has been unhooked, the gaff could damage its gills. If you choose that option, do it carefully. I prefer to grasp the fish's "handle" with my right hand, then after it quits kicking either cradle its belly just behind its pectoral fins with my left hand. I then either unhook it (or cut the leader) while it is in the water or slide the fish aboard with both hands. To release a fish that is cradled and held at boatside for unhooking, simply push him forward vigorously and turn him loose. A fish that has been boated is best released by sharply thrusting the fish headfirst back into the water, sort of like you were throwing a spear.

A 12-weight outfit is heartily recommended for this opportunity, both for facilitating casting the quite large flies, which are most productive, and for quickly taming the fish. The reel should hold a lot more 30-pound Dacron backing than you would ever imagine necessary, and its drag should be nothing short of the best available—otherwise you will be needing a new reel in very short order! Set the drag at about 25 percent of the class tippet's rating. (A good practice for all occasions!) An intermediate sinking or sinking-tip line and a 9-foot leader tapered to 20-pound class and finished with around 8 inches of 60-pound, single-strand wire should do the job.

A really simple and effective way to work with single-strand wire while fly fishing is to take a piece of it about a foot long, attach the fly to one end with a Haywire twist, and create another Haywire twist in the other end. Your class tippet is then created with the combination Bimini Twist/doubled double-surgeon's loop in one end and a size 3 black interlocking snap on the other end. Then all you have to do is loop one end of the class tippet to the leader's butt section and snap the other end to the wire. It's a simple rig, and it has accounted for kings up to 36 pounds.

Thankfully there is no need to match your flies to a foot-long mullet. However, the best choices are large, bulky, flashy, and tied on size 4/0 hooks—sharp 4/0 hooks! Since a single strike from a king will likely as not mangle the fly, the patterns should be simply created. A good choice is a Clouser-type about 5½ inches long tied with medium brass hourglass eyes. From top to bottom it consists of a half-dozen peacock herls, green bucktail, chartreuse bucktail, and white bucktail, and it is finished with a dozen strands of Krystal Flash running full length on each side. The kings love it!

Kings can provide an excellent big-fish target for fly fishermen. At times—especially during autumn—when they hem a school of mullet up against a jetty, the ensuing madness has to be seen to be believed. Try it; catch some decent conditions and it could be an experience you will not forget!

And the chances of that occurring will increase tremendously if you choose to work the east jetty of the Mississippi River's Southwest Pass in November and early December!

As a staunch southern ultraconservative, I have well-entrenched philosophies on certain stuff and things and shall not waver from them. Since many of you may not share some of those particular points of view, I will not burden you with them, and if you prefer your sour mash with a Coke, that's your business. I like mine with a little water—the way it always has been, and the way it will continue to be.

The jetties at the mouth of the Mississippi River create an ideal setting for a fly fisherman to catch king mackerel, especially during autumn.

As a fly fisherman one of my most steadfast convictions is: "If it's there, fly fish for it." At first thought that might appear to be some pretty liberal politics. Yet a conservative is one who usually does not especially care for changes, and I have no intention whatsoever of changing that philosophy after more than 45 years of fly fishing by it.

During that time it has led to some interesting encounters. Because of them, along with the fact that most have occurred in Louisiana—a state once not too well known for an overabundance of fly-fishing opportunities, much less fly fishermen—I have received some recognition as a pioneer of sorts—hereabouts, anyway.

"Pioneer Pete"—it has a nice ring to it. Nevertheless, I did not set out to become one; it just worked out that way because of my political orientation. Take king mackerel, for instance.

I have never gone very far out of my way to fish for kings. They are present year-round in our waters, and during November and December the biggest of the beasts move in from all over the Gulf to spawn here. Catching them is fun, even on relatively stout trolling gear. The smaller ones—up to 20 pounds or so—rate only as "pests." Most of my share have been taken while trolling for tarpon, a fish held in much higher esteem, and were super-pests—well, not quite as bad as crevalle jacks. And I don't really care for the way kings taste. Still, they are known for giving quite a spirited first run, and many of the more "liberal" types fish for them—and eat them, and as I said, the big ones are fun.

Of course, if you've never caught one, any of them would be fun. . . .

And that's what started the venture into this heretofore-unexplored wilderness. A nephew and his wife from Missouri came down to the Delta for a Thanksgiving visit. Besides seeking to escape winter and overly indulge in great piles of fresh seafood (and nuts to the turkey!), they wanted to fish. Our first trip however was disappointing.

Upon returning to the marina that evening, I ran into my friend, Dave Ballay, and related the day's sad efforts. The next morning I was awakened by his phone call; it seemed his son Brent—who was a charter skipper at the time—had a no-show, wanted to fish, and had a gang of king mackerel hemmed up along the Southwest Pass jetties. Did I think my guests would like to go catch some? So since neither of them had ever caught a king before, we shortly sallied forth.

And a little after noon we returned to the marina, both Dan and son were beat to the bone from all of the kingfish festivities.

At this point it would be expedient for me to explain a bit about just where and what this place is.

Southwest Pass is the main route for major shipping traffic entering and exiting the Mississippi River. In order to preserve adequate depth in the channel for the big ships, the natural banks of the pass were extended well offshore by jetties made of granite boulders. They maintain the river's current—which carries the sediments that would otherwise settle to the bottom and create sandbars—to a point well out to sea where the sediments disperse harmlessly.

Within the river are numerous prey sources—which are often carried in the current past the ends of the jetties where they suddenly find themselves in the realm of great saltwater predators. Within the Gulf are also numerous prey sources that in their travels hither and yon come upon the jetties, find them impassable, and collect there, often in great numbers. For king mackerel—and a variety of other predators—the rocks at Southwest Pass constitute a five-star restaurant.

The first step into this particular wilderness came with the innocent thought that I should have taken my 12-weight outfit along that morning with my guests. Two days after their departure, a weak cold front blew through. That evening—Wednesday—our friendly and reliable (and often rather "liberal") weatherman forecast that Friday would be "The Day."

Down here in the Delta, "The Day" comes when it's still cool (if it's too warm, there is the threat of sea-fog) and the wind is light and variable from northeast to southeast. It is precious time, for there are lots of great fishing opportunities: yellowfin tuna and wahoo off the deep-water platforms—trolling, bull redfish—fly fishing the surf at the Chandeleur Islands, and maybe this time, fly fishing for king mackerel at Southwest Pass. They were there, why not?

At the time, I knew of only two kings having been taken from our waters on flies—both of which were quite small and both caught incidentally to other targets. I knew of no one who had ever intentionally even tried to fly fish for them locally; I knew I never had. But I knew Bubby—a good friend who had fly fished for them in Florida—had chummed. So I called him—radically.

"Hey Bubby, I've found some kings. Do you want to go fly fish for them?"

"You ain't gonna do any goddamn chumming, are you?" he asked.

"No, I guess not."

"How are you gonna catch 'em, then?" Bubby asked.

"Hell, I don't know." I said. "There was a bunch of 'em skyrocketing along the Southwest Pass rocks the other day. Just drift along and cast, I guess—like fishing specks over oysters."

"That might be fun. Got any flies?" he asked.

"No." I said.

"We used big ones—all white."

"Okay, see you Friday at eight."

The only "white" on my tying desk is bucktail and Krystal Flash. I am averse to single-colored saltwater flies—and realize these will probably be the "one fly, one fish" type. So I create a handful of size 4/0 Clouser Minnows—dark green-over-chartreuse-over-white and with lots of flash. Hairy monstrosities, but easy to tie.

Friday was indeed "The Day": the sea was flat, the air was only cool, and there wasn't a cloud in the bright December sky—a fine time to explore a wilderness. A friend is anchored at the end of the jetty and hooked up conventionally when we arrive, but there is not a sign of bait or feeding fish. We begin our first drift a couple of hundred yards up the rocks and a hundred yards out.

And blind-casting size 4/0 Clousers with a 12-weight outfit, by the way, is work, friends! The drift only results in well-fatigued right arms.

Over the VHF, I check with my friend; he was steadily catching them—tag and release. Perhaps we are too far out. I make a circle back to our original starting point, move to within 30 yards of the rocks, and begin another drift—and Bubby is immediately on a fish, only to lose it to a pulled hook moments later. King?

We cast toward the rocks—I am quite contented with reaching out only 50 feet or so—allow about 15 seconds for the sink-tip and fly to settle a bit, and strip like hell. There is no "strike;" one instant I am rapidly stripping in line, the next the line is whistling back through the guides—and I mean whistling!

A little after noon we had caught five to 36 pounds, lost a half-dozen others, and wrecked everything suitable for them in my box. Bubby had extras, but with the same arm being used to blind-cast a 12-weight as well as fight large, strong fish, we decided to quit and go home—the conservative approach. And I must say that our "discovery" was quite self-satisfying.

The next day a friend who I hadn't seen in a while called, said he was in the area and that he would like to come down for a visit. When I mentioned the kings, he responded that he just happened to have a brand-new 12-weight outfit in the car. That's a bit liberal for up-the-country folks!

That night I was able to tie three flies and put together three leaders. The next morning he caught three fish, the largest about 28 pounds—his first kings and his biggest fish on fly.

"Radical!" he said.

That sums it up pretty well.

CHAPTER 7

Close Combat

The previous chapter on king mackerel began to illustrate the big-fish potential that the Louisiana Coast offers fly fishermen. Big fish do a lot of things little fish cannot do—or normally don't do—like destroy tackle. This chapter is dedicated to what I feel is the most crucial time of the contest, the time when your tackle—and the capture of your prize—is most at risk. Take heed, reader, and remember.

You stand on the bow's casting platform, 10-weight in one hand, fly in the other, a short bow of slack between it and the rod's tip, and plenty of shooting line coiled neatly on the deck. As you search beneath the patches of sargasso scattered along the current line, you get that strange, familiar feeling that something is about to happen. It does: a suspicious-looking shadow suddenly transforms into a sizeable cobia. The cast is quick but on target, and the fish strikes without hesitation—and you now wish you had armed yourself with your 12-weight outfit. But the 10—plus the knowledge you have of how to properly fight a big fish with it—has done the job before and does so again. Within 20 minutes the fish—somewhere around 35, you figure—is on the surface near the boat. Now you watch his movements closely to ensure he is indeed whipped and not playing 'possum—a ploy he will sometimes use to lull you into complacency, then tear away unexpectedly. But now you can turn this one's head—he appears to be yours.

If at all possible, you don't want to gaff him. If you do you will risk him destroying the contents of the cockpit once he has been boated—and then he will bleed all over everything! So you instruct your boat-mate to take up the big landing net you recently bought for this exact purpose; the cobia then avoids three of your friend's passes with it. Ready for the contest to come to an end, you tell your friend to go ahead and gaff the fish, but the first pass with it also fails to connect. By now you are concentrating more on catching the fish than fighting it, and in an attempt to draw it a little closer to the boat, you raise the rod tip. The rod then takes on a deep bend, and under the sudden load it snaps just beneath the ferrule: the classic butt-section failure caused by overloading the rod at a short distance. What could you have done to prevent it? After all, a 9-foot fly rod becomes awfully unwieldy when you are trying to maneuver a big fish that is quite close at hand, and most of that unwieldy length is absolutely worthless for applying pressure on the fish at that point!

In all probability if you fish for them long enough (and that doesn't nec-essarily mean over a long period of time!), you will eventually break a rod in close combat with a beast. It's simply the nature of the thing—the fact that a fly rod is designed to cast line instead of a lure (or troll one). As such it is the least efficient fish-fighting tool ever devised by mankind. Still, there are ways to postpone, if not totally eliminate, breaking one.

The first is a mental thing: You must remember that once a large fish is nearby, you—and your fly rod—have just entered the critical stage of the con-test, so maintain your concentration on proper rod-handling techniques.

You can lose that concentration easily. Over a long fight, a "Let's hurry-up-and-get-this-over-with" attitude may arise. I recall an angler involved in a lengthy scrap with a big crevalle jack, and in an attempt to end the battle his fatigue overrode his better judgment. He hauled back on the rod with the fish nearby, and that was that. To be sure, occasionally a big fish will tire you, but don't let the condition of your muscles affect that of your brain!

A 12-weight stick I once knew was broken on what the angler assumed was a "small fish" which was hooked in a melee of king mackerel and big jacks and which he wished to rid himself of quickly in order to get back in contact with the big boys. He got rid of it all right, and in the exact manner I once did with another 12-weight wand on a dolphin that could not have weighed eight pounds! It struck as I was trying to get a cast on a nearby bull that remained plainly visible throughout the fight with the small fish. In these cases we were both in a hurry to get back at the larger fish and over-loaded our rods trying to hustle the smaller fish to the boat. It may be hard to believe someone can break a 12-weight rod on an 8-pound fish; trust me when I say we both wish we hadn't! And we wouldn't have if we had fought

The most critical time in a contest with a big fish is when it is close at hand.

them properly. Be patient; a small fish hooked on a big stick can often be brought in quickly enough without "horsing" it for you to get back to any larger ones that are about.

The last example of the correct mind-set is to not let yourself get rattled— like I did when my friend continued to have trouble capturing the cobia I had hooked at the front of this chapter. Keep your cool; at short range a mistake on your part is compounded exponentially and very quickly, and you cannot concentrate on doing things the right way if you are all shook up!

One of the "right ways" is to take the length out of the rod. For example, if the fish is circling beneath the boat, lower the rod into the water to the point where it is nearly vertical. With your reel hand firmly on the spool, follow the fish's movements with the rod's tip, giving line only when you feel it's absolutely necessary—you'll be able to tell—and quickly taking in what line the fish gives you. This will eventually cause the fish to plane toward the surface, which is highly desirable. While that is taking place, strive to keep the rod and line on as straight a path as possible between you and the fish—and keep up the heavy-handed palming!

Once the fish has surfaced he will be attempting to swim off fairly slowly but still with some strength. With the rod held low maintain a strong a pull on him in a direction away from that in which he is going and with as little bend in the rod as possible. No, that won't look "classic," but you are not protecting tippet here—you are trying to whip that fish before it whips you! It can also require a step or two backward on the casting platform, so watch your footing! Should a sudden flurry occur simply release your grip on the reel; the class tippet will then only feel the reel's pre-set drag, and since a straight rod is not loaded, you would be sorely pressed to break it.

However, it is quite possible to remove a guide or two from it—or to snap the class tippet—if the connection between the leader's butt-section and the fly line is not gut slick! Just prior to and during the landing process that connection can be inside the guides, and a knot with a long tag end tied in heavy mono can foul on them. Incidentally, the odds of that disastrous event occurring increase with the amount of bend in the rod!

And personal experience has proven that once the knot has fouled and a beast is pulling on it only seven or eight feet distant, your chances of freeing the knot are next to none. At that point any flurry will end the contest. The rod might not break, but it will need some repairs if the class tippet does not part first!

So you have had the foresight to either cover your leader-to-fly-line knots with sewing thread and pliobond cement or make them as slick as possible. The fish is ready, but it is a big fish, and its weight alone now creates a problem for moving it the final inches to the point where it can be captured. And that is well inside the span of your 9-foot rod! Now is the time when the temptation to raise it in order to bring the fish closer is at its greatest, and yes, sometimes you simply must do it. If that is the case, do it very slowly and deliberately—in other words, think about what you are doing. And be ready to drop the tip in a heartbeat to counter a flurry!

The author having just whipped—and been whipped by—a 40-pound cobia on a hot, still August afternoon in West Delta, his favorite offshore waters.

Still, it is much better to maintain as little bend in the rod as you can, creating the pressure you are putting on the fish with your reel hand. If the boat is fairly low-sided, back away from the fish across the deck, allowing the man with the net or gaff to get between you and your prize, but don't let him get into a position that will keep you from quickly returning to your fighting position near the gunwale should the fish suddenly dive.

Similarly, on a high-sided boat—or one whose bow or stern decks are too narrow or cluttered for you to back far enough away from its sides, it's best to back up or down the boat's length, in effect slowly towing the fish alongside it and within easy capturing distance. Once the gaff finds the mark—or the fish is well within the net—give it a little slack, but remain prepared for the unexpected. The gaff may tear out or the fish may flop itself out of the net. Both cases demand immediately lowering the rod and pointing it toward the fish to apply only minimal instantaneous drag on it. There is no room for complacency at any time during close combat. "Almost" does not count—he's not yours until he is aboard or you have intentionally released him while he was in the water at boatside. Then, with your fly rod and class tippet in the same number of pieces as they were before the affray, you can celebrate the event—and then go look for another fish.

CHAPTER 8

Cobia

Saltwater fly fishing has gained many advocates over the past decade. Typically the initial stages of their newfound sport are devoted to the pursuit of the smaller, inshore species. Then, as their expertise and enthusiasm increases, fly fishermen seek out larger targets. Cobia are made to order for them.

The fish is common from late spring into autumn throughout the nearshore reaches of the northern Gulf. Cobia reach a weight of 40 pounds or more with regularity, frequently exceed 60, and 100-pounders are captured every year—on conventional gear—and they are often be quite aggressive. Though cobia may not be as flashy as tarpon (they will jump on occasion), they may not be as spooky or finicky as permit. But sight-fishing for them is the best fly-fishing tactic, and that's exciting! They may not run as far as a comparable king mackerel (but they might!), and it may not be as prestigious to catch as a billfish (but they taste a damned sight better!), but they are a strong, challenging boot in the butt to fly fish for!

That statement would be heartily verified by any of the folks who, over the years, have taken their first fly-caught cobia from my boat. Nevertheless, when you're fly fishing for them—as Mr. Murphy so aptly put it, "If anything can go wrong it will." Believe it! It took five years of major malfunctions before I caught my first legal cobia on a fly!

Since the object of the exercise is to catch them, I'll begin by describing where to find a cobia in a fly-fishable setting.

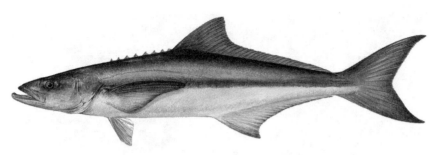

cobia (Rachycentron canadum)

The first is beneath nearshore buoys, channel markers, and such. However, these fish can receive a lot of pressure and can actually become rather finicky. If you see one beneath a buoy, by all means cast at it, but a much better opportunity occurs offshore.

The first of two specific patterns here involves shrimp trawlers and can arise when the boat is fishing, dumping the contents of its nets' tails on deck between "drags," or culling, its catch after the day's final drag (the latter being the mode preferred by most conventional in-the-know anglers). Cobia—along with king mackerel, crevalle jacks, and a variety of sharks, among others—are frequently found around these vessels, panhandling for lunch in the form of discarded by-catch. To target cobia specifically in this setting would be quite difficult, but if you see one cast a size 3/0 green-and-white Deceiver right at its nose and let the fly dead-drift. Likely as not, though, that will result in a big jack!

The second pattern is usually much more productive. Cobia can also be found beneath or beside such "structure" as castaway cardboard boxes and ice-chest lids, wooden pallets and logs, 5-gallon buckets and 55-gallon drums, coils of rope, lost life jackets and shrimpers' salt sacks, dead fish and turtles, and a variety of vegetation, oceanic or otherwise. Any of those objects, and numerous others found randomly in open water, are always worth a quick look. Find such flotsam gathered along a current line, and you've discovered a spot worth at least an hour's investigation. It's not at all unusual for one rip to provide action for most of the day.

Work a current line at dead idle some 40 feet distant on the side that offers the best subsurface visibility—and watch for fish on both sides of the line, even if the water is somewhat grungy on one side! Ideally, the swells should be following; side-seas are tolerable, but if at all possible avoid heading into them. That makes it difficult for the angler on the bow's casting

Cobia are abundant in Louisiana's nearshore waters during the warm months and provide fly fishermen with an excellent big-fish opportunity.

platform to maintain his balance, and in trying to do so he could end up standing on his line at a critical moment. It also can create excessive boat noises. And always check the water behind the boat before you take off for somewhere else, especially if your outboard has been out of gear for a while. Cobia appear to be quite attracted to lower units!

A cobia that is sighted patrolling the flotsam along a current line is looking for something to eat. Period! Here, prey come in many forms, some of which will hold tightly to a floating object in an attempt to hide, then bolt for freedom at the last moment. To mimic this action, the fly should be presented just ahead of the fish and near the edge of the flotsam, then immediately retrieved with moderately fast, 6-inch strips. That's a highly effective technique—for single fish. However, cobia often come in twos and threes—or more.

With a little good luck, that presentation just might account for the larger of a pair of fish, but when three or more are involved a small one will almost invariably beat a beast in the race to the fly. Here you must forget the natural presentation, resist the urge to flock-shoot the school, pick your target, and place the fly right on its nose, retrieving it immediately. Sounds easy, doesn't it? Just wait!

Okay, a fish strikes. You will see it all happen, and you could be inclined to try to set the hook by what you've just seen. Don't! Keep stripping until you feel the fish's weight, then strip-strike it hard several times. That should be simple enough.

The problem, though, arises when the fish has followed the fly for some distance toward the boat before striking, and afterward it continues on the same course. In effect it thus outruns your efforts to tighten the line for a strip-strike. Do not attempt to catch up with it by pulling back on your rod, as that will result in the rod being out of position for an effective hook-set when the line finally does come tight. Keep stripping; at some point the fish will either turn or sound. Then you will feel him and can set the hook.

Notably, failure to follow that practice in my excitement has cost me more lost cobia than all the other reasons combined! If you worry that the fish will eventually detect the fly as a fraud and then spit it out, be assured that your fly probably feels just fine compared to some of the things these fish eat!

Once the fish is hooked one or two things usually happen. Either it will take off like the proverbial striped ape—which is good, since that act will assist you in clearing your slack line, or it won't do anything at all, apparently not realizing something is amiss. That's bad, as the longer the line remains on the deck, the more likely it will become tangled or fouled. With a slow-starter it is critical to reel in that slack line as quickly as possible, because sooner or later the fish will take off!

Assuming the hook was well set and the slack line was cleared successfully—and the ensuing contest ended up in your favor—the fish will eventually be at boatside. Here, another pair of scenarios often arises. The first will be that the fish is truly whipped and landing it creates no significant problems; if you can turn its head, it is ready for boating. More likely, though is the second—and if you cannot turn its head, the fish is just waiting for you to screw up so it can make its last bid for freedom!

Here you must be patient while keeping maximum pressure on the fish. Keep the rod low, and palm the reel heavily. Watch the fish; when you can lead it at will, it is ready.

On that note, in a fly-fishing setting a big net has proven more effective than a gaff for fish to 40 pounds or a bit larger, since it provides better control of the fish after capture. Once the fish's head and shoulders are within the net, give it a little slack line so the netter can work all of it into the meshes. Lift the fish aboard by holding the net's rim with one hand on each side of the handle, and lift it vertically. Never, never try to lift a netted cobia aboard by the net's handle!

While the first legal-sized fly-caught cobia to come onto my boat was captured by Bubby with an 8-weight outfit that was mistakenly grabbed on the way out of his house, and though several in the 30- to 40-pound class have been taken since on 10-weight outfits, a 12-weight is a much better choice. That's because of the hump-and-pump routine demanded in deep water—and because of the potential for catching a really big fish in these waters. Be sure the rod has a foregrip on it!

Reels should have a decent disc drag, a capacity for line, around 200 yards of 30-pound Dacron—no more, unless you also plan to use the outfit for king mackerel and "blue-water beasties" (see chapter of the same name). Then you'd be wise to get a high-end reel with a really good drag and a lot more capacity. For cobia alone a floating braided monocore line is best, though a "compromise" clear intermediate sinking monocore line works just fine. A 9-foot leader with a 20-pound-class tippet and an 80-pound fluorocarbon shocker has proven to be more than adequate.

Since so many types and sizes of prey are consumed by cobia, attractor patterns are recommended over those that depict a specific type. Size 2/0 or 3/0 green-and-white or green-and-yellow Deceivers work well in many areas. My size 3/0 Flashy Chartreuse Thing has been seldom refused over the past eight years; it is a combination of green-and-chartreuse hackles, marabou, and bucktail and sports lots of Krystal Flash and big doll eyes (see page 235). I have no doubt a big popper would also work, but I recommend that you catch a few on streamers before speculating one. As with king mackerel, expect each fish to wreck a fly; cobia don't have teeth to shred flies like a king does, but they can chew 'em up pretty thoroughly. Bring plenty!

That said, take advantage of the opportunity these fish offer saltwater fly fishermen along the Louisiana Coast. You may end up getting hooked on them worse than I am!

Nah, I doubt that . . .

CHAPTER 9

Tarpon

You stand on the stern platform, 12-weight in hand and ready for the cast. You have done this before, but familiarity does not calm the excitement building within you. Your legs are like rubber and are trembling uncontrollably, your throat is dry, your pulse-rate is off the scale. You hear nothing; all your senses are funneled through your eyes toward a small patch of Gulf 100 yards away where a school of tarpon just broached, moving directly at you. It is indeed a thrilling moment, even though you know that your efforts with the fly rod will probably be futile.

They surface again, barely 50 yards away and coming dead on. A very unfamiliar voice in the back of your mind screams "Cast, man, cast!" You respond, and as the fly touches down, you wonder if this could be the one. Experience says it's very doubtful, but you pause anyway to allow the fly to sink a bit, then begin to retrieve it with short, fast strips—just for the hell of it.

Three fish porpoise in a close-knit pod not 50 feet behind the boat. Damn—you should have waited! Strip, strip. Now they are all around you, silver sides flashing in the morning sunlight—so many fish, but so much water, and so little a fly. Strip, strip—this is a stupid waste of time. Then suddenly and very unexpectedly the line comes tight. Holy . . . gotta be a jackfish. But you strip-strike anyway—once, twice, three times, and the placid surface of the West Delta is shattered as six feet of silver king vaults skyward. Totally stunned with amazement, you do not bow to him, and the knot between the class tippet and the shocker parts. Oh well, at least you got to jump him.

And along the parts of the Louisiana Coast where tarpon spend the summer, that is no mean task on a fly. But it can be done.

On any given day from May through September, a school of tarpon could be encountered in these waters. Those surrounding the Mississippi River Delta offer the best opportunity, but even as good as that is, it is extremely marginal for fly fishermen. Fishing for tarpon here is nothing like it is in other well-known tarpon destinations. Most of the fish will be found in open and relatively deep water, and they are almost always on the move—and that's a tough nut for a fly fisherman to crack. I include tarpon as available species because they are, and if more people who knew what they were doing would fish for them with flies, assuredly more of these great fish would be caught. No, it's not sight-fishing in the truest sense of the word, but picture yourself in the setting I just related—or find yourself there—and try to convince me you don't get at least a small bunch of butterflies flittering around in your tummy!

I am no authority on fly fishing for tarpon, but I have paid my dues, having caught one and jumped off four others in these waters. However, all that took place over a period of time when I had quite a few other opportunities that resulted in only casting practice. Why?

Possibly because some of those fish were simply not hungry at the time. But there is a basic tenet in all types of fishing that I feel is the critical element in this topic, and it involves timing: to hook a fish, you must first make it strike, and in order for it to strike, it must first see the lure. I have little doubt that the great majority of the tarpon in the schools I have cast to never saw my fly.

That's because in most cases I have waited for fish to appear on the surface within casting range before I made my presentation. Assuredly there are times when that procedure will be effective; three of the fish I've jumped and lost—and the one I caught—were hooked in that manner. But even then the fish are usually moving too fast to see the fly if it is cast after the fish themselves were seen.

Better chances arise in melees when the fish feed on the surface—staying up and staying put. I have witnessed several of these glorious events, but because of extenuating circumstances (like having seven trolling lines running off the stern and two guys casting conventionally from the bow), I was never able to get a fly into one. I will one day, Lord willing, and I'm certain I'll hook one of the great silver beasts when I do. The problem, of course, will be stumbling across the melee, something that requires a bit of luck.

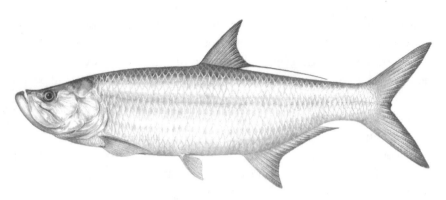

tarpon (Megalops atlanticus)

But as I mentioned earlier, on any given late-summer day you may come across any number of schools rolling along on the surface. If they are not in a particular hurry—and if you are very cautious in the way you position your boat ahead of them, you can get a cast into them. The timing of that cast appears to be the key when the fish are in this setting.

The common tendency to cast "at" something is the fatal flaw here. If you wait to cast at fish that have just surfaced, they will pass well beneath the fly as they sound. And all those fish that you are certain are below those on the surface will have passed beyond the fly before it has come even close to sinking to their level. And if they can't see it, they won't strike it.

There wasn't any doubt that the school of fish I mentioned earlier was going to pass nearby, all around the boat. But to be entirely honest, I cannot say I even thought about all the particulars as I made that uncharacteristic cast—at nothing but the direction in which the school was approaching and in time to allow the fly to sink deeply enough to be seen by them. Such thoughts usually arise after I have returned to the house. And I must admit that in three subsequent and almost identical setups on that aforementioned morning, I did not think of those particulars again—and I did not get another strike. It's awfully hard to break an old habit—and overcome the fear that the cast might end up being outside the fish, resulting in the loss of valuable time.

Should you have the opportunity to fly fish for Louisiana's tarpon—and that can come on a trip targeting cobia or any other nearshore species as well as on a directed effort, trust that with proper boat handling, a school of slow-rolling fish will probably maintain their heading. Make your cast soon enough to allow the fly to sink, and, if you feel a fast-sinking line would be more of a help than a headache, then by all means use one; Louisiana's first known fly-caught tarpon was taken on a high-density line worked through fish marked on a depth recorder. But above all, unless you're quite fortunate, do not expect—or wait—to cast "at" a fish. In most cases that would be just like stopping your shotgun's swing as you blast away at a passing duck, and we all know what that will result in: a miss behind him.

And tarpon do not see—or eat—with their tails.

Should you decide to try your hand at fly fishing for tarpon in these waters —or should you want to be prepared just in case a school of them pops up nearby while you are hunting cobia along a current line—here are some spots to consider. The fish usually appear first in the West Delta south of Venice. As summer progresses the "flat" off Southwest Pass, the part of East Bay west of the South Pass mud-lumps, and the area north of Northeast Pass are consistently productive. During summer tarpon are also regularly encountered between Little Gosier and the Curlew Islands in the Chandeleurs and in the Gulf just north of Chandeleur Island itself.

A 12-weight rod—a stout 12-weight rod!—is appropriate for our tarpon. There are a lot of 12-weight opportunities available in Louisiana waters, so buy the best outfit you can afford, and if your dollars are limited, let the reel take priority.

I prefer a clear intermediate sinking line for all my 12-weight work. I create a loop into the backing-end of it by doubling back around 3 inches of line and wrapping it securely and tightly with black size A nylon thread. The resulting loop is about a ½-inch long while the length of the wraps should be at least 2 inches long. After coating the thread with a thin layer of Sally Hanson Hard-As-Nails fingernail polish and allowing that to dry, it is looped to a Bimini Twist at the end of the backing. A quarter-mile of 30-pound Dacron or one of the superbraids a bit heavier is enough. If it appears it won't be, use the outboard to chase him.

For the leader end of the line I first tie a small perfection loop in one end of a 10-inch piece of 50-pound mono, tie the other end to the fly line with a 10-turn Albright knot, trim the tag ends very closely, and coat them with a thin film of superglue. The leader's butt-section—a 5-foot length of 50-pound mono with a small perfection loop in each end—can then be looped onto the line. The 20-pound class tippet is connected to the butt section with a combination Bimini Twist/doubled double-surgeon's loop, and the 80-pound fluorocarbon shock tippet is connected to the class tippet with a 12-turn Albright knot.

A tarpon fly

Size 3/0 or 4/0 flies about 4 inches long and in color combinations of chartreuse and orange, orange and yellow, or green and chartreuse have been effective. Use the most webbed feathers for wings you can find, supplement them with bucktail to increase their silhouette, and don't skimp with the flash material. Flies with weighted, medium brass hourglass eyes may help.

So will a lot of luck!

A while back I was invited to be a member of the panel at one of Salt Water Sportsman's National Seminars. Mark Sosin was the moderator of a tarpon-fishing session, and he mentioned that I had caught one on fly in Louisiana waters—a very rare event. His following question was something like this: "Pete, just how did you catch that tarpon?"

My response, after some consideration, was something like this: "Lots of blind, dumb luck!"—and the audience, all 500 strong, busted out laughing! Hell, I was serious!

While tarpon provide an established summer opportunity for conventional fishermen, fly fishing for them is very difficult. Still, it can be done.

Not that tarpon are scarce off the Louisiana Coast—far from it, and I do know a little about how to catch them—conventionally. Fact is, I've been smitten by them since I met my first on trips to the Texas coast as a teenager: three dear but very brief relationships. Several years ago, when I had more money than sense, I even bought a boat especially for tarpon fishing around the lower Delta, and after four years of mostly burning gas and drinking beer, I actually caught one—a big sucker, too! But most of my experiences with them, and all but two of those that I have caught, have been with at least one member of the Ballay family—Dave, Debbie, and their sons, Brandon and Brent—each and all crackerjack tarpon fishermen.

I had known Dave for many years when we both worked in the oil field and each of us had more money than sense. We both made "career moves" at about the same time: He forged a marina out of a piece of southeastern Louisiana swamp, and I became a writer—and for a while both of us had neither sense nor money. That aside, we began to fish together, mostly for tarpon.

I had long since sold my boat, so initially our trips were made on his: a 24-foot Topaz. It was the top boat in Louisiana—and possibly the entire Gulf Coast—one year, accounting for 107 fish, tag and release! But Dave eventually sold it for the down payment on a charterboat for his son Brandon, who became the youngest captain in the state. He caught fish, too, and on the days when he didn't have a trip, we would go out with him. But because of Brandon's job—and his reputation as a tarpon ace—that didn't happen very often. At least, it didn't happen often enough for Dave. So he finally broke down and bought another boat—an old 24-foot Wahoo, and dropped a big new diesel into it. By the time the fish arrived, the boat was shipshape, and we were ready.

And after burning several hundred gallons of fuel, we discovered the damned thing couldn't pull a strike on a dare! Bad vibes, I guess—some boats catch fish, some don't. That one didn't, so late in the season and desperate with only two fish in the tag-book, Dave replaced the diesel with a gas motor and caught the last fish of the year—not much consolation for his worst season ever.

The Mississippi River Delta is a gathering ground for these great fish. They migrate there from both south Florida and Mexico, usually arriving some time in early May, and from that point into early autumn when they depart, their numbers grow phenomenally. Indeed, the Delta is the premier destination for tarpon in the entire world during the months of August and September, and they are big fish; the next strike is as likely to come from a "150" or larger as from one less than 100!

They are also normally found in some pretty deep water—50 to 100 feet or a bit more, and with one notable and fairly infrequent exception—a surface melee—they usually feed deep and on the move.

Trolling heavy jigs has become the proven tactic; casting jigs to surfacing fish is done when the opportunity arises. Fly fishing for them is not a very worthwhile endeavor.

Oh, I had tried it before. A friend and I had found a school in what seemed to be an ideal setting—the fish slow-rolling and wallowing on the surface—and followed them with the trolling motor for some distance, casting a variety of patterns into them without as much as a sniff. Since a dedicated Louisiana tarpon nut cannot tolerate much of anything that isn't working when poons are present, I eventually broke out a big casting rod I had smuggled aboard, made one cast with a jig, and caught one—some two hours later—which we estimated to be in the 180-pound class.

That fish mauled me. It took three full days for the pain in my left forearm to subside. And that led to a lot of negative conditioning about fly fishing for our deep-water tarpon—which often sulk at some depth and require some heavy-handed pumping to bring back up. Thoughts of having to pump up that 180-pounder—that was taken in 75 feet of water—with my 12-weight were not very appealing. Besides that, those fish—which were in one of the most fly-fishable settings I had ever witnessed—had showed no interest whatsoever in our flies. So the fleeting fancy of catching a Louisiana tarpon on fly quickly faded—but the 12-weight still accompanied me on trips with Dave, should we have a chance encounter with a cobia or any of the other beasts found around the Delta.

I doubt Dave's new gas engine had 50 hours on it by the time April rolled around, but he and Debbie had received many hours of ribbing about their bad year and the apparent loss of their tarpon-fishing expertise.

It all culminated one night during a roast at the monthly meeting of the New Orleans Tarpon Club. Finally, having taken all the verbal abuse she could tolerate and in what has to be one of fishing's all-time greatest boasts, Debbie rose from her chair and proclaimed long and loudly that she and Dave would show them about any "lost expertise" by catching the first tarpon of the year—tomorrow! That would be April 22—slightly less than prime time for our fish—not too good for reclaiming lost expertise. Or for saving face after a boast like that!

Dave phoned me at eight the following morning, asking if I would like to participate in the capture of the year's first tarpon. I don't believe I'll quote my response, but the gist of it had something to do with the trip's question-able timing. Still, I hadn't been offshore in a couple of months, and the day promised to be nice, so I gathered up the 12-weight—just in case—and it wasn't long before we set the season's first trolling spread.

By mid-afternoon the light breeze had died, leaving the surface of West Delta as flat as a duck pond. We had seen only one fish—apparently an early-arrival stray; for over four hours we had trolled aimlessly—blindly—alone on the hallowed grounds of high summer. Then they came.

They appeared as tiny vee-waves, barely brushing the surface in 50 feet of water. They never broached, never sounded, their courses identical—southwest to northeast—the vanguard from Mexico. Here there was one or two, over there maybe three or four—everywhere we looked. They were in no hurry, and although they showed no signs of feeding, they were hungry—and as fly-fishable as I have ever seen them!

A lot more happened within the next hour than I could ever recall. Dave and I swapped shots from the bow's casting platform while Debbie posi-tioned the boat ahead of an oncoming school, killed the engine, and then waited until the fish set themselves up for a cast—time after time. And a cast on target—by either of us—brought an immediate response—every time! It was the stuff that dreams are made of.

Besides several short strikes and near misses that we both had, I put three in the air, losing the first to a pair of loops in the shooting line fouled on a bow cleat and the second—well, let's just say I went into a trance at the fish's first jump and broke it off; buck fever was running amok that afternoon! But Dave "leadered" the third—the Louisiana way of counting coup with a tarpon; about 90, he said. And a little later he got his—a bit larger—after jumping off five others. And that was more than enough.

We just drifted along for a while after that, watching the parade continue—an absolutely awesome event. There sure were three happy tarpon fishermen aboard the old Wahoo that afternoon; "face" had been saved, "expertise" regained, and I had claim to my first fly-caught tarpon—at the time only the second known to have been taken in that manner in Louisiana waters. Needless to say, some serious celebrating ensued after we returned to the marina, not only in commemoration of the fish, but of the day.

April 22, 1994, was the rarest of days for those of us who pursue tarpon around the Delta: perfectly fly-fishable during the unsettled weather of spring and at the exact instant the fish arrived. Then there was the way the tarpon did arrive, where the slightest breeze ruffling the water's surface would have masked their presence—behavior that is so out of character for them during the "normal" times of summer, anyway. And of course, there was the fortune of being invited to go out on that particular day during such an unlikely time. Maybe it wasn't blind, dumb luck. Maybe Debbie had some premonition the fish would appear that day. Still, she sure couldn't have manipulated the weather—or the way the fish acted.

The next morning Dave and I made another run, had one strike while trolling, tagged and released it, and never saw another fish. That afternoon a screaming norther ripped across the Delta—residual winter. Over three weeks would pass before the next fish would be taken. Yeah, my first fly-caught tarpon really was the result of a lot of blind, dumb luck. But that doesn't bother me a bit, especially when I know that luck can repeat itself. . . .

Like it did a few summers later for a friend who got number three. . . .

CHAPTER 10

Crevalle Jacks

An elderly gentleman from Arkansas who used to come down to the lower Delta to fish several times a year made a tarpon-fishing trip one day with Dave and me. After several hours of complete boredom—a regular result of slow-trolling seven "Coon-Pops" (named after its inventor, Capt. Lance "Coon" Schouest) through tarpon-less waters or waters inhabited only by tight-lipped tarpon—a rod decked. Our Arkansas guest took it up, and after a signature tug-of-war that left no doubt as to the fish's lineage, we boated, unhooked, and released a crevalle jack of nearly 25 pounds.

The ole boy had to tolerate an appropriate amount of ribbing about his great catch and the great job he did in capturing it.

For a tarpon fisherman a hook-up with a jack means lost tarpon-fishing time, and that's quite serious for a tarpon junkie. For a speck angler it leads to a grueling contest that seems to have no end and results in aching muscles and nothing to show for them in the ice chest.

But, for a fly fisherman, jacks—in small doses—can provide great sub-surface action—a long run and dogged determination along with enough size to back it all up. They're relatively common throughout the northern Gulf for most of the year, and with only a few exceptions they will greedily strike a decently presented fly.

While I have stumbled across acres of these fish in the open Gulf as early as mid-March and have caught them there from that time well into No-

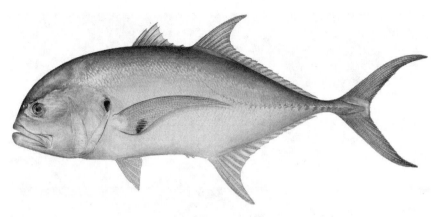

crevalle jack (Caranx hippos)

vember, most anglers will have their initial annual encounters with them in and around the surf sometime in late March to early April. Conventional-minded folks seem to have no difficulty getting these fish to strike. I wish I could say the same about flies, but although over the years I have presented patterns quite similar to my buddies' jigs at numerous fish in that setting, I have yet to entice one. One of these days I will, but until then I'm rather reluctant to offer any specific "how-to" information for this scenario other than to use appropriate gear when catching them is a possibility (a good 9- or 10-weight outfit and a leader with a 16-pound-class tippet and a 40-pound fluorocarbon shocker), and don't be intimidated by them. Some folks I know won't even make a cast at them! And as an afterthought, it is possible that I have not been retrieving my flies fast enough.

Three situations arise that can lead a fly fisherman to all the action he can stand with these fish. The first occurs around jetties and breakwaters. The second is a surface melee in the open Gulf, and the third involves shrimp trawlers.

Jetties and breakwaters are best worked from a boat that can be handled safely and efficiently with a bow-mounted electric trolling motor. Blind-casting the length of the structure in depths of roughly 5 feet or more is the technique. Casts made parallel to or at a slight angle to the structure cover the strike zone best, that being the water out to 30 feet or so from it. Areas where bait is concentrated should be worked more thoroughly.

Here as in anywhere else big jacks are found, a 10-weight outfit will suffice, but if you don't have a thing for long-term relationships, you really should use the 12-weight outfit that you (hopefully) bought for cobia, king

Crevalle jacks are plentiful in Louisiana's coastal waters almost to a fault, and they're usually quite willing to give a fly fisherman much more than he really wanted!

macks, and the blue-water beasties. And I'd also recommend using a short trace of #6 single-strand wire, just in case a king takes a liking to your fly. That is a frequent occurrence around a jetty in water of sufficient depth!

I have used size 4/0 Clouser Minnows between 5 and 5½ inches long for almost all my jetty fishing, and I have caught a lot of big, nasty jacks with them there—along with some big and not so nasty kings and bull redfish. It's a great choice, but I've never seen one that large offered in fly shops or mail-order catalogs. You'll have to tie them yourself (see "The Monster Clouser" on page 238). With a clear intermediate sinking line let the fly sink for various countdowns starting at around 10, and retrieve it with short, moderately fast strips.

And keep a real good grip on that rod!

Offshore surface blitzes will arise virtually anywhere—or they won't, so don't waste a lot of time running around the Gulf looking. Just be ready for one while you're searching for other fish or working other patterns. You will have absolutely no trouble recognizing a blitz, so there's no need to describe one to you Lots of white water and diving, squawking gulls are a fair indication of such blitzes.

Offshore shrimp trawlers probably create the most consistent action with big jacks. That can occur in three fashions, and in order to fully understand them a brief description of the character and operation of these boats is necessary.

The boats are equipped with an outrigger-type boom on each side, both of which can be raised and lowered with a winch—raised and upright while the boat is in transit, down and outstretched while it is trawling. Another winch stores a long cable that runs out through the outrigger and back to a bridle. The bridle is attached to two large, heavy "doors" that keep the mouth of the net open and on bottom. The net is relatively flat and tapers from its wide mouth—50 feet or so—back to its tail where the catch collects.

Each net is set behind the boat far enough for it to tag bottom, then it is dragged along at a slow to moderate speed. A test trawl—much smaller but rigged the same way and a great deal easier and quicker to set and retrieve—is also deployed. Its contents are checked regularly—a good catch demands making another pass through the area just worked, a meager catch dictates another spot should be tried.

The shrimp—and everything else that enters the nets' mouths—do not all end up in the tail. Some get caught in the nets' meshes along the way, and some even manage to escape, though usually worse for the wear, throughout the duration of the drag—the length of time they are pulled before being re-trieved and dumped. Is it any wonder that jacks—and a host of other fly-fish-able targets—follow these boats like a pack of wolves after a herd of starving deer?

There are three ways to work an offshore shrimp trawler. First, find one that is fishing in depths greater than 50 feet or so and idle up behind it be-tween the cables leading from the ends of the outriggers to the nets. Then you should determine which side of the boat the test trawl is being deployed from, and then move to the opposite side. Now close to within a short cast of the trawler's stern, go to neutral—having established a safe distance be-tween your boat and the cable as it passes you, and from the bow make a quick cast. Your boat's momentum will prevent you from retrieving the fly very enticingly, but that's no problem, as it will look just like a piece of by-catch (for example, a small croaker, menhaden, white trout, and the like) that just fell overboard. The strike usually comes right at your feet, so you'll have to do some scrambling in order to clear enough line to set the hook. Ex-citing? You'd better believe it! And it's no danger to your boat or the trawler's crew if you're careful. Just don't hang the fly on the trawler and expect him to stop so that you can retrieve it. If that happens, break it off.

The second productive mode you will find an offshore shrimper in is when he is picking up his nets to dump their contents for separating and then icing down the shrimp. This act can be predetermined by the boat raising its nets' doors from the water, so if there are any in the area you are fishing, keep an eye on them, and, when this indication is made, get over there quick!

Again, approach from the stern. By the time you reach him the doors will be hanging from the ends of the outriggers, the net draping from their ends down into the water, then up again above the trawler's deck. During the time the nets' tails are being retrieved, untied, dumped, and then retied, the jacks that have been following the boat feast on the by-catch that is stuck in the nets' meshes or is falling from them. This is a melee you must see in order to believe, and a hook-up is a foregone conclusion! Frequently, though, dead-drifting the fly is much more effective than actually retrieving it. Once you have hooked up—or when the trawler begins to reset his nets, back away from him quickly.

The trawler usually culls his catch while he is making another drag. However, at day's end he and some of his cohorts might anchor in a group and cull their catches together while they visit. This typically takes place in the evenings, though trawlers who work at night often create the same opportunity in early morning. And it too can lead to a real jackfish melee as well as encounters with cobia, kings, sharks, and others. In truth, though, one of those would have to be moving pretty fast to beat a jack in a race to the fly!

In either of the last two settings a fly with a slower sink-rate than the big Clouser—but still size 4/0 and big!—should be used. Then there's the time when a little more, uh, "enticement" is required.

This slight aberration in the fish's normal personality might have never been discovered had the Gulf not been gut-slick one hot August afternoon. With a trawler, nets again deployed, having moved well away from us, a small swirl in its wake a hundred yards or so distant caught our attention. Idling up to the disturbed area we noticed a very sparse trail of by-catch that was scattered along the trawler's wake, and a pair of jacks were patrolling it, occasionally rising to pluck a morsel from the surface like a trout sips a spent mayfly. And the damned things wouldn't even look at a big streamer! Very uncharacteristic behavior!

But not uncharacteristic at all once a buddy had lobbed the streamer he had "sweetened" with a dead croaker that we had salvaged from the trail of by-catch, and one of them immediately ate it! Hey, when you want to bend a fly rod you do what you gotta do!

And jacks are a sure means to that end!

CHAPTER 11

The "Lesser Types"

I use that collective description above for several very fly-fishable creatures not derogatorily—not completely, anyway—but because they are
"lesser," both in size and in angler interest than the other fish profiles in
this book. Most of the following fish that I've caught, on flies or otherwise,
have been incidental to other targets, and, with one exception, they have been
greatly outmatched by the gear I was using. That's a partial result of my
adamant refusal to carry anything lighter than a 10-weight outfit on offshore
trips. In truth, in most of my experiences with all but one of these fish,
they've been nuisances.

But they will bend a fly rod—at least for a while!

The lesser types inhabiting Louisiana's inland and offshore waters, for
our purposes, include ladyfish, blue runners, bluefish, Spanish mackerel, and

ladyfish (Elops saurus)

little tunny. Assuredly there are others that will occasionally strike a fly. Some of those—like sea catfish and stingrays—are not especially appreciated when that occurs; others—like pompano and southern kingfish—are always a welcome bonus to a day's catch. Nevertheless, most of those you will catch—intentionally or otherwise—will be members of the following five.

Ladyfish

The only serious efforts I've made toward this group of fish have involved ladyfish, and each of those efforts was initially directed at redfish. However, I just love to catch fish that jump, and redfish don't. So on those hot, late-summer afternoons when ladyfish appear, I immediately abandon my search for the reds and launch Plan B. And it just so happened that on every occasion in which I've met the ladies in that setting, I was using my 5-weight outfit for the reds. Talk about a boot!

Being creatures of warm water, ladyfish usually begin to appear in late spring and in the surf, where your chances of catching a 20-inch trophy are best. As summer progresses the smaller fish move into interior areas, even coastal rivers that have adequate clarity and salinity. There they stay until cool weather or a surge of fresh water causes them to retreat offshore. Where do they go for the winter? I haven't a clue, as I'm not aware of any tagging study that has been done on ladyfish.

The fish found in surf zones readily strike the same types and sizes of flies which are best there for specks, even poppers when conditions permit their use. Fish in interior areas are most susceptible to smaller offerings—size 4s and 6s—and they, too, will strike scaled-down poppers with a vengeance. And a 5-weight outfit is just right for them! All you have to do is convince yourself to carry one along when you make a redfishing trip!

While surf fishermen should already be prepared for a ladyfish's raspy jaws by their steadfast use of a shock tippet for resistance to fraying from speck-teeth, inshore redfishermen often tie the class tippet directly to the fly. If that's the case with you and ladyfish suddenly appear—especially should you be using a class tippet of 12 pounds or less, quickly adding a foot of 20-pound fluorocarbon will prevent you from losing too many flies. Still, retie it after every fish!

Unless you know of a ladyfish honey-hole where these fish regularly gather—and I know of only one, and it is not within the scope of this book—if you set out to intentionally catch a ladyfish, you probably won't. On the

Several species of little local acclaim inhabit Louisiana waters and will provide a fly fisherman with a good scrap. Ladyfish are one.

other hand, if you find a school of specks in the surf or in the open waters of any given large coastal bay or sound, it's just about a foregone conclusion that a gang of party-crashing ladyfish will eventually appear. Most folks cuss them for that—personally I don't see how anyone could cuss a fish that jumps like they do!

Blue Runners

I take great pride in having avoided these fish quite successfully throughout my lifetime. Typically they have been encountered while I had a 12-weight outfit in hand, armed with a labor-intensive fly and a single-strand wire bite-guard, both of which are prone to being wrecked by a single strike from one of the greedy little devils! Therefore I must admit I've had little experience in actually catching them.

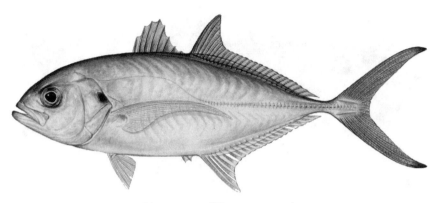

blue runner (Caranx crysos)

However, in avoiding them so well I have become an authority on where and when they are likely to be found, and that's damned near anywhere and any time from outside the surf to depths of 2,500 feet and probably beyond!

Covering that much area would require more time and expense than most folks would want to spend in an effort to catch one of these diminutive jacks on a fly; like ladyfish, a 2-pounder is a really good one. (If there is such a thing!) But although blue runners are readily found in large schools in the open waters of the nearshore Gulf, the fish's fatal flaw is an attraction to structure—jetties and petroleum platforms being literal magnets. If for some reason you feel you must catch a blue runner on a fly, make a trip to one of those on a nice, sunny morning any time between March and November. If the fish aren't boiling the surface around it like a school of piranhas in a feeding frenzy, toss a size 2 Clouser Minnow up against the structure, let it sink a bit, and just try to get it back without a fish on it!

Bluefish

Unlike a lot of Louisiana anglers, I'm a lot less anti-bluefish than anti–blue runners, probably because I don't encounter many of them. That's not their fault, as they are reasonably plentiful in these waters, and like the blue runners, they have a fondness for jetties and platforms and can be found around them throughout much of the year. Still, they don't seem to come in the numbers the little jacks do, and in a way I guess that's good. Bluefish are eating machines, and since they reach considerably larger sizes than the runners do—and therefore eat much more and larger prey—the Gulf might

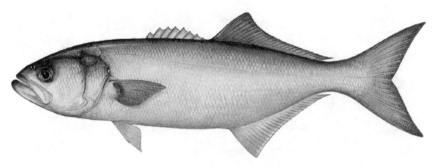

bluefish (Pomatomus saltatrix)

become a little more dangerous to everything in it if there were as many blue-fish around as blue runners!

If you target bluefish, you can avoid a lot of bite-offs by using a long-shank hook. Personally, I don't like to use them, as I tend to bend them on reasonably sized fish of numerous species, so I tolerate the minor hassle of using single-strand wire bite-guards. Clouser Minnows in size 1 or 1/0 are simple and cheap enough to tie or buy so that replacing a dozen or so of them shouldn't be much of a problem. And, oh yes, you'll probably wreck that many! Remember, to catch a bluefish you usually have to get your fly past a rather thick layer of blue runners first!

If you feel that life simply won't be complete without your catching a blue-fish from the Gulf on a fly, finagle a red snapper trip with some conventional-fishing buddies to some platforms in appropriate depth. With a 10-weight outfit and a Class III sinking line, toss out your Clouser Minnow and let it sink—forever! Then, when a buddy has worked a snapper or some other bottom-type almost to the surface, begin to rapidly retrieve your fly. Besides bluefish, with a little luck you just might get a snapper too.

Spanish mackerel (Scomberomorus maculatus)

Spanish Mackerel

Of the not-so-fabulous five, the Spanish mack rates second to the ladyfish in popularity in the Cooper household. It is much more attractive than the steely bluefish and blue runners, it's fast, and some find the fish delicious (though with a freezer well stocked with speck fillets and cobia steaks, I'd have to pass). The bigger ones put up a very nice accounting of themselves, and they don't seem to care to associate with blue runners. My kind of fish!

Spanish macks, like ladyfish, are frequently taken during summer from the surf using speck-fishing flies and tactics, though the fish are usually found out past the second bar. Summer is also the time when they can be found in schools marauding silversides and sardines in the open Gulf. But a jetty can be the best bet for a fly fisherman's efforts.

These fish, like ladyfish, are often difficult to specifically target with flies. A jetty helps to concentrate them in a limited area, increasing the chances for one to detect the fly. An 8- or 9-weight outfit with a Class III sinking line, and the previously recommended bite-guard, are adequate for any Spanish mack you will ever encounter, but jetties hold beasts, too. Because of that— and the potential for an encounter with one of them in many of the settings found along the northern Gulf—I am convinced it should be against the law

Spanish mackerel can often be caught with ease along jetties and in open-water blitzes.

for anyone to venture onto the ocean with anything less than a 10-weight! But that aside, the size 1/0 Clouser Minnows you use for specks—and the size 4/0 Clouser Minnows used for kings—will attract fish found near jetties, even when you don't want them to!

Little Tunny

This is the archfiend of the lesser types—the largest, the fastest, the most likely to expose backing, and the most aggravating in my humblest of opinions. Yet there are folks, even a few from Louisiana, who really get their bells rung by fly fishing for them! They are present in nearshore and offshore waters throughout most of the year, and they can be taken in a variety of settings.

To be sure, I have made many casts into them as they attempted to completely annihilate schools of silversides, and I have little doubt that my rather consistent failure to catch them in that setting is a result of the quickly presented cobia-directed fly I was using at the time (too big) and its retrieve rate (too slow).

On the other hand, my successes with them while on chunking trips for tuna have led me to believe that dead-drifting the fly might be the solution—it sure works on the ravenous little pests when one is trying to entice a tuna, anyway! So here, too, is another fish that I often have trouble catching when I want to and am often eaten slap up by when I'd prefer not to be!

Matching the chunk is a very productive method for taking these fish—lobbing out a fly similar in size and color to the chunks of fish-flesh being dispensed overboard and allowing it to drift and sink at the same rate as that

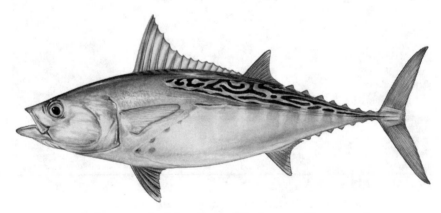

little tunny, aka false albacore (Euthynnus alletteratus)

The archbeast of the "lesser types" is the little tunny, and there are more of them in Louisiana waters than some folks care to have around!

of the chunks. So is working anchored shrimp trawlers who are culling their catches—provided you can get your fly through the jack, and so forth. Surface melees can erupt anywhere and at any time on the open Gulf and can be differentiated from those caused by other types by the tunny leaping clear of the water's surface. And as with many other fly-fishable creatures, a jetty can provide outstanding action, dependant, of course, on what other types—lesser or greater—happen to be around at the same time. On that note, if your intended target demands the use of wire, and you desire to catch some of the tunny that have suddenly begun to churn the water all around you to a froth, losing the wire often leads to the best results. Finally, size 1 and 1/0 Clouser-types are a good bet—retrieve them fast or not at all.

And if a gang of them appears in your tuna-directed chunk-line, you'd better have brought along a tube of Ben-Gay!

As I mentioned at the beginning of this chapter, there are other lesser types you may encounter. One that you may not consider but may offer a excellent sight-fishing opportunity, especially along sandy, clearwater shorelines of barrier islands, is the ignoble sea catfish. Hey, they'll bend a rod—and they sure bust up the slow times when your primary targets have a case of "tight-lip."

And, in my humblest opinion, that's the main purpose the lesser types serve.

CHAPTER 12

The "Blue-Water Beasties"

The first time that you see blue water, especially if it's across a strong "rip" (a sharp change in current directions and water temperature and color) on a bright, warm day when the ocean is friendly, you will assuredly be astounded! Its color, its clarity, and the sudden realization that you have just entered the realm of great beasts—"inappropriate fly-fishing targets," one might say—will be mesmerizing, perhaps even a little intimidating to a fly fisherman. However, those creatures don't abruptly become great beasts, and in their smaller sizes some of them make quite appropriate—albeit sometimes rather brutal—fly-fishing targets. Others are just downright fun to catch!

Most of these fish can be found along the rip—which is frequently packed with sargasso grass and assorted flotsam. As this serves as cover for various types of prey species, grass-packed rips are prime hunting grounds for the four major players in this drama.

Other blue-water opportunities can be found around Louisiana's deepwater petroleum platforms and floating—"semi-submersible"—drilling rigs. These massive, state-of-the-art steel creations can stand—or float—in upward of 3,000 feet of water, and they attract pelagic prey and predators of all types like magnets.

Another opportunity that primarily involves tuna (and can lead to more little tunny than you'd ever want to see, much less catch) is created by the snout of a salt dome. An excellent example of oceanic benthic structure pierced the floor of the Gulf some 16 miles south-southwest of the mouth of the Mississippi's Southwest Pass and has risen some 250 feet above the surrounding seabed. This is Sackett Bank—"The Midnight Lump" to those who fish there—and it is possibly the best place in the entire Gulf of Mexico for a fly fisherman to destroy a perfectly good 14-weight outfit!

But that's another story.

Dolphin

This very fly-fishable, blue-water target is dolphin, not dolphinfish, not mahi-mahi, not dorado. Dolphin! Got that?

Okay.

Probably more dolphin have been taken on flies in Louisiana's offshore waters than all the other pelagics combined. One reason for that is they are extremely prolific breeders and mature very early in life, making their numbers quite large, even though practically every fish in the Gulf that is a tad bit larger than they are preys upon them constantly. Another reason is that dolphin are fairly easy to locate and usually come in bunches—the smaller ones, anyway: "chickens."

For a fly fisherman the best opportunity the rip offers is dolphin. These come in all sizes ranging from 1-pound-ish chickens—which are great fun to catch on a 5-weight outfit, should you have the courage to carry one to these far-off waters—to "bulls" of 20 pounds or much more: 12-weight stuff. For fly-fishing purposes, most encounters with dolphin of any size are almost invariably initiated by sight-fishing while idling along the clear side of the rip, though they can be found associating with anything floating randomly

dolphin (Coryphaena hippurus)

Small dolphin ("chickens") and school-sized fish are often abundant along offshore current lines and occasionally venture into clear nearshore waters.

on the water's surface. Show the big ones—the bulls, though they may be females—a big size 4/0 green-and-yellow Deceiver (dolphin are cannibalistic), and strip it fast. Once you hook a big one, the ensuing aerial display is guaranteed to be entertaining! Smaller fish will readily strike the size 1 Clouser Minnows you use inshore for speck. Dophin like it fast, too, but sometimes a dead drift is a better choice.

Dolphin are a warm-water fish and are therefore mainly caught during summer or at other times in suitably warm water across the rip. Small fish—up to 5 pounds or so—are occasionally found fairly close to shore during the summer, and the water there doesn't have to be blue in order to hold them, just clear—or "clean green." These fish are most often found around random flotsam and which has been collected along nearshore current lines.

While they're not members of the open ocean's fearsome foursome, a couple of other fish that are quite susceptible to fly fishing can often be found with dolphin or near the same types of flotsam that commonly hold them in suitable conditions. Almaco jacks are one and are a rather recent acquaintance of mine. Admittedly neither of the pair I caught on a rip one gorgeous

Bull dolphin provide an exciting warm-month sight-fishing opportunity along Louisiana's offshore current lines and grass patches.

June afternoon was 12-weight-worthy, but they frequently reach that size. Typically, jack are strong fighters with lots of stamina, and I've heard they are decent table fare. If you notice a darkish, jacklike fish lurking beneath the sargasso grass, it is probably an almaco. Take a shot at it—it will probably strike.

Rainbow runners are also often found in "dolphin territory." Also a member of the jackfish family, they are quite streamlined, colorful, and reputed to be delicious. I have never caught one—though I once saw a bunch holding deep beneath a huge sargasso "island" one day, but I couldn't get the fly through the layer of dolphin that was on the surface in order to catch one! (Life is tough on the far-off grounds!) On another occasion I had a perfect setup on a school of them following a conventionally hooked comrade to the boat, but I fouled my back cast in an outrigger's cable. (Need I say that it's really tough trying to fly-fish on a conventionally rigged boat loaded with a bunch of jig-chunkers!) Anyway, one of these days I'll figure them out—or find some when there aren't so many dolphin or fly-fishing hazards around. They are really neat fish.

But not nearly as neat as catching dolphin!

Tuna

While little tunny may be the archfiends of the lesser types, tuna are the overall archbeasts. The latter can be found on the warm side of the bluewater rip throughout the year, and a fly fisherman should always be ready for a school of tuna that may suddenly appear nearby while he's sight-fishing for dolphin. Normally you have to be pretty quick to get a cast into these fish, but it can be done. And that quick opportunity is one very good reason why I do my fly fishing for dolphin with a 12-weight outfit.

During fall their numbers begin to increase in some areas—primarily the waters off the Mississippi River Delta that are deeper than 200 or so feet. This is probably the result not of a migration but from the cooling water that causes more comfortable feeding conditions on the surface than those that are present during summer.

Also during this time a fly-fishing opportunity occurs that involves shrimp trawlers. Assuredly, blackfin can be caught around those at anchor in suitable depths culling their catches, but the most exciting encounters with them take place while the boat is trawling. The water around it doesn't have to be blue—again, clean green is sufficient! The setting and technique are exactly the same as for one of the crevalle jack opportunities, though the water

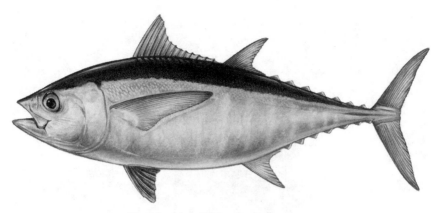

blackfin tuna (Thunnus atlanticus)

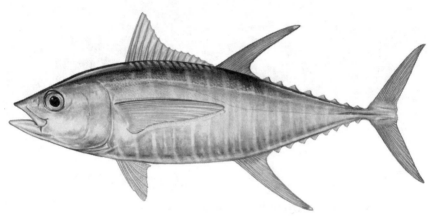

yellowfin tuna (Thunnus albacares)

should be at least 200 feet deep for blackfins, much deeper if you are on a quest after yellowfins. As with jack, you should idle up behind the trawler—approaching its stern on the quarter opposite the one deploying the test trawl—go to neutral, make the cast, and begin quickly stripping in the slack line that your boat's momentum has created.

Once you've hooked up, say a little prayer that the fish's run is outside of the cable leading from the outrigger to the net. And unless you are a glutton for punishment, you might add to that prayer a plea that the fish is either a blackfin or a reasonable-sized yellowfin, as those commonly reach triple digits in Louisiana waters!

When fighting a tuna, my experiences have shown that unless the fish is threatening to dump your entire amount of backing, it's best to let it run,

Tuna, both blackfin and yellowfin (shown here) respond to chunking efforts and can be caught—hooked, anyway—on chum flies.

then once it has stopped begin to move toward it with the boat in order to regain line. If you try to pump back even a 20-pounder that has run 100 yards, sounded in 200 feet of water, and has begun to flat-side you like an overgrown bluegill, you won't catch many of them before you become beat to the bone! Moving up on them after that first run allows you to pump the fish up much more efficiently than you could from a distance.

I use a 12-weight outfit for trawl-boat chasing, both for tuna and for jacks and other possibilities. The reel is top of the line and holds a clear intermediate sinking line and a quarter-mile or so of 50-pound small-diameter backing. So far it has performed adequately on blackfin and small yellowfin, but sooner or later I am bound to hook a brute that will probably wreck either it or me. If you think dueling with tuna could become your thing, invest in a good 14-weight outfit, the rod being no longer than 8 feet—a bit shorter would be better!

During autumn the number of tuna of both types also increase around deep-water petroleum platforms. I've never caught one on a fly in this setting, but while conventionally fishing for them schools have surfaced within fly-casting range numerous times. Those fish were assuredly fly-catchable—the smaller ones, anyway, though they may require chasing in order to keep the line clear of the platform's legs. Personally, though, when I fly fish for the archbeasts I want as much going for me as possible, and that does not include chasing a hooked tuna around a platform!

During winter and early spring Louisiana's "Midnight Lump" provides excellent fly-fishing potential through "chunking"—a form of chumming involving solid appetizers as well as scent. All sorts of chunk material may be used, with menhaden, mullet, little tunny body parts, and boiled crawfish heads being favorites. Yeah, boiled crawfish heads! If you use them, though, you'll need some red flies!

That brings up a good point. For fly fishing a chunk line, it is best to use several types of chunk material at one time. Tuna can become quite selective when only one type is used, and need I say "matching the meat" is not easy! Give 'em a variety, and your fly will normally only need to be "close enough."

Much that concerns fly fishing for tuna has changed for the best since that day, years ago, when I caught my first—a yellowfin just under 23 pounds—on a chunking trip to the Lump with Dave and Brent Ballay. Many of those changes have been a result of the efforts of Venice's Capt. Peace Marvel, who has chunked up yellowfins exceeding 70 pounds and blackfins to 27 pounds for his fly-fishing clients. Notably, some of those anglers have come down from far northern states to sample this opportunity. Many of them come back every season now—the fishing's that good.

That is, it's that good if you want to subject yourself and your fly rod to the rigors that are typically imposed on both by a tuna!

Wahoo

The wahoo—the super-mackerel—are included in this list because they have been taken on flies. (The fact that those deeds were accomplished in the Pacific Ocean has no bearing here!) I know of only one caught on fly in Louisiana waters, and it was rather small for the species. But there are enough of these fish around for them to constitute a viable fly-fishing opportunity hereabouts.

While wahoo, like tuna, can appear at any time along a rip, a fly fisher should always be ready for a quick cast at one. With few exceptions these fish are always on the move; you'll probably have only one shot, so make it good.

wahoo (Acanthocybium solandri)

Flies suitable for bull dolphin should also work on wahoo; a 12-weight outfit with a 9-foot rod is preferable to a shorter 14-weight tuna-stick, as longer casts may be required. Also, wahoo don't normally grow to sizes as large as yellowfins, though 40- to 50-pounders are common. They also fight in a more gentlemanly fashion than the archbeast—much quicker and to the point than tuna. Still, they can go from here to way over yonder faster than you would believe possible!

And there's not much that swims, walks, crawls, or flies that tastes better!

Wahoo can also be found around random flotsam, though not as commonly as dolphin. Unlike dolphin, though, they may be deep and undetectable. If there is no visible fish holding to a promising piece of floating junk, that's a real good sign the ole bad boy is down there somewhere. Prospect for him with several blind casts; let the fly sink a good ways and strip it back fast!

The problem with all that is the wahoo's teeth, which are formidable! If you are rigged for bull dolphin, prepared for tuna, and manage to get a 'hoo to strike, you will almost assuredly and probably quite quickly be snipped. If you take precautions for that unhappy event and utilize a single-strand wire bite-guard, you may deter any tuna you encounter from striking.

Then too, wahoo often appear atop the Midnight Lump in a chunk line, especially during early spring and when the water there is blue. At this time these handsome, swift, open-ocean predators will slowly move from chunk to chunk—eating them quite deliberately, and they won't even look at one with a hook on a short wire trace in it! The same goes with a fly, and guess what happens when you lose the wire?

I've been told that black titanium wire is effective on chunked-up wahoo. I'm not certain of this, but what I do know is that I have a severe case of the hots to catch one of these prizes on a fly, and Lord willing, one day I shall.

Of course, that's provided the archbeasts haven't beaten me slap up before I manage to hook one!

Billfish

While the numbers of sailfish and white marlin present in the northern Gulf no longer appear to be enough to make a directed effort toward them, blue marlin, a stray white, or sailfish could appear in the teasers at any time. Throughout much of the year these fish are taken along the blue-water rip by conventional anglers, so there's no reason why they shouldn't be by fly fishers. I know of no billfish having ever been caught on a fly in the northern Gulf, but there should have been!

Again, the waters off the Mississippi River Delta probably provide the best chance for this monumental event, since the deep-water petroleum platforms as well as the blue-water rip hold these fish, thereby providing a greater opportunity than other areas. Nevertheless, it could occur along the blue-water rip virtually anywhere. The drill is "bait-and-switch," a technique used with consistent successes on the Pacific side of Central America. Here's the deal: A spread of "teasers"—normally hookless surface lures—is deployed a short distance behind the boat and pulled at a desired speed. They create a commotion, which, when combined with the boat's wake, attracts the billfish.

The fly rod—a state-of-the-art 14-weight being a good choice—is placed in the boat's port quarter if the angler casts right-handed, the starboard quarter if he's left-handed. About 30 feet or so of line, which has first been cast and retrieved, is coiled in a bucket nearby. The fly resembles half of a young and rather gaudy chicken and is equipped with a popper head.

A billfish appears in the teasers. The angler takes up the fly rod, while a companion retrieves the teasers to a point where they can be quickly removed from the water. Hopefully the fish follows, "lighting up" as they do when they are excited. At that point the guy on the teaser-line hollers "Stop!" The boat's

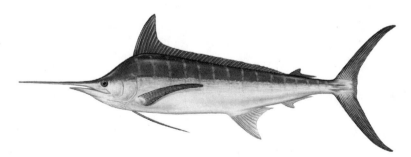

blue marlin (Makaira nigricans)

skipper then slams the motor's gears into neutral. The teasers are snatched from the fish, and the fly is cast, the teasers taking their place. The fish immediately strikes, then turns away, and at that point the angler gives it three or four firm strip-strikes. And then the festivities begin!

At least, that's how it's supposed to work.

There are a lot of blue marlin in the Gulf off Louisiana that can rightly be classed as "inappropriate fly-fishing targets," but there are also a lot of them in the 150- to 200-pound class that would make a challenging but very doable target. It will take a suitable boat—or a lot of money for charter trips. Or, with a little luck, it could be done on your first attempt.

As it's been said, when it comes to fishing, you never know. . . .

Part II

Destinations

For this book's implied purposes, the Louisiana Coast is divided into eight distinct areas. Some of those may have similar opportunities; others may have opportunities that are unique to that area alone. Now that you know what species are available in Louisiana and where and how to catch them in general, the following describes the state's separate areas and their specific opportunities—fly fishing or otherwise!

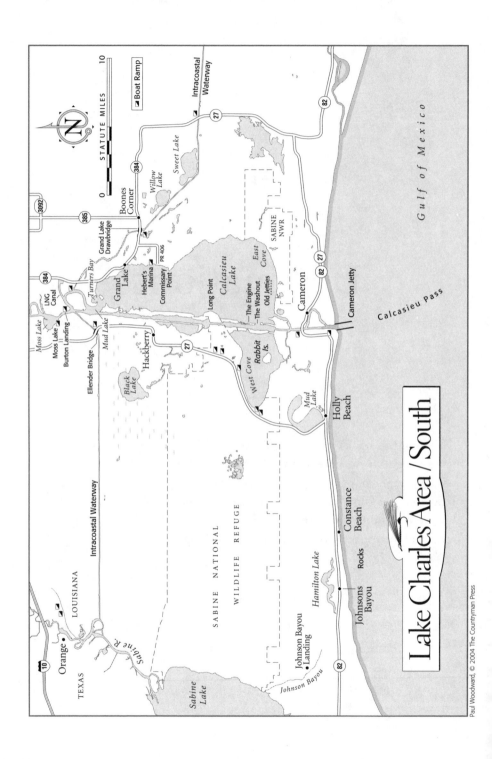

Lake Charles Area / South

Paul Woodward, © 2004 The Countryman Press

CHAPTER I

The
Lake Charles Area

Beginning Louisiana's coastal coverage in the west, the first significant body of water you will notice is Sabine Lake. It's an excellent fishery for speck and flounder, and redfish and striped bass are far from scarce in its waters, but access to it from Louisiana is limited to a pair of remote launch sites off LA 82. Because of that we'll have to concede it to Texas. However, if you happen to find yourself in Beaumont, Orange, or Port Arthur with time to kill and an itch to fish, contact Capt. Chuck Uzzle in Orange (he can be reached at 409-886-5222). He's young, personable, a fly-fishing fool, and a highly recommended guide.

LA 82 is very near the Gulf of Mexico, from Constance Beach through Holly Beach and on toward Cameron (in the parish of the same name). Throughout this stretch of the highway, if you can find a spot to park your vehicle, you should be able to access the surf. And during periods of calm or moderate offshore breezes, the fishing can be quite good, especially on a rising tide with a range of foot or more.

Seasonal action is representative of wadable surf-zones across the state. During the cool months redfish predominate. Speck normally begin showing up in numbers around the spring equinox, and from the first of May through mid-June is the best time for the biggest fish. Summer action with school-sized specks, along with the occasional ladyfish and Spanish mackerel, can be very good. And the end of summer and the beginning of autumn finds bull reds prowling the troughs and bars.

While those forms of structure are typical of a sandy surf-zone in Louisiana, there is another form found here that is not, and it can provide the best action around. In order to slow beach erosion—which was getting awfully close to undermining the highway, a series of walls made of granite boulders were created just offshore of, and parallel to, the seashore. They are reachable by wading, and need I say a fly dropped anywhere near one of them will very likely be eaten by something!

As in any other surf setting across the Louisiana Coast, that fly should be a Clouser Minnow or something similar. Size 1/0 versions around 3 inches long will appeal to both reds and specks, though during the big-speck time of spring and the bull red time of early autumn a size 2/0 about 4 inches long will better attract the beasts' attentions.

A 9- or 10-weight outfit is appropriate for all of Louisiana's surf settings; its reel should have a quality disc drag and a capacity for an intermediate sinking-tip line and at least 150 yards of 30-pound Dacron backing—more is better. The combination of a 16-pound-class tippet and a foot of .021 or thereabouts (40-pound) fluorocarbon make for adequate beast insurance.

Most Louisiana surf fishermen keep their daily quotas of what they catch, retaining them on a cord stringer while they continue to fish. There's certainly nothing wrong with that, though a fly fisherman should remove the float commonly affixed to a wading-stringer, as it will snag loose fly line. Other must-haves are either flats boots or slip-on tennis shoes, a wide-brimmed hat, and, of course, sunscreen.

When onshore winds make the surf here a little too lumpy and stirred up for your liking, it's time to hire a guide and try Calcasieu Lake. This is southwestern Louisiana's pride and joy and could very well be the premier big-speck spot on the entire northern Gulf Coast. Here, as in most other areas where specks are found, the biggest fish are normally taken during spring, but a "wall hanger" is possible at any time, and good fishing with "standard-sized specks" can occur on virtually any day throughout the year when the lake's clarity and salinity are favorable.

There are several techniques that are productive on Calcasieu Lake. Fan-casting the oyster reefs around Commissary Point, Nine-Mile Cut, the Washout, and West Cove with chartreuse-and-white or olive-and-white size 1/0 and 2/0 Clouser Minnows has accounted for many specks, working small, fresh slicks caused by the fish's feeding activities is also productive. Always keep an eye out for slicks! During the warm months—and occasionally during warm periods in winter—specks drive shrimp and various other prey species

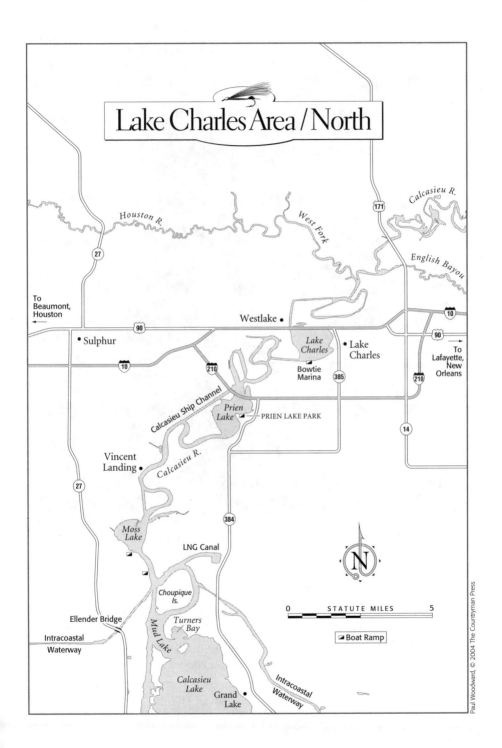

Lake Charles Area / North

Calcasieu R.

Houston R.

West Fork

English Bayou

171

10

To Beaumont, Houston

90

Westlake

90

To Lafayette, New Orleans

• Sulphur

Lake Charles

• Lake Charles

10

210

Bowtie Marina

385

210

Calcasieu Ship Channel

Prien Lake

PRIEN LAKE PARK

14

Vincent Landing •

Calcasieu R.

27

384

Moss Lake

LNG Canal

Choupique Is.

N

Ellender Bridge

Turners Bay

STATUTE MILES

0   5

Intracoastal Waterway

Mud Lake

Boat Ramp

Calcasieu Lake

Grand Lake

Intracoastal Waterway

Paul Woodward, © 2004 The Countryman Press

Calcasieu Lake offers great speck fishing almost year-round and is one of the best spots on the Louisiana Coast for a fly fisherman to catch a trophy.

to the surface, where their presence is announced by squawking, diving gulls. Pitch a 4-inch-long, size 1/0 green-and-white popper into one of these melees—which, like the slicks, can occur literally anywhere on the lake, and it's doubtful you'll be able to retrieve it without a speck being attached! Notably, the lake's big specks have an affinity for conventional surface lures, so a big popper just might be the best way to go for a fly-caught trophy here.

Calcasieu Lake also holds a lot of redfish and flounder, both of which are possibilities when you're blind-casting the reefs for specks. There is little sight-fishing potential here for redfish, though. On the other hand, during the summer tripletail move into the lake—not many, but enough, and some pretty big ones, too—and they do offer a sight-fishing opportunity. Keep your eyes open and a smaller fly—something like a size 1 Deceiver—ready to be quickly swapped out should a tripletail appear.

Nine- and 10-weight outfits are recommended for Calcasieu Lake. The lighter one should be matched with a sinking-tip line and used with sinking flies; for the 10-weight, which is intended for the big, bulky poppers—the line should be full floating. For your leader a 16-pound-class tippet with a short 30-pound fluorocarbon shocker are recommended. Calcasieu Lake can be accessed from Hebert's Marina, located in Hebert's Camp about midway down the east side of the lake, or at several locations off LA 27 near Hackberry (directions are provided by your guide or marina personnel).

Prien Lake and Lake Charles itself lie within Lake Charles's city limits and both can provide creditable action, especially with specks, in late summer and early autumn—the dry season. Their banks—lined with everything from rolling, pine-topped backyards to tall buildings to docks for ships—can protect nearby waters from winds that have Calcasieu Lake white-capping, and their proximity to urban pleasures make them highly popular fishing spots in season.

The technique here is blind-casting the shoreline drop-offs, docking areas, and any open-water indications of fish like diving gulls and slicks. The same flies and gear recommended for Calcasieu Lake are suitable here, though an extra spool holding a Class III sinking line might come in handy on days when the fish are holding near bottom, a common occurrence during autumn.

Access to these lakes is from a public ramp on the Prien Lake Road at the base of the I-210 bridge and from the Bowtie Marina. Guided trips usually originate on Calcasieu Lake.

On calm days the big lake's guides will make offshore trips. Fishing can begin right at the Cameron jetties and involves year-round action with bull redfish and a hot spring bite courtesy of outsized black drum, then progresses seaward into the realm of cobia, tripletail, crevalle jack, and the lesser types. These waters are comparatively shallow—20 miles out it's only around 55 feet deep, but from late spring into autumn—the time of most offshore opportunities—it can be quite clear, offering some very good sight-fishing around the ship-channel buoys, patches of sargasso, and odds-and-ends flotsam. There's a very limited offshore charter fishery in Cameron that opens in May and runs into autumn, but it is not geared for fly fishermen. Nevertheless, the skippers can be coerced; just tell them what you want.

Lake Charles has all the amenities one would expect of a small southern city, along with a few one might not expect. There's McNeese University where you could send your kid to school and go fishing when you come down on the pretext of visiting him.

There are a couple of floating casinos, though personally, I'd rather risk my dollars on another guided trip, gambling on catching one of Calcasieu Lake's trophy specks. And in a land famous for seafood and Cajun dishes, it might seem surprising that Mazen's—an upscale Mediterranean restaurant—is a popular spot and the favorite of my good friends Capts. Jeff and Mary Poe.

Airport

Though there is a regional airport present, you'd be better off to drive to the Lake Charles area after arriving in New Orleans or Houston.

However, if you wish to fly to the region, Continental, Delta, American, and Northwest Airlines operate commuter flights to Lake Charles, flying out of large Texas cities and New Orleans.

Motels

The following is a list of motels found in Lake Charles proper. Several of the guides who fish Calcasieu Lake offer overnight accommodations on the lake in a package deal. The Hackberry Rod and Gun Club in Hackberry, Big Lake Guide Service in Hebert's Camp, and Calcasieu Charter Service, also in Hebert's Camp, are some that do.

- Best Suites of America, 401 Lakeshore Drive, 337-439-0903
- Best Western Richmond Suites, I-10 East, 337-433-5213
- Comfort Inn, 921 N. Martin Luther King Highway, 337-437-9785
- Highway Day's Inn, 1010 N. Martin Luther King Highway, 337-433-1711
- Deluxe Inn, 3900 Highway 90 E., 337-433-1024
- Econo-Lodge, 2700 Broad Street, 337-433-8291
- Economy Motel, 1512 Broad Street, 337-439-0020
- Holiday Inn, 402 N. Martin Luther King Highway, 337-433-2812
- Howard Johnson, 825 Broad Street, 337-436-4311
- Inn on the Bayou, 1101 W. Prien Lake Road, 337-474-5151 (A great place!)

- Lakeview Motel, 1000 N. Lakeshore Drive, 337-436-3336
- La Quinta Inn, 1320 N. Martin Luther King Highway, 337-436-5998
- Melrose Motel, 2429 Broad Street, 337-436-3608
- Motel 5, 3407 Broad Street, 337-439-6113
- Motel 6, 335 Highway 171, 337-433-1773
- Players Island Hotel, 505 N. Lakeshore Drive, 337-433-7121
- Players Lakefront Hotel, 507 N. Lakeshore Drive, 337-433-0541
- Rose Weave Motel, 1408 Booker Street, 337-433-3681
- Siener Motel, 818 Moss Street, 337-436-9584
- Sleep Inn & Suites, 3211 Venture Park Drive, 337-480-0898
- Sunrise Inn, 5390 Highway 90 E., 337-437-8339
- Super 8 Motel, 1350 E. Prien Lake Road, 337-477-1606
- Travel Inn, 1212 N. Lakeshore Drive, 337-433-9461
- Treasure Inn, 351 N. Martin Luther King Highway, 337-721-8001
- Walter's Attic Bed & Breakfast, 618 Ford Street, 337-439-6672
- Yogi Bear's Jellystone Park, 4200 Lake Powers Road, 337-433-1114

Restaurants

There isn't enough ink to print a list of all the eateries in and around Lake Charles, much less in the other destinations across Louisiana. Therefore, I'll only make note of those serving seafood—and, typically, comparatively good steaks, and groceries with a local flair. Again, the aforementioned guide services on Calcasieu Lake who offer overnight accommodations can also provide meals, and very good ones, too. By staying on the lake (and not getting into an all-night game of bu-ray, a popular Louisiana card game) you'll be fresher and more ready to confront the spotted beasts in the morning than you would after getting out of bed earlier to make the drive down from Lake Charles. I strongly suggest you yield to the call of the casinos only after your fishing trip is over!

- C'est Bon Seafood, 7383 Gulf Highway, 337-478-1703
- Crab Palace, 2218 Enterprise Boulevard, 337-433-4660
- Cravin' Cajun, 3425 Fifth Avenue, 337-479-2936
- Mazen's, 217 W. College Street, 337-477-8207
- Mr. D's on the Bayou, 3205 Common Street, 337-433-8644

Sporting Goods Stores

I know of no fly shops in Lake Charles, and there are, surprisingly, few sporting goods stores around. If you intend to fly fish, you'll have to be self-supporting.

If you bring along a casting rod—just in case the wind is blowing a bit too hard for you to cast and retrieve a fly effectively—the marinas usually have a selection of locally productive lures and a smattering of tackle. Otherwise try these:

- Lake Charles Tackle, 310 W. McNeese Street, 337-479-2999
- Pelican Pawn & Jewelry, 1704 Gertsner Memorial Drive, 337-436-7296
- Sulphur Wal-Mart Supercenter, 525 N. Cities Service Highway, 337-493-3245
- Wal-Mart, 4501 Nelson Road, 337-477-3785; 3415 Gertsner Memorial Drive, 337-474-3503; 140 Highway 171, 337-855-1348
- Wal-Mart Supercenter, 3451 Nelson Road, 337-474-2696

Marinas and Launch Sites

Lake Charles Metro Area

- Bayou Marina, 337-439-2794
- Bowtie Marina, 337-478-0130
- Nalmar Landing, 337-494-1959
- Launches can be found at Westlake and the Prien Lake Park

Calcasieu Lake

- Hebert's Marina, 337-598-5850
- Launches are located beside the Ellender Bridge on LA 27, at Davis Sea-food, Dugas' Landing, and a parish launch, all near Hackberry, at the LA 27 nature center near West Cove, at the LA 27 west landing for the Cameron ferry, at the head of the east Cameron jetty, and at Hebert's Marina.

Guides

A couple of years ago, while I was on a trip over to Jeff and Mary Poe's, Mary mentioned that there were around 60 licensed guides working Calcasieu Lake. That's a bunch! Not all of them fish at the same time, and some do come and some do go. And I'd bet that somewhere around three of those who have stayed know more than a little about fly fishing!

Jeff is one who does, and I know some of it has rubbed off on Mary. Both are great guides and are highly recommended for fly fishermen. Their once-upon-a-time residence on the shore of the lake, and a lodge in nearby Hebert's Camp, provide ample overnight accommodations, and if you talk nice to her, Mary will cook your dinner for a modest sum. Their operation is called Big Lake Guide Service, and the guides who help them on days when they are both booked are also first-rate.

Across the lake you'll find the Hackberry Rod and Gun Club, which was established many years ago and has become a tradition of sorts. It is a full-blown lodge and was made famous by its founder, Terry Shaughnessy, with whom I've fly fished and who is quite good at it. Terry moved to Florida to become a guide over there, and the club is now run by his son, Kirk Stancel. As many as 18 guides work out of the club now, but only one, Dane Viator, specializes in fly fishing. Note: If you catch a day when he's already booked, don't worry about the ability of who you draw. Just let the guide know you'll be fly fishing and that you would prefer for him or her to not pound the water with conventional tackle ahead of you!

I've never fished with Capt. Eric Rue, but I've stayed in his lodge overnight, eaten his groceries, and passed company with him, all of which was way more than satisfactory. He, like Jeff and Kirk, run a crew of guides that will do their best to make your trip a good one. Again, just let them know you'll be fly fishing. Eric's operation is also in Hebert's Camp, just around the corner from Jeff's and within a reasonable double haul of Hebert's Marina.

While the lake guides will take you offshore on appropriate days, Capt. Dan Swanson works out of Cameron for strictly that purpose. He looked like he was going to have a stroke when he saw me break out my 12-weight outfit during an August trip with him a few years ago. He specializes in rig-fishing, but he knows the sight-fishing drill for cobia and tripletail quite well; just let him know what you want—and again, bring everything you'd expect you'd need and a little more!

- Big Lake Guide Service (Capts. Jeff and Mary Poe), 337-598-3268
- Blue Water Expeditions (Capt. Dan Swanson), 337-775-2834
- Calcasieu Charter Service (Capt. Eric Rue), 337-598-4700
- Hackberry Rod and Gun Club (Capt. Kirk Stancel), 337-762-3391

And if that's not enough to put you on the right track to a great saltwater fly-fishing experience in the southwest corner of the state, then maybe Lafayette's highlights will. Me, I doubt that, but I am compelled to tell you about them anyway.

Ever since Barbara and I moved to Buras down in the Mississippi River Delta back in 1968, I've felt that as a fisherman, I had it made. Eight launch sites are within a 20-minute drive of my home—the closest being about 5 minutes, and from several of those points there's excellent fishing for speck, redfish, and, at times, even flounder begins within a distance of mere yards. But years ago, when I first turned into Jeff and Mary Poe's driveway, I realized that as fishermen, they had it made in the shade! At the time, their home lay about midway down the east bank of Calcasieu Lake, and by then Jeff had taken several specks in excess of 6 pounds from the pier of his boathouse, which was literally in his backyard! When I first saw their spread, I was eaten up with envy!

Jeff and Mary are both licensed charter captains and have built a reputation as top-of-the-line speck guides by the time I met them. I had just become the Louisiana regional editor for *Salt Water Sportsman* magazine, and had driven over there to check them out for future writing data. We only had a few hours to fish that day, and I insisted on doing so with a fly rod—with which I caught nothing. Still, we hit it off well together, and although three or four years would pass before we again shared a boat, we stayed in touch.

Jeff had enjoyed fly fishing during his youth in the lakes and ponds near his home in Alabama, but a full schedule of guiding conventional fishermen left little time for him to learn the saltwater aspects of the sport. So he honed his skills with soft-plastic and big surface lures—with which he caught specks up to 9 pounds! And he and Mary did very well for themselves.

He called me one morning in the fall of 1994. Thoughts of fly fishing for the lake's big specks had grown in number and intensity, reaching the point where they could not be ignored, so he and I had an extensive question-and-answer session on what tackle, flies, and such would be most appropriate for them. I ended up sending him some flies I had tied that had produced well at my end of the state. He bought a very nice and suitable outfit, and shortly thereafter, while he was practice-casting off his pier, he caught a speck that weighed 6.33 pounds! That fish vaulted past my 4.84-pounder, which, at the time, held the top spot in the newly formed fly-fishing division of the state's fishing records. Not a bad speck for a "practice session"!

Being the sympathetic guy that he is, Jeff invited me over later that month to try to regain my "title." The wind whistled and the lake had taken on the semblance of café au lait, so we had to pop plastics in the marsh of the Sabine National Wildlife Refuge to catch anything at all! So he invited me back again in late May—prime time for the lake's big specks.

There are a lot of popular spots in the lake: Turner's Bay up north, West Cove, The Engine and Nine-Mile Cut near the ship channel, and Commissary Point just below Jeff's house, to name a few. All are time proven—as was The Tank Battery: a derelict petroleum platform in the southeastern corner of the lake, which has since been removed. When I arrived Jeff had just sent his day's clients on their ways home with an ice chest full of speck fillets from fish that had been caught around The Tank Battery. The afternoon breeze was light, the lake was as clear as I'd ever seen it, and he was as ready as I was to go fly fishing. And as we raced down the lake toward the old platform, he mentioned the fish were still biting when he and his clients had left a couple of hours earlier.

They were still biting when we arrived. He quickly caught a pair of small ones on a fly I'd given him: a flashy size 1/0 green, chartreuse, and white Clouser Minnow. I soon caught a fair one on the same type of fly. Jeff then eased down the anchor, made a cast, and proceeded to catch a 4-pounder. He then made another cast, and while he watched me wrestle in another "fair one," the boat yawed, and his fly snagged the anchor line.

While he was retrieving his fly, I made a couple of fruitless casts at a particular spot along the platform's walkway. Then Jeff—back in action and with an exact duplicate of the fly I was using—cast at the very same spot and caught a speck that weighed 6.56 pounds! At least I got to net it.

The next morning we managed only a few fair ones, though Jeff had "something" break off after a spirited battle. And I missed a huge strike on a big popper. Then the wind picked up, so we went in, tied flies, yakked, and soaked up some cold ones during the afternoon. Mary and I tried for a couple of hours the next morning in a building gale, caught one fish, and that was that.

I wasn't able to fish with Jeff and Mary in 1996. I had planned to go again in May, but some out-of-state business came up at the same time. Then

Capt. Jeff Poe with a 6-pound-plus beauty of a speck he caught on my fly from a spot I just worked!

their busy season began, as did my cobia and tripletail season. We chatted over the phone from time to time, and Jeff was sneaking out occasionally after a charter trip, developing his fly-fishing skills as well as testing some flies he had created. One of those—a big, olive Deceiver-type streamer with red flash material and that closely mimicked a popular soft-plastic in avocado with red glitter—accounted for several specks in the 6-pound class. But Jeff wanted a truly big one, and he worked hard after it.

Ask any of the dedicated few who specifically target big specks—fish of 8 pounds and more—all across the Gulf Coast, and they will tell you those fish are the most difficult of all our inshore species to catch. They are relatively rare, they have become conditioned to every warning signal imaginable and are therefore quite spooky, and they feed rather infrequently, preferring one or two large mullet or menhaden—which sates them for some time— over a number of smaller prey. To catch one you must first find it—no mean feat in itself. It must be hungry at the time, it must not sense your presence, and it must find your offering worthwhile. Combine all that, and the odds of catching one are unfavorable at best. Add to it the element of fly fishing, and a big speck becomes the ultimate trophy for an inshore Gulf Coast fly fisherman.

But perseverance, knowledge, and his newly acquired fly-fishing skills— along with a whole lot of good luck—finally came together for Jeff on the afternoon of December 5, 1996. And I'll tell you this: I would have given a fly rod to have had a tape recorder on my phone when he called me the next morning—he was one happy puppy! The fish weighed 9.31 pounds, and he caught it—after his day's charter trip—on his olive Deceiver on an 8-weight outfit up in Turner's Bay. Besides the fact that it soon adorned a prominent place in his living room, it now rests in the top position in the state's fly-fishing records, and it is one that will be quite difficult to beat.

But with Calcasieu Lake you never know. Historically, and in the years since Jeff's spectacular catch, these waters have annually produced for recreational anglers several specks surpassing 9 pounds. Now, since commercial netting in the lake has ended, the promise of big fish is even greater.

Still, the indiscriminate take of the largest specks—which, as I've mentioned, are a strain genetically superior to others along the coast—is assuredly a hazard to the fishery. Jeff seldom keeps a big one now, and he asks his clients to release all but one of the big ones for a trophy. That's a fine idea; after all, one speck of more than 2 feet long, per day, is something I can usually only dream of in these parts, but over there many more than that are possible—but for how long?

Jeff's clients—and Mary's—still regularly catch their limits of fair ones. Most often that is done conventionally, but Jeff has a growing number of fly-fishing clients. And besides all that—and that sow of a fly-caught speck he has hanging on his wall—he has remained a really great guy. He wouldn't have become a buddy otherwise.

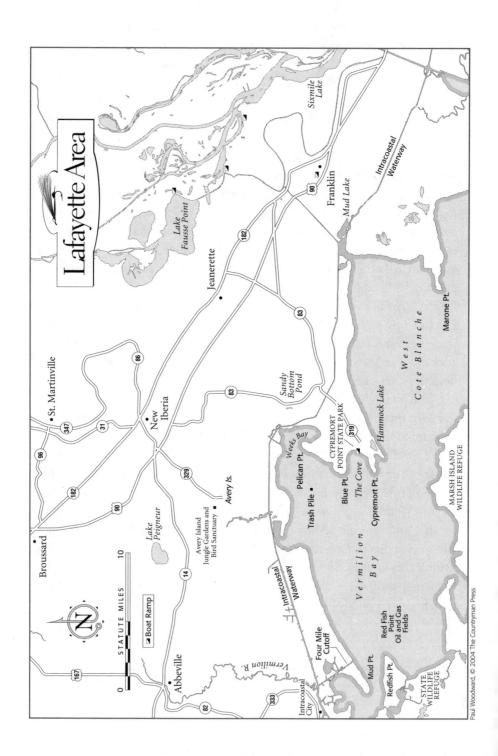

Lafayette Area

STATUTE MILES

0   10

■ Boat Ramp

Paul Woodward, © 2004 The Countryman Press

CHAPTER 11

The Lafayette Area

There's a lot of Louisiana between Calcasieu Lake and Cypremort Point, southeast of Lafayette, that could offer some decent fly fishing, but access to this area is very limited and quite remote. There is a launch in Grand Chenier, which is east of Cameron on LA 82, on the Mermentau River—normally a muddy waterway that leads to nowhere for a fly fisherman. There is also a marina of sorts on Freshwater Bayou off LA 82 east of Pecan Island. It isn't much, and I've been told its owner doesn't care if it ever amounts to more than just that. I've been there once to check it out as an access point to the Gulf and surrounding marshes, couldn't find anyone to talk to, and left with absolutely no intention of ever returning.

The last time I was in Intracoastal City—south of Abbeville—was more than 20 years ago, and the town seemed to be entirely created for the petroleum industry. In truth, that's why I was there, supervising some oil-well remedial work in what was then Gulf Oil's Redfish Point field. But that aside, I have never heard a word about anything pertaining to sport fishing of any type in Intracoastal City.

From there to Cypremort Point, any launch-site you might discover would be in freshwater and a long way from salty environs. Cypremort Point is indeed *the* saltwater access point readily available to Lafayette anglers, and the area it serves is rather limited. I include it because of all the other fun and games to be had in Lafayette and the surrounding area. First of all, though, there's the fishing.

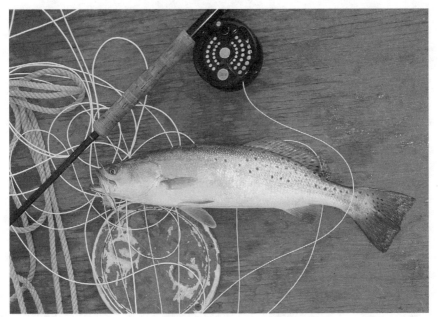

Lafayette relies on Cypremort Point to provide local saltwater fishing opportunities, and then usually only during late summer and fall, but there is a lot of lagniappe *(Cajun for "extra") in the area.*

That is mostly confined to the reefs in Vermilion and Cote Blanche Bays, and the canals, bayous, and ponds in Marsh Island—a wildlife refuge. Bay fishing has improved in recent years as a result of the Department of Wildlife and Fisheries (DW&F) adding shells to damaged and subsiding reefs. These reefs provide good fishing for all the popular inshore species found along the northern Gulf as well as an autumn run of bull reds. However, they are fairly deep—up to 12 feet or so—and will require a full sinking line to fish effectively.

Another popular open-water spot is north of Cypremort (Cajun French for "dead cypress") Point and is fondly known as the Trash Pile. It is a submerged field of cypress stumps in around 7 feet of water, and when that is clear, it provides good action with specks and reds. The Cove—a pocket inside a line between Cypremort Point and Blue Point to the north—has good redfishing along the stump-lined shoreline, and to the east Hammock Lake can provide good catches of both redfish and flounders. And even though my son-in-law, Chris Disher, of Lafayette, occasionally fishes out of Cypremort Point and even catches something every now and then, I must thank Paul

Cook, inland fisheries biologist at the New Iberia office of the DW&F, for that information.

Cook also related that the ponds within Marsh Island offer some excellent sight-fishing for reds—when the water is clear! And during much of the year it, like the adjacent bays, isn't—a result of Atchafalaya River runoff through its Wax Lake outlet. This is almost exclusively a summer and autumn fishery, and if you want to go offshore, it can be an awfully long run to water clear enough for sight-fishing.

For sight-fishing in the Marsh Island ponds, bayous, and such, an 8-weight outfit and full-floating mono-core line is adequate. There, flies like 3-inch-long, size 1 green-over-yellow poppers, weedless size 1 Roadkills (a black and purple "SeaDucer" of sorts which is quite effective on shallow reds when they are a little tight-lipped), and ice-chenille-bodied bucktails that ride hook-point up are good choices. For blind-casting the deeper reefs and stump-fields in the bays, a 9- or 10-weight outfit would be more appropriate, the Class III or IV sinking line a must, and size 1/0 Clouser Minnow–types more appealing, especially to any bull reds that might be present.

Louisiana assuredly offers a lot of saltwater fly-fishing opportunities that are much better than what is available off Cypremort Point. (Otherwise I doubt this book would have been published!) Nevertheless, these waters are a viable option, especially if you like to combine fishing-time with a little road-time, scoping out the local color and sampling the local goodies.

Must-sees include Avery Island, its gardens, and its wildlife. This is the snout of a subterranean salt dome and is located at the end of LA 329 a short drive southwest of New Iberia. It is owned by the McIlhenny family of Tabasco brand pepper sauce fame and requires a modest admission fee, but there aren't many places on this planet that are like it. It is worth seeing.

In New Iberia itself is "Shadows on the Teche"—an antebellum plantation home that has been maintained as a tourist attraction. It is a place of true southern finery, and, if you are into that kind of thing, it is definitely worth seeing!

St. Martinsville can be reached by taking LA 96 off US 90 in Broussard—a Lafayette suburb, or from New Iberia via LA 31. It offers the Longfellow Evangeline State Commemorative Area and the Evangeline Oak, along with a lot of historic Acadian (or "Cajun") stuff.

Henderson lies right on the edge of the Atchafalaya Floodway and is best reached by taking I-10 east from Lafayette. It is the home of Pat's—a seafood restaurant that has been in my life since 1964. Sure, there are other restaurants in Henderson and that are probably as good as Pat's, maybe even better. I really wouldn't know, because I've never eaten in any of the others. Unless turtle sauce piquant is on the menu, shame on you if you eat anything but crawfish—boiled, fried, étouffée, bisque, pies, or whatever. Bon appetit!

Lafayette offers a lot of Acadian centers. One you might check out is the Acadian Park Nature Station and Trail, which is situated on a 5,000-year-old Indian campground. Others here and elsewhere can be found in *The Roads of Louisiana* (Fredricksburg, TX: Shearer Publishing, 1998)—an atlas of sorts that is available at Louisiana bookstores or at 1-800-458-3808.

All that and some decent fishing, but it gets better, too!

Motels

- Acadian Motel, 120 N. University Avenue, 337-234-3268
- Alexander's, 1521 W. Pinhook Road, 337-235-6111
- Bendel Executive Suites, 213 Bendel Road, 337-261-0604
- Best Suites of America, 125 E. Kaliste Saloom Road, 337-235-1367
- Best Western Hotel Acadiana, 1801 W. Pinhook Road, 337-233-8120
- Blue Moon Guest House, 215 E. Convent Street, 337-234-2422
- Calloway's Inn, 1605 N. University Avenue, 337-232-6131
- Comfort Inn, 1421 SE. Evangeline Thruway, 337-232-9000
- Comfort Suites, 2300 NE. Evangeline Thruway, 337-291-6008
- Courtyard by Marriott, 214 E. Kaliste Saloom Road, 337-232-5005
- Cypress Tree Inn, 2501 SE. Evangeline Thruway, 337-234-8521
- Days Inn, 1620 N. University Avenue, 337-237-8880
- Executive House Hotel, 115 Sycamore Drive, 337-988-1750
- Extended StayAmerica, 807 S. Hugh Wallis Road, 337-232-8313
- Fairfield Inn, 2225 NW. Evangeline Thruway, 337-235-9898
- Hampton Inn Hotel, 2144 W. Willow Street, 337-236-6161
- Hilton Lafayette, 1521 W. Pinhook Road, 337-235-6111
- Holiday Inn, 2032 NE. Evangeline Thruway, 337-233-6438
- Holiday Inn Central Holidome, 2032 NE. Evangeline Thruway, 337-233-6815
- Homewood, Inc. 2503 SE. Evangeline Thruway, 337-234-2000
- Lafayette Hilton & Towers, 1521 W. Pinhook Road, 337-235-6111
- Lafayette Inn, 2615 Cameron Street, 337-235-9442

- Lafitte's Inn, 1801 NW. Evangeline Thruway, 337-233-5500
- La Quinta—Lafayette, 2100 NE. Evangeline Thruway, 337-233-5610
- Lighthouse Inn, 2111 NW. Evangeline Thruway, 337-235-4591
- Motel 6, 2724 NE. Evangeline Thruway, 337-233-2055
- Plantation Motor Inn, 2810 NE. Evangeline Thruway, 337-232-7285
- Ramada Inn, 2716 NE. Evangeline Thruway, 337-233-0003
- Ramada Inn, 120 E. Kaliste Saloom Road, 337-235-0858
- Red Roof Inn, 1718 N. University Avenue, 337-233-3339
- Rodeway Inn, 1801 NW. Evangeline Thruway, 337-233-5500
- Shoney's Inn, 2216 NE. Evangeline Thruway, 337-234-0383
- Sleep Inn Hotel, 2140 W. Willow Street, 337-264-0408
- Travel Host Inn, 1314 NE. Evangeline Thruway, 337-233-2090
- Travelodge—Oil Center, 1101 W. Pinhook Road, 337-234-7402

Restaurants

If you're not quite sure how much south Louisiana folks enjoy eating, get on the Internet, call up Yahoo's yellow pages, locate Lafayette, La., and then search for restaurants. If I had to transfer all of them by typing them onto a floppy disc for my editor, I have no doubt my fingers would fall off, and that would make fly fishing difficult for me. No thanks! Again, the establishments listed here serve seafood and local goodies. I don't think you'll be disappointed!

Those establishments highlighted by a "*" are regularly enjoyed by my daughter and her husband, Christi and Chris Disher.

- Alexander's, 1521 W. Pinhook Road, 337-235-6111
- Cajun Boilers, 6803 Johnston Street, 337-993-3614
- *Don's Seafood and Steak House, 301 E. Vermilion, 337-235-3551; 4309 Johnston Street, 337-981-1141
- Evangeline Steakhouse & Seafood, 2633 SE. Evangeline Thruway, 337-233-2658
- Gator Cove Restaurant, 2601 SE. Evangeline Thruway, 337-264-1263
- Guidry's Reef, 1508 W. Pinhook Road, 337-237-2860
- John's Seafood, 405 NW. Evangeline Thruway, 337-269-9117
- Julien's Famous Cajun-Style Poboys—Store #1, 1900 W. University Avenue, 337-232-5168; Store #2, 4400 Ambassador Caffery Parkway, 337-981-8162

- Kajun Kitchen & Lounge, 2111 NW. Evangeline Thruway, 337-233-3098
- *Lafayette's Restaurant, 1025 Kaliste Saloom Road, 337-216-9024
- La Fete du Lafayette (Cajun and seafood buffet), 4401 Johnston Street, 337-981-9979
- Lagneaux's Restaurant, 445 Ridge Road, 337-984-1415
- Miss Helen's Cajun Seafood, 101 Vital Street, 337-234-8586
- Oxford Street Restaurant & Pub, 3561 Ambassador Caffery Parkway, 337-989-8017
- *Poor-boy's Riverside Inn, 240 Tubing Road, 337-235-8559
- *Prejean's Restaurant, 3480 I-49 N, 337-896-3247 (also features live Cajun music)
- *Randal's Restaurant and Cajun Dance Hall (also features live Cajun music), 2320 Kaliste Saloom Road, 337-981-7080

And for those who have an inordinate fondness for Mexican food (like I do!), there's

- *Posado's Café, 3822 Ambassador Caffery Parkway, 337-988-0835

There are also a lot of creditable eateries in Lafayette's neighboring cities. In New Iberia a few of note are

- *Bon Creole, 1409 E. St. Peter, 337-367-6181 (Note: My wife, Christi, relates that Bon Creole looks like a hole-in-the-wall, but it's a local favorite, and the meals are great! She ought to know!)
- Landry's Seafood & Steakhouse, 2318 Highway 90 W., 337-369-3772
- *Little River Inn, 833 E. Main Street, 337-367-7466

Finally, if you'd like to experience a culinary adventure, make the trip to Henderson.

- Pat's Fisherman's Wharf, 1008 Henderson Levee Road, 337-228-7512

Mangez!

Good Eatin'

Since a lot of this chapter is dedicated to eating and I find absolutely nothing illegal, immoral, or unethical about occasionally practicing a little catch-and-keep with a fly rod, I thought it might be apropos here to include some recipes that reflect a little, uh, local color—mine, anyway.

Grilled Redfish

1 20- to 22-inch redfish filleted, but with the skin and scales still
    attached (if not available, striped bass fillet would be a suitable
    substitute)
2 shallots, finely chopped
½ tablespoon minced garlic
½ stick of margarine (4 tablespoons)
garlic salt (to taste)
cayenne pepper (to taste)
small handful chopped parsley (dried or fresh)
Preheat broiler at 450 degrees.

Place the fillets scales side down on a cookie sheet. Make three or four diagonal cuts through each fillet, ensuring the skin is not cut through. Dust the fillets lightly with garlic salt and cayenne pepper and set aside.

Place fillets in broiler at 450 degrees. Melt the margarine in a small saucepan. Add the shallots, minced garlic, and parsley and cook on low heat for about 15 minutes.

Baste the fillets with half of the sauce before placing them in the oven. Broil until the meat flakes easily. When they are done baste the fillets with the remaining sauce.

Serve with a green salad and either a small baked potato or French bread.

Makes 2 servings.

Redfish Soup

This may actually be redfish "court bouillion" (a well-known Creole fish dish), but when I got inspired to create one I had forgotten what it was supposed to taste like, and I had no recipe for it. So I had to ad-lib. It turned out pretty tasty, whatever you choose to call it!

2 22- to 24-inch redfish—filleted, skinned, and cut into bite-sized
    chunks with all the red meat removed
⅓ cup corn or vegetable oil; ⅓ cup flour
1 large yellow onion, finely chopped
1 tablespoon minced garlic
1 tablespoon basil (smashed)
¼ tablespoon thyme (fresh or dried)
1 tablespoon onion salt
1 tablespoon white pepper
1 can (12 oz.) petite diced tomatoes
2 cans tomato sauce
4 cups water.
2 bay leaves.
chopped parsley (fresh or dry)

Make a *roux* (see below) with the corn oil and the flour, then sauté the onion and garlic for 5 minutes. Add all the other ingredients except the fish and parsley and simmer covered for about a half-hour.

Add the fish and parsley and simmer covered for another half-hour or until the fish flakes easily.

Oh, so you don't know what a *roux* (pronounced roo) is? Literally, it's a Cajun word for flour browned in oil and used as a thickening agent for gravies, soups, and the like. It serves as the base for many fine recipes.

For a dish that will serve up to four people, you create a roux by pouring ⅓ cup of the oil into a large iron or steel pot (use half-cup portions of flour and oil for recipes with more servings). Flick two or three drops of water into the oil and heat it on high. When the water begins to "pop" add ⅓ cup of flour and turn the heat down to medium. Now the fun (work?) starts.

With a large wooden spoon begin to stir the flour into the oil. Now you cannot stop, as the roux will either burn or quit making if you do, so don't answer the phone, the door, or any call of nature until the roux is done. After it has reached a dark-brown consistency, has begun to smoke a little, and smells like it's about to burn, quickly add the onions, peppers, celery, garlic, or whatever, and sauté them, still continuously stirring the mixture. Once the veggies are soft you can either put it aside for later use—even freeze it—or continue on with the recipe. But I must reaffirm: Once you have started the roux and for some reason have to leave it, you cannot restart it. Throw it away and begin again.

Serve over rice—remember this is a soup and not a stew—with French bread.

Makes 4 servings.

Perhaps this red will find its way to the table!

And if you're really brave—and happen to have a couple of tripletail fillets handy, you simply must try some of the following:

Pete's Scintillating Ceviche

1 4- to 5-pound tripletail filleted, skinned, and cut into ¼-inch strips
with all the red meat removed
juice from at least 5 limes (enough to cover all the strips)
1 tablespoon salt
1 tablespoon Tabasco Sauce
3 shallots, finely chopped

Thoroughly mix all the ingredients except the fish and place into a shallow, wide bowl. Add the fish, ensuring it is all covered with the juice. Place in the fridge and let sit for about 6 hours. The strips are done when they are white and without any opaqueness. If, after 24 hours, there are any leftover strips, pour off the remaining juice and keep covered to prevent them from drying out. I promise they won't last long!

And yes, the fish is cooked—the lime juice does it!

An appetizer or a light main course for 2.

Sporting Goods Stores

Come entirely well supplied to this area!
- Academy Sporting Goods, 4533 Johnston Street, 337-984-9868
- Wal-Mart Supercenter, 3142 Ambassador Caffery Parkway, 337-989-2120; 2428 W. Pinhook Road, 337-231-1992

New Iberia hosts even more.
- Blue's Archery & Tackle, 684 E. Admiral Doyle Drive, 337-369-9280
- Gary's Sporting Goods, 224 Center Street, 337-367-2310
- Holiday Sporting Goods, 805 S. Lewis Street, 337-365-2763
- Lipari Sporting Goods, 958 S. Lewis Street, 337-364-9891

Marinas and Launch Sites
- Cypremort Point State Park, 337-867-4510
  Here you will find rest rooms, picnic areas, group shelters, fishing, swim-

ming, and a launch for nonmotorized craft. In light to moderate easter-
lies the shoreline of the Cove can be fishable from canoes and such.

- Bay View Marina, 565 Bay View Drive, 337-867-4324
  Guides are intermittently available during the season (summer and au-
  tumn). Virtually everything shuts down here during winter and spring.
  It's best, if possible, to bring your own boat.

Bay Name	Reef Name	GPS Coordinates
Cote Blanche	Nickel Reef	29°25.16'N 91°42.45'W
Cote Blanche	Rabbit Island #1	29°35.62'N 91°35.80'W
Cote Blanche	Rabbit Island #2	29°30.57'N 91°33.87'W
Vermilion	Cypremort Point	29°43.33'N 91°52.37'W
Vermilion	Redfish Point	29°40.62'N 92°07.08'W

Now let's move on to a really great fishing area, though the local color may
not be quite so, well, "colorful."

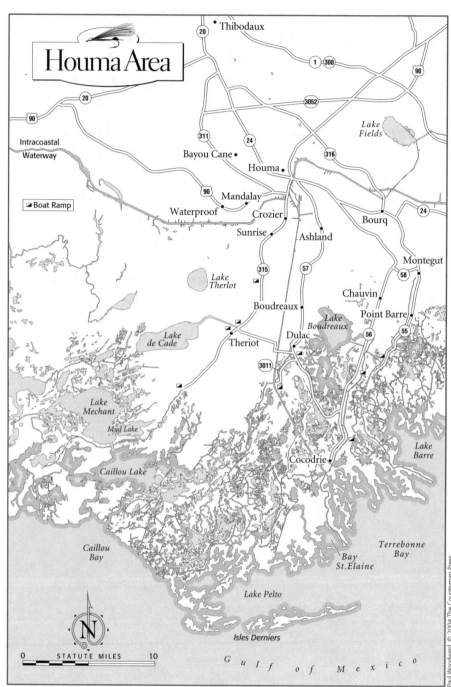

Houma Area

Thibodaux

20

1 308

90

3052

Lake
Fields

20

90

Intracoastal
Waterway

311

24

316

Bayou Cane

Houma

24

Boat Ramp

90

Mandalay

Bourq

Waterproof

Crozier

Sunrise

Ashland

Montegut

58

315

57

Lake
Therlot

Chauvin

Boudreaux

Point Barre

Lake
Boudreaux

56

55

Lake
de Cade

Theriot

Dulac

3011

Lake
Mechant

Mud Lake

Lake
Barre

Caillou Lake

Cocodrie

Caillou
Bay

Terrebonne
Bay

Bay
St. Elaine

Lake Pelto

N

Isles Derniers

0   STATUTE MILES   10

G u l f   o f   M e x i c o

CHAPTER III

The Houma Area

Houma (pronounced Home' ah) is a midsized city about 60 miles southwest of Louis Armstrong International Airport in New Orleans and is named after an Indian tribe that once inhabited the area. Its economy is very dependant on the petroleum industry and the area has few must-sees for tourists. However, it is a pretty town, and as it is in the "Cajun belt" its residents know how to eat—and how to cook! Therefore there are some fine seafood and Cajun restaurants scattered around (see listings at the end of the chapter). There is also some excellent saltwater fishing a short drive to the south!

Houma has just about everything you'd expect to find in a city of its size. Like Lake Charles and Lafayette, it has a big hospital and medical center, though not as big as those in the first two destinations. It also has an airport, though it is comparatively small. At least it was years ago, when I was flying offshore and back out of the nearby heliport that, incidentally, was quite large!

It seems strange, but after all the years that have passed since I was last there, I can clearly recall the heliport's logo printed on T-shirts that they sold: an airborne Bell "Lone Ranger" with the inscription beneath it, "Avoid the rush; fly to work."

I did that for more than a year when I was a drilling representative for Gulf Oil, logging a great deal of helicopter time. I caught my first decent cobia (on a shrimp) off the South Timbalier Block 37A platform (while I was supposed to be working) during my tour of duty out of Houma. And ongoing reports from friends, guide-buddies, and a certain son-in-law indicate that the fishing south of Houma continues to be excellent, and there are plenty of places to access it. There are also a few folks of the fly-fishing persuasion here and there! True, the specks may not reach the size of those found in Calcasieu Lake, but they—and the redfish—are much more plentiful. There are also bull reds along the barrier island beaches and their passes almost year-round, and the platforms in Block 37, which are really good for cobia, are less than 10 miles offshore.

The area around Houma is unlike that near Lake Charles and Lafayette because it is unaffected by runoff from a large river. However, the bays can become roiled from trawlers during the inshore shrimp seasons in spring and fall, and summer algae and plankton blooms can turn the water quite turbid in places. Here, as in anywhere else along the Louisiana Coast, locating reasonably clear water is of primary importance to a fly fisherman. Here, there's plenty of it; you just have to find some!

Speck fishing usually begins in earnest in March. School-sized fish then quickly become plentiful in interior areas like Lake Boudreaux, Lake de Cade, Lake Mechant, and Lake Barre, though they are certainly not confined to those waters. A real fete with poppers arises when schools of these fish herd shrimp to the surface; look for slicks and diving gulls as indications of that festivity. Somewhat slower but often longer-lasting action takes place with Clouser Minnow–types worked across the numerous shell-beds in the area.

Early on, an 8-weight outfit is suitable for this time and place, as size 1 flies are about as big as you'll need and the largest red you're likely to encounter will not demand anything heavier. However, by the beginning of the big-fish time of May and June, larger flies, like size 1/0 Clouser-types and poppers, will better your chances. Personally, I now exclusively use a 9-weight for inshore work in all seasons but summer, as it allows me to cast big flies and bulky poppers as well as smaller ones with relatively ease, plus it's more effective in a breeze.

During May and June when the potential for a trophy is best, the petroleum facilities and reefs in the open waters of Timbalier and Terrebonne Bays are good bets. Most of the big fish will be taken deep—"near bottom" might be a better description. However, during early-morning calm spells these fish can be coerced to hit a big popper. Steady retrieves of moderately paced soft pops are best unless a fish acts like it wants to initially stun the popper rather than eat it. If that's the case, after a missed strike allow the

*The waters south of Houma offer very good inshore and offshore fly-fishing
for a variety of popular species.*

popper to rest for three to four seconds, then give it the slightest twitch. Just
thinking about the result sends me into acute withdrawal!

Typical of the Louisiana Coast, by the first of summer the best action
with specks below Houma normally moves toward seashore waters, like Lake
Pelto, the lower reaches of Terrebonne and Timbalier Bays, Bay St. Elaine,
and Caillou Bay.

Incidentally, a local chapter of the Coastal Conservation Association
funded the construction of a reef made of crushed Kentucky limestone in
lower Lake Pelto during early 2002. It is at the one-time site of Bird Island,
is well marked, will be maintained by the Department of Wildlife & Fisheries, and should be self-sustaining with a building accumulation of oysters

on it. Situated in roughly 6 to 12 feet of water, it should become a real hotspot shortly!

During summer the outside waters are usually where you will find the largest specks. As in spring, these fish can be caught over shell-beds and chasing open-water prey, but now some of the most consistent catches are made around oil-field structures—platforms, wells with clamshell "pads" that rise a few feet off the bay's bottom to provide firm support for the rig that drilled the well, and the like—and in the surf. Again, big flies normally take the biggest specks; don't worry if it takes a 10-weight outfit for you to cast a size 1/0 3-inch-long Clouser Minnow in order to catch these fish—do what you gotta do!

Summer finds school-sized speck all over the middle and outer bays and occasionally in the surf. In more interior waters, oyster beds and schools of fish detected while feeding in open water produce much of the action. Nevertheless, fishing for them beneath the lights of a petroleum platform—with poppers, *s'il vous plait*—is a real boot and is a fine way to beat Louisiana's stifling summer heat!

In interior areas—and at night—smaller flies can be productive and allow the use of much lighter outfits in calm conditions. The nighttime opportunity is created by the platform's lights attracting small shrimp and minnows, which, in turn, draw the predators, usually specks. Quite a few guides working out of the marinas at Cocodrie offer abbreviated night trips. (Frequently that's all that's required for amassing a limit; if you want to practice catch-and-release a while longer, be sure your guide knows your wishes beforehand!)

Some time in October specks will begin to move back inside to congregate in the same waters in which they are found in March. Some of the best action of the year—along with some of the shortest boat runs—can come in November and early December, and good catches are quite possible during moderate winters. However, redfish provide a better opportunity at that time.

Reds are abundant throughout this area. The best way to catch them—sight-fishing, *merci beaucoup*—is exactly like it is anywhere else. Find a shoreline that is sheltered from the wind and has water a foot or so deep against it and start looking! The shorelines of interior ponds and broken marsh are usually better than the banks of larger bays, and spring and fall are the best times for all-day action. During summer look for them in early morning and mid- to late afternoon; midday is best for sight-fishing in winter. Avoid abnormally high tides for sight-fishing at any time of the year; remember, "The less water there is, the fewer places a red can go, so the more likely you will be to see it." That's Pete's Law of the Low Tide, in case you didn't know. The

9-weight outfit and flies that are productive elsewhere work just fine here.

While bull reds lately have been prowling the barrier island beaches and passes year-round, their numbers have historically tended to increase from July into October. Mullet heads and half of a blue crab are popular enticers. Size 2/0 chartreuse-and-white Clousers (Hey, if it ain't broke, don't try to fix it!) and Class III or heavier lines on a 10- to 12-weight outfit are required for fly fishermen when the fish are deep in the passes through the Timbalier and Terrebonne Island chains. Lighter gear and intermediate sinking or sinking-tip lines suffice when bull reds are running the surf. This opportunity will normally provide the best action on a guided trip.

Offshore opportunities in this area are most often confined between May and October. For a fly fisherman they involve cobia, tripletail, crevalle jack, and the lesser types, and action takes place around platforms, along current lines, beneath flotsam, around open-water schools of baitfish, and behind shrimp trawlers. True, these are nearshore opportunities and are more easily reached from Grand Isle and Venice. And yes, that nearshore potential here is very good, but the marsh, bays, and barrier islands south of Houma are what make this destination shine so brightly.

From Houma LA 315 leads to launch sites at Theriot (a favorite of Chris's) and at the end of the road; these provide access to Lake de Cade, Lake Mechant (and Chris's secret spot in Mud Lake) and the marshes on the western side of this area. LA 57 and a ramp at Dulac provide access to the central marshes and Lake Boudreaux. LA 56 leads to Cocodrie—the most developed access point and the most popular jumping-off spot for the barrier islands and offshore grounds. It also has some great spots to overnight and eat!

Motels

- A-Bear Motel, 342 New Orleans Boulevard, 985-872-4528
- Audrey's Lil' Cajun Mansion, 815 Funderburk Avenue, 985-879-3285
- Economy Inn, 224 South Hollywood Road, 985-851-6041
- Fairfield Inn, 1530 Martin Luther King Jr. Boulevard, 985-580-1050
- Hampton Inn, 1728 Martin Luther King Jr. Boulevard, 985-873-3140
- Holiday Inn, 210 S. Hollywood Road, 985-868-5851
- Holiday Motel, 802 LA 182, 985-879-2737
- Honduras House, 1023 Saadi Street, 985-868-1520
- Lake Houmas Inn, 955 LA 182, 985-868-9021

- Plantation Inn, 1381 W. Tunnel Boulevard, 985-868-0500
- Ramada Inn, 1400 W. Tunnel Boulevard, 985-879-4871
- Red Carpet Inn, 2115 Bayou Black Drive, 985-876-4160
- Sugar Bowl Motel, 8053 Park Avenue, 985-872-4521

Restaurants

Again it behooves me to list only the seafood and Cajun restaurants in the area. And for sure, don't overlook the lodges in Chauvin and Cocodrie for your meals, should you choose to overnight closer to the action than Houma. They can be awfully hard to beat!

- A-Bear's Restaurant, 809 Bayou Black Drive, 985-872-6306
- Bayou Delight Restaurant, 4038 Bayou Black Drive, 985-876-4879
- Boudreau & Thibodeau's Cajun Cooking, 5602 W. Main Street, 985-872-4711
- Cajun Treasures, 2927 LA 311, 985-868-0680
- Copeland's of New Orleans, 1534 Martin Luther King Jr. Boulevard, 985-873-9600
- Dave's Cajun Kitchen, 6240 W. Main Street, 985-868-3870
- Doogies on the Bayou, 3254 Little Bayou Black Drive, 985-872-9073
- Dupree's Seafood, 5511 W. Main Street, 985-868-2828
- Eastway Seafood, 1029 W. Tunnel Boulevard, 985-876-2121
- J&M's Boiled Crawfish & Espresso Hut, 6914 W. Main Street, 985-876-6925
- 1921 Seafood, 1522 Barrow Street, 985-868-7098
- Rick's Cajun American Restaurant, 1023 W. Tunnel Boulevard, 985-879-4386
- Savoie's Louisiana Cooking, 1377 W. Tunnel Boulevard, 985-872-9819

Jouirez!

Sporting Goods Stores

Houma

- Capt. Allen's Bait & Tackle, 4325 LA 56, 985-868-2204
- Champ's Sports, 5953 W. Park Avenue, 985-872-3038
- Danny's Sporting Goods, 9642 E. Main Street, 985-872-4011
- Dinger's Outdoors, 307 N. Hollywood Road, 985-873-8644

- Duncan Sports, 1056 Grand Caillou Road, 985-876-6891
- Sharky's Bait & Tackle, 3194 Grand Caillou Road, 985-872-3474
- Songy's Sporting Goods, 3044 Barrow Street, 985-857-8929
- Sports Avenue, 5953 W. Park Avenue, 985-868-2589
- Wal-Mart Supercenter, 1633 Martin Luther King Jr. Boulevard, 985-851-2745

Chauvin

- Bayou Bait & Tackle, 7681 LA 56, 985-594-9462
- Sandpiper Bait & Tackle, 7211 Shoreline Drive, 985-594-1800

Marinas and Launch Sites

Theriot

- Falgout Canal Marina, LA 315, 985-782-1636
  There is a back-down ramp at the end of the highway.

Dulac

- Boudreaux's Marina, 1711 Four Point Road, 985-563-4356
- Defelice Marina & Seafood, 163 Old Bridge Road, 985-563-2100

Chauvin

- Sportsman's Paradise, LA 56, 1-800-906-5484

Cocodrie

- Cocodrie Charters and Lodge, 7255 Shoreline Drive, 1-877-524-3474
- Co-Co Marina, LA 56, 985-594-6626

The last three marinas are full-blown destinations in themselves, offering great cooking, nice overnight accommodations, plenty of atmosphere, and a host of capable guides. While most of those are not really "fly-fishing guides," many of them know the drill. They will put you on fish; you'll just have to catch them. That also means here, too, you'll have to be entirely self-supportive.

Guides

Besides the conventional guides who are available through the Chauvin and Cocodrie lodges, there are actually three in the area who are competent fly-fishing guides.

- Danny Ayo, 985-868-7208
- Gerald Bryant, 985-868-2353
- Blaine Townsend, 985-594-7772

There's enough fly-fishing potential in this area, along with all the other things that create an enjoyable trip, to make the days you spend in and around Houma hard to forget. I know a lot of those guys over there, and besides knowing their stuff, they are also fun!

Passez un bon temps!

If a state's recreational possession limit for a particular fish is any indication of the abundance of the species in its waters, then Louisiana must assuredly host a tremendous population of spotted sea trout—speck in local patois. Here, an angler can keep—if he so chooses—25 of these tasty gamesters per day. That's many more than he can keep in any other state bordering on the Gulf of Mexico, and during much of the year doing so is not all that difficult a task.

Sure, for fly fishermen as well as for those with conventional mind-sets, the productive techniques change with the seasons. And during spring and fall—those times that are usually considered best for these fish, and no matter how good the action can be—two factors arise that combine to adversely affect much of the sport of those who fish with flies. The first is the fact that large flies are usually most effective. In spring—normally the best time for really big fish—large flies are the surest way to tempt a trophy. During autumn they should more closely match the size of the various prey species that speck then pursue.

The second factor is the wind—the often persistent 12- to 15-knot breeze, a condition in which the waters are still fly-fishable but demand 8- or even 9-weight sticks in order to cast those large flies. So here's the rub: In the inland bays, bayous, and canals across the Louisiana Coast, a 9-weight outfit is far too heavy to provide any real sport with most of the specks that you'll encounter during the prime times. However, if you fly fish for the specks of summer, you can often use gear that allows them to really strut their stuff.

While there will be a lot of fish around during summer, this is not the season considered to be quality time. Many specks will be short of the 12-inch minimum-size restriction, and fish of 20 inches or more are uncommon in most of the areas where fly fishing is a viable option. During the dog days of late July, August, and September an average size of 15 inches would be creditable, though on a torrid August afternoon a while back I caught over two dozen that averaged a bit larger. Some folks contend that even speck like those are too small to be much fun to catch. I would agree—if I happened to be wielding an 8- or 9-weight stick at the time. That day I was using a 6-weight, the gear of choice for summer speck for half a decade now, and believe me, I had a ball!

Two factors that lead to the need for heavier rods during much of the remainder of the year are absent during summer. First, it is, typically, fairly calm, so casting a 6-weight the normally required 60 feet or so is no chore. And second, the prey species are now fairly small, so the flies that mimic them best are quite suitable for use with the lighter rod. Size 4s are just right. While a smorgasbord of appetizing morsels awaits the specks during summer, one of the primary sources of protein at that time is small white shrimp. However, in the typically dingy waters of the season in many areas, an exact match is not necessary, and Clouser Minnows and poppers in chartreuse over white or green over chartreuse suffice as "near-nuff" imitations of the shrimp as well as small menhaden and bay anchovies, which are also on the specks' menu. Tie them a tad on the bulky side, tie 'em tough, and carry a bunch of them with you—if you find fish as I have a few times, it's possible to catch more than 100 on a good tide. And on that note, remember to flatten your hooks' barbs; you may lose some fish when they surface and perform their familiar head-sloshing routine, but you will injure far fewer of those you intend to release.

The outfit I normally use could be deemed more appropriate for river-dwelling smallmouth bass than for saltwater applications, but it has proven ideal for summer specks. The rod is a fast 9-footer, the reel a beefed-up and corrosion-resistant trout model holding 100 yards of 20-pound Dacron backing and a floating braided monocore line. The leader is around 8 feet long, tapered to 12-pound class, and finished with a foot of 20-pound fluorocarbon for resistance to fraying by the specks' raspy teeth. As it is, the outfit is light enough to prevent undue fatigue from several hours of nonstop casting in the broiling heat; it casts the aforementioned flies with ease; and it allows the fish to show their spunk while still being capable of handling a

*During summer, the bays south of Houma provide a fine example of
the speck fishing found along the Louisiana Coast.*

decent-sized redfish should one of them make an appearance—a fairly
common event. Remember that the largest inshore redfish I've ever taken,
which weighed almost 15 pounds, was captured on a 6-weight outfit, so fear
not an encounter with a red while using one.

There are two tried-and-true ways to enjoy the spectacular light-tackle
action that summer speck offer: Either hire a guide or time your own trip to
coincide with the falling tide. Along much of the coast low tide often occurs
near dark. That causes some of the best time to fish to take place during the
hottest part of the day, so carry a lot of water and sunscreen along with your
bunch of flies; you will need them all!

On the other hand, the heat doesn't seem to bother the speck too much,
provided there is current present. That is the factor that generates the bite.
Here's how it works:

As the tide falls, it drains the shallow ponds and cuts through the marshes surrounding the bays. The shrimp and various minnows that inhabit these havens during high tide are thus drawn into deeper waters where they become affected by the current. Since none of these prey species are particularly strong swimmers, they're carried along with the flow in a highly vulnerable state. Find a place that tends to bottleneck the flow, thereby concentrating the bait, and you have found a prime feeding spot for the specks. Notably, the best of these are usually found closer to the seashore than the hotspots of spring and fall.

One of my favorite spots—but only on a falling tide with a range of a foot or more—is the point where a moderate-sized and fairly deep tidal cut enters a shallow bay. Here, the bottleneck is the water's depth: The bait is constricted within the water column as the bottom of the cut rapidly rises to meet the bay's bottom. Finding one like it is an easy task if you pay attention to what your depth recorder is telling you. (Or if you get lucky like I did and have it given away by a flock of squawking gulls diving onto shrimp being driven to the surface by the specks!)

Current passing around a grassy point along a bay's shoreline creates another good feeding opportunity for speck, since the bait becomes concentrated as it's swept around the point. Also, clamshell dams and wooden bulkheads that once isolated canals but over time have become washed out at their ends by the current are great bunch-up spots for bait and speck alike. Find any of these that are attended, and you won't need to be told where to cast! The falling tide is best here, too, as it pulls prey from inside the canal into the waters on your side of the dam or bulkhead.

One last bit of local inshore structure that tends to gang up specks is an oyster bed. Once again, these are privately leased sections of the bay's bottom and are marked by willow branches or lengths of white PVC pipe. Once you locate one of these—preferably in around 3 feet of water at mean sea level— fan-casting across it is the proven tactic. Here, too, the falling tide is best during summer, and as the water will probably be a little dingy as it flows across the bed, the darker Clouser Minnow is the best choice. Of course, here, as anyplace else, if the fish are active on the surface, then try the popper; even a 15-inch speck will strike one of those with so much gusto that you surely wouldn't want to miss out on it! Remember, don't try to set the hook until you actually feel the weight of the fish.

In truth, on the days when poppers are effective—and that's most of them during the summer—this opportunity becomes even sweeter. Imagine this: More than 100 specks in one afternoon, all of them smashing, gulping, and jumping all over poppers, often three or four times on a single cast! Then, when they finally manage to get themselves stuck, they were on a 6-weight outfit. That's hard to beat in my book. Get yourself some of it and you'll see way.

Chapter IV

The Grand Isle Area

rand Isle is the only barrier island along the Louisiana Coast with a permanent human population. Almost all of its residents are employed in some fashion by the petroleum industry, in fishing—both commercial and recreational, or in tourism. It boasts over 6 miles of public beach where surf-fishing for specks, among others, can be outstanding, and the marsh on the north side of the island and on the nearby mainland, the islands in and at the mouth of Barataria Bay, and the open Gulf offer plenty of other fly-fishing opportunities.

However, before these are described in greater detail, I'd like to make a few points. If you take US 90 west from New Orleans, stop at the Chevron station by the stop light in Boutte and treat yourself to a couple of links of hot *boudin*, or Cajun sausage. Either crawfish or pork, this boudin is out of this world!

Bayou Lafourche (pronounced la foosh) is commonly referred to as "the longest street in the world." Because of that—and the traffic, school zones, shopping centers, and so forth alongside LA 1 on the bayou's west bank, it is best to exit US 90 on the less congested LA 308 at Raceland. Head south on it until you notice a big shopping center on your left in Galliano. Cross the bayou on the drawbridge there, then continue across LA 1, and you will shortly arrive at a nice little 4-lane bypass (LA 3235) of both Galliano and Golden Meadow that will put you back on LA 1 just south of the latter. And as a word of warning, throughout this area the speed limits are strictly en-

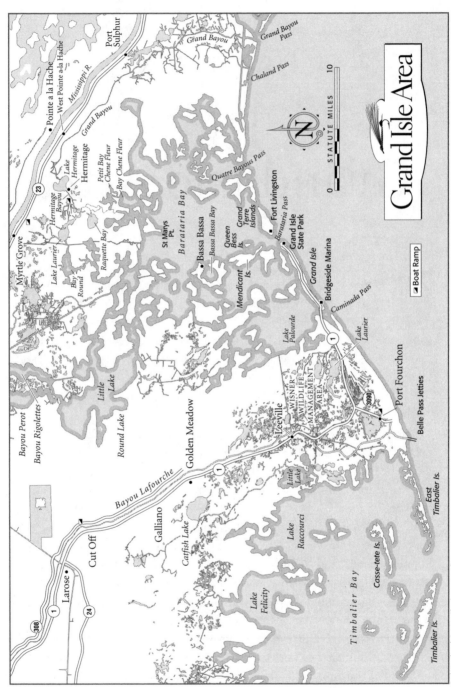

Grand Isle Area

STATUTE MILES

0   10

Paul Woodward, © 2004 The Countryman Press

■ Boat Ramp

Port Sulphur

Pointe a la Hache
West Pointe a-la Hache

Grand Bayou

Grand Bayou Pass

Chaland Pass

Mississippi R.

Grand Bayou

Hermitage
Lake Hermitage
Hermitage Bayou
Hermitage Bayou

Petit Bay Chene Fleur
Bay Chene Fleur

Quatre Bayous Pass

Myrtle Grove

Lake Laurier

Raquette Bay

Bay Round

Baratatia Bay

St Marys Pt.

Bassa Bassa
Bassa Bassa Bay

Queen Bess Is.

Grand Terre Islands

Fort Livingston

Baratatia Pass

Grand Isle State Park

Grand Isle

Bridgeside Marina

Caminada Pass

Mendicant Is.

Little Lake

Round Lake

Lake Palourde

Lake Laurier

Bayou Perot
Bayou Rigolettes

Golden Meadow

Leeville

WISNER WILDLIFE MANAGEMENT AREA

Port Fourchon

Belle Pass Jetties

Bayou Lafourche

Catfish Lake

Galliano

Cut Off

Larose

Little Lake

Lake Raccourci

Lake Felicity

Casse-tete Is.

East Timbalier Is.

Timbalier Bay

Timbalier Is.

forced; traffic tickets are a source of major income for Golden Meadow, especially, so take heed!

Below Golden Meadow on LA 1 you will follow the bayou to Leeville, and the first signs of recreational fishing amenities you will probably have noticed. From the marinas here there is access to Bayou Lafourche and thus Belle Pass and the offshore grounds, and Timbalier Bay with all its petroleum platforms—and all its specks. The surrounding marshes are loaded with redfish, and during winter some huge specks are taken from the bayou just below the bridge. Depending on where the action is presently the hottest, several guide services work out of the Leeville marinas.

Timbalier Bay, Lake Raccourci, and Little Lake offer good speck fishing, and the seasonal patterns and opportunities, effective techniques, and productive flies are the same as they are in areas south of Houma. The nearby marshes are full of redfish, which are fly fishable under the same conditions and with the same gear as they are elsewhere across the coast.

The jetties at Belle Passe occasionally offer good action with bull redfish as well as the lesser types, the best of which normally occurs during summer and fall. As in fishing for the bulls along any jetty, a big stick (10- to 12-weight) and a sinking line of intermediate or Class III density is the best choice. My favorite pattern for them in this setting is a size 4/0 bucktail around 5 inches long with an ice-chenille body and weighted brass eyes tied Clouser-style. Try various count-downs and retrieve rates until a strike indicates you've got it all together.

The winter deep-water opportunity below the Leeville bridge will require a 9- or 10-weight outfit, sinking line, and size 1/0 or 2/0 Clouser Minnows, and a guide who works out of Bobby Lynn's Marina would be a wise investment. As the offshore opportunities out of Fourchon are a mirrored image of those available from Grand Isle, they will be covered shortly.

About 5 miles below Leeville, turning south on LA 3090 will take you to Port Fourchon. About three miles down that road you will come across a public launch on your left. This "park"—besides giving boating access to the surf and the wells in the Bay Marchand oil field just offshore—is graced with restrooms and a fishing pier.

Specks inhabit nearshore waters as well as those found inshore, and the Bay Marchand field is a great place to fish for them. The opportunity is roughly from late April through October, and the best conventional technique is usually bottom-bumping with either jigs or live baits. I have yet to connect with offshore oil-field specks on flies, and I know of no one else who has caught them thusly in Louisiana waters with consistency. If you simply must try, I suggest a day with current but very little of it, a full sinking line, and size 1/0 weighted flies worked as deep as possible and relatively slowly—at least, that's how I intend to do it whenever I decide to make a full-blown effort. That pattern should also produce the lesser types, which are common in this area.

Beach access at Fourchon is across the old swing bridge; be sure to turn right at the white fence and avoid getting hemmed in by the anti-trespass pilings. Surf fishing here is available all the way to the cut separating the Fourchon beaches from Elmer's Island, and the species involved—and the times they are available—are consistent with other areas of Louisiana's wadable surf.

Elmer's Island, located between the Fourchon beaches and Grand Isle, and once a popular place for surf-fishing and camping, is presently for sale, and all access to it is denied. But the surf there is accessible by boat, and I'm told the cut between the island and Fourchon, where Dr. Jim LaNasa caught the great southern flounder a while back, is reachable by boat from the surf. At around 7¼ pounds, that fish is not likely to be unseated from its top spot in the state's fly-fishing records, but it's possible, and that cut is worth prospecting for a bigger one.

The eastern end of Elmer's Island butts up against Caminada Pass. A large, moderately deep flat extends from the bank out into the pass for some distance, and during late summer and early fall schools of bull reds prowl this flat. Beach your boat on the flat, and wade cautiously around Caminada Pass, as the current there can be quite strong, and the water deepens suddenly!

Once you're on the island proper and beyond Bridgeside Marina, you'll notice that almost all of the buildings on the Gulf side of the highway are built between the highway and the dunes. They are all on private property, so respect that. Access to the beach—which is public to the state park—is gained through small parking areas and stiles over the dunes that are scattered along the length of the island. This is a popular retreat for simple family fun as well as for fishing, so it is best fished in early AM, late PM, and on weekdays, especially if you're limited to wade-fishing the surf.

Inland action with specks and reds, and offshore opportunities involving cobia, tripletail, bull redfish, crevalle jack, and the "blue-water beasties," can range from very good to excellent, and there is no difference from taking them out of Grand Isle than from other areas of Louisiana Coast. During high summer—normally the last weekend in July and the beginning of the

Grand Isle is more of a family-friendly spot than other Louisiana destinations; but its waters are well known for good fishing for a variety of species.

peak time of tarpon—the country's oldest saltwater-fishing contest, the Grand Isle Tarpon Rodeo, is held. (Go to www.grand-isle.com/events.htm for specifics of this event, and other information concerning fishing Grand Isle.) You probably won't catch one on a fly, but there are lots of other categories, even a few for fly fishing. The competition is quite intense as there are many ardent contestants in a number of specific categories. There are also a lot of non-fishing visitors on the island during the rodeo who come solely for the atmosphere, the groceries, and the general good time. Book ahead if you're traveling here as it can get pretty crowded!

So if the rodeo sounds like it's not for you, charter a big boat and spend those three days fishing offshore!

If you trailer your own boat to the island, buy a chart of the area you intend to fish—that's an excellent move anywhere you fish in Louisiana. Be forewarned that charts of inland areas can be outdated within a year of their issuance due to the rapid erosion of coastal marshes in certain places. Your surroundings may look nothing like your chart implies. Use charts for references only, and like the old bayou boy once said, "If ya ain't sure where y'at, stop!"

And always carry along a cell phone and a push-pole!

In Barataria Bay try such time-proven hotspots as Mendicant Island, Queen Bess Island, and Bassa Bassa for specks, and always keep an eye and an ear out for squawking gulls diving on surfacing shrimp. Across Barataria Pass is Grand Terre Island, the remains of historic Ft. Livingston, a Department of Wildlife & Fisheries biological station, and frequently lots of specks on both sides of it. Farther to the northeast is Quatre Bayous Pass—a summer bull redfish spot of the first order. (And one that can hold a bunch of big jacks with bad attitudes, too!) Here fish the edges of the offshore bars from the boat, and wade-fish—quite cautiously—the surf and the edges of the pass, using flies and gear appropriate for other areas of the Louisiana surf.

The Grand Isle surf has been a popular spot for speck fishermen for decades and on days with decent conditions begins to provide good action in late March. That's also a time your party may be crashed by a hook-up with a big jack, and that's a very good reason for a 9-weight outfit with a well-made reel sporting a quality disc drag and a capacity for a bunch of 30-pound Dacron backing! Fish can be encountered literally anywhere along the surf, but areas with unconformities like jetties, the edges of submerged points, deep troughs, and such are prime prospects. The action with specks picks up as spring waxes along with the promise of big fish in May—by June and vacation time if you want a trophy, be in the water before daylight to beat the arrival of beach bunnies! Summer typically offers early morning and late evening action with school-sized fish and the lesser types, though by mid-July the potential for bull reds begins to increase as it does in the Elmer's Island surf. By the time school begins again and the water becomes far less crowded with swimmers, the number of bulls—and the size of the specks—begins to increase, though the specks are not likely to reach the size they do in spring. By mid-autumn mostly just a few in-the-know residents are fishing the surf, and not long thereafter most of them have hung it up for most of the winter.

With one exception, which will be discussed shortly, offshore fly-fishing opportunities reachable from Grand Isle realistically begin in late April with the appearance of cobia. Early on these fish are normally taken around petroleum platforms and must be teased away from them before a fly fisherman makes a presentation; otherwise he is quite likely to lose his line as well as the fish as it dives into the platform's barnacle-encased legs. Here it's a three-man job—one on the rod, one on a casting rod armed with a big natural bait or popper "teaser," and one on the helm to move the boat into safe water as the fish is being teased away from the platform. By the end of the first week in May cobia—as well as tripletail—will be found along flotsam-laden rips where they pose much less of a danger to your fly line!

The lesser types also become more evident around May 1. These fish can offer bang-up action in open water, in the surf zone, and around jetties, but in my experience they have usually been pests, impeding efforts toward larger creatures, and, because those were almost always being pursued with a 10- to 12-weight outfit, not really much fun. Of course, if enough little tunny are around, you can wear yourself slap out with them if you so choose. I did that once—unintentionally—and wish I could figure out a way to prevent it from happening again under the same conditions!

That event occurred on a chunking trip for tuna on the Midnight Lump—the snout of a subterranean salt dome about 16 miles SSW of the mouth of the Mississippi River's Southwest Pass and as accessible from Grand Isle as it is from Venice. Catching tuna here is a fine opportunity for fly fishermen in late winter and early spring, and as it can involve quite sizeable yellowfins, your gear—and your back and forearm muscles—must be in top-notch shape. I wouldn't rush out and buy a $1,500, 14-weight outfit for it, but a 12-weight is the absolute minimum, and you should use the shortest rod possible for its superior pumping ability.

On that particular day the chunk-line brought little tunny to the boat in droves, and they weren't at all bashful about eating my flies! Fact is, if there hadn't been a bunch of yellowfins and blackfins around, too, catching the lesser types would have been fun. However, as is frequently the case, they quickly became pests.

Yeah, all right, perhaps I'm spoiled. . . .

The best fly-fishing opportunity blue water offers in summer is for dolphin. Like cobia and tripletail, these fish have an affinity for flotsam, and they are commonly found beneath that which is randomly encountered; a rip loaded with varied and sundry types of it can provide all the action one can stand!

In schools of mixed-sized fish the larger ones normally hold beneath the smaller ones. In order to get your fly through the smaller fish before it is eaten by one of the greedy little beggars, a weighted fly and a fast-sinking line are recommended. Fast retrieves are best, even for single bulls. A friend who knew something I didn't know once carried a 5-weight outfit on an offshore trip and had a ball with some "chicken" dolphin (small ones) we found beneath a patch of sargasso. However, a 12-weight would be a much wiser choice since you never know what opportunity might suddenly arise along a rip. Personally, I'd leave the little ones alone and be ready for a quick shot at whatever else might come along.

The area of lower Lafourche Parish between Leeville and Grand Isle offers just about anything a saltwater fly fisherman could ask for—well, except the exotic tropical species and places of "fine" dining. Still, you can experience the challenge of sight-fishing—both inshore and offshore; you can suffer through brutal bouts with big deep-water species; and you can get into schools of others so thick and so willing that your arm will end up sore to the bone! And if you don't get your fill of great-tasting, if not fancy, seafood while you're there, blame no one but yourself!

That said, *Allez!*

Motels, Apartments, and Cabins

Leeville

- Boudreaux's Motel, 985-396-2215

Grand Isle

- Anchors Away, 985-787-3378
- Angelette's Rentals, 888-323-8117
- Anna's, 985-787-3701
- Barefoot Inn, 985-787-2294
- Bill's Shady Lawn, 985-787-3170
- Blue Dolphin Inn and Cottages, 985-787-3697
- Breakers, 985-787-3169
- Bridgeside, 985-787-2418

- Bruce's Apartments, 985-787-3374
- Cajun Cabins, 985-787-2767
- Cajun Holiday, 985-787-2002
- Cajun Tide Resort, 888-248-4611
- Cigar's Cajun Riveria, 985-787-3220
- Gulf Breeze Bed & Breakfast, 985-787-4703
- Gulfstream Apartments, 985-787-3566
- H & M Cabins, 985-787-3753
- Landry House Bed & Breakfast, 985-787-2207
- Offshore Hotel, 985-787-3178
- Poche's Cabins & Apartments, 985-787-3444
- Rainbow Motel, 985-787-3515
- Richoux's Rentals, 985-787-2381
- Ricky's Motel, 985-787-3532
- Rusty Pelican Motel, 985-787-2665
- Sanddollar Motel, 985-787-2893
- Sandpiper Shores Motel, 985-787-2020
- Seabreeze, 985-787-3180
- Sun & Sand Cottages, 985-787-2456
- Tropical Motel, 985-787-3321
- Wateredge, 985-787-2329

Campgrounds & Trailer Parks
- Bridgeside, 985-787-2418
- Cigar's Cajun Riveria, 985-787-3220
- Duet's (pronounced do' way's) Camper, 985-787-2378
- Louisiana State Park, 888-787-2559
- Offshore Camper Park, 985-787-2452
- Pat's Trailer Park, 985-787-2207

Restaurants
Grand Isle
- Cigar's Cajun Cuisine, 985-787-2188
- The Lighthouse, 985-787-3331

- Sarah's Diner, 985-787-2955
- Starfish Restaurant, 985-787-2711

If, by any chance, you take US 90 back through Boutte after your trip to Grand Isle, plan on suppertime to coincide with your arrival there, and treat yourself to a meal at Sal's. The turtle soup and fried frog legs are out of this world! But then, it's all pretty good eating!

Sporting Goods Stores & Fly Shop

Most of the marinas in both Leeville and Grand Isle will stock a limited amount of gear, but expect absolutely nothing relating to fly fishing. Again, bring everything you think you will need and a little more!

- Blue Water Sports, 985-787-2212
- Charlie's Live Bait (Hey, it's there!), 985-787-3704
- Gulf Coast Outfitters, 225-926-3597
- Minnow Bucket II (Likewise!), 985-787-2381
- Red Tag, 985-787-2130

In Baton Rouge, Richard Whitner keeps up with what's biting where in the Grand Isle area and can recommend productive flies and such; 225-926-3597.

Marinas

Leeville

- Griffin's Station & Marina, 985-396-2415
- Bobby Lynn's Marina, 985-396-2678

Grand Isle

- Bridgeside Marina, 985-787-2419
- Camardelle's Marina, 985-787-3222
- Cigar's Marina, 985-787-3220
- Gulfstream Marina, 985-787-3566
- My Favorite Marina, 985-787-3179
- Pirate's Cove Marina, 985-787-3880
- Sanddollar Marina, 985-787-2500

(Notice that several of those establishments offer restaurants and overnight accommodations as well as marina facilities.)

Guides

I know of only one outfit in this area who might offer bona fide fly-fishing guides. The others are typically knowledgeable about their waters, the fish in them, and how to find them, but you will have to catch the fish yourself. As anywhere else, let them know you will be fly fishing, and if you don't want them beating the water to a froth with conventional gear ahead of you, just tell them. Also, if you decide to head offshore in a big boat, tell the skipper to lose the outriggers, center-rigger, and any lines that would be hazardous to casting a fly.

Leeville

- Marsh Masters Guide Service, 985-936-2411
- Marsh Rat Guide Service (These guys actually do offer fly-fishing trips!), 985-632-8156

Port Fourchon

- Cajun Made Offshore Adventures, 985-638-6740
- Capt. Frankie Hardison, 985-396-2422

Grand Isle

I—Inshore; C—Coastal; O—Offshore

- B&B Postman Charters (O), 985-626-9290
- Bay Coast Charters (I), 985-787-2067
- Bon Chance Fishing (I,C,O), 985-787-2602
- Charis Charters (I,C), 985-382-6253
- Cherece IV (O), 985-787-2200
- Coastal & Inland Charters (I,C), 985-787-4850
- Fill It Up (I,C,O), 985-787-2639
- Gotcha Charters (O), 985-787-2481
- H & M Charters (I,C), 985-787-3753
- Hard Times Charters (I,C), 985-787-3529
- Hook 'Em Fishing (I,C,O), 985-787-3247
- Island Charter (I,C), 985-787-4765
- Mirage Charters (I,C), 985-787-2625
- Pro Guide Services (I), 985-787-2316
- Rig Runner Charters (C,O), 225-695-3451
- Tucker's Tolly (O), 985-837-4947

Lafitte, our next destination, offers inshore fishing as good as it gets, and to spice up that sauce, the marinas there are only a half-hour or so drive from all the fine dining and debauchery you could ask for in the New Orleans Vieux Carré (the French Quarter or "Old Square").

AEEIYAA!

It is the morning of the first Saturday in May. You arrived at Grand Isle late last night, checked into your motel, and managed to get five hours of sleep before the chatter of the alarm clock announced the beginning of another season. You are still quite groggy as you dress, but through the mist of your mind you recall the same sensation on past first Saturdays in May spent at the island—and at Cameron—and camped out on the Chandeleurs. It's just another part of the tradition you and your buddies have established over the years: The season for wade-fishing for specks opens this morning—unofficially, of course, but traditionally.

Dressed now, and with fly rod in hand, a stringer stuffed into a back pocket, a box of flies and a couple of small Ziplock bags containing extra tippet and shocker material crammed into a shirt pocket, and wearing your good-luck wide-brimmed hat and with a pair of sunglasses hanging from an 80-pound mono "croakie" around your neck, you join your friends, cross the highway and the grass-topped dunes, and disperse at the beach. Finally, after months of abstinence spent reflecting on past days here and in wistful anticipation of those to come, you reach the edge of the sea. The excitement of being there, and the promise of the first day builds rapidly within you.

It is a gorgeous morning—"island perfect." The sun has yet to crack the eastern horizon, but the sky is already pale blue and cloudless. The light southeasterly breeze is just strong enough to fan your cheeks; the smallest of swells slosh easily onto the beach. Even in the low light, you can plainly tell the Gulf is "speck-green."

Yes indeed, it is a day handmade for fishing the surf, but with your first step into the still somewhat chilly waters, a lot of factors governing the final weight of your stringer will come into play. And that is true anywhere you are wade-fishing the surf along the Louisiana Coast.

That "first step" is a good starting point, especially in early morning on a rising or high tide. Along much of the area's wadable surf a series of troughs and bars extend seaward from the beach, beginning with a trough right at land's end. During this time of high water and low light, some of the biggest specks around can be found in the first trough and caught by standing well back on the beach and casting across it. Yet many anglers, in their excitement and their rush to get wet, plow through this prime water like a herd of stampeding cattle in order to cross the first bar and work the second trough—the area most surf-fishermen prefer. Believe me, the second trough isn't going anywhere! And the specks that might be in it will probably stay there much later into the morning than will those in the first one.

Low light, high water, and a calm, clear surf is also a combination that is made to order for a popper—say, size 1/0 in dark green-over-chartreuse or -white and around 4 inches in length. With these flies, it will only take a couple of casts to determine if fish are present, so don't spend a lot of time pounding a particular area, be it in either the first trough or the second.

Once you have become convinced that there are no fish nearby in the first trough, wade easily through it and cross the first bar to the point where the water has become about mid-thigh deep. From that position make a cast parallel to the bar, a couple of casts at about a 20-degree angle to it, a couple of more at 40 degrees, and if you have had no strikes then move along the bar —remaining in the same depth of water—a short distance and repeat the sequence. And take your time while wading, always dragging your feet to the ever-popular Stingray Shuffle rather than taking regular steps; besides giving the little nasties plenty of time to get out of your way, slow wading is less likely to alert any nearby specks of your presence.

Soon you locate a small school and quickly string three nice ones that engulfed the big popper in their typically rowdy ways. Now a question arises: are you in search of fillets or are you seeking a trophy sow at this time of year when your odds of encountering one are at their best? If you want a big fish, move on; the commotion caused by the antics of the fish you have hooked may not spook a sow that is close at hand, but it will put her on guard. In the surf you almost always catch the biggest speck in a given spot either first or not at all.

So you decide to seek a sow, and that is always best done alone. As you slowly wade away from your buddies, the specks on your long cord stringer swim around your legs, and as you reach down to clear the stringer from them, you notice a 5-foot shark checking out your catch from an uncomfortably short distance. Now what?

Knock on wood, but I have never lost a strung speck to a shark. However, I did meet up with one—a bull shark about 6 feet in length—that did its best to prevent me from crossing a narrow trough, and I had every intention of crossing it, as I could see redfish working on the other side of it. So I tried to swat the shark on the tip of his nose with my rod. Bad move—he tried to eat it! More than a little concerned now—me being a tad too far from the bank to make a run for it, I decided to try a trick I had heard about but had never used before and gave the sandy bottom a sharp thump with the heel of my right foot. Man, that shark took off like the proverbial striped ape! Since then, so has every other one that was becoming a nuisance. The only problem is that the thump will also scatter any nearby specks, so while the Stingray Shuffle should be practiced at all times, do the Shark Thump at your own discretion.

So you got nervous and thumped, the shark hauled butt, and you waded along another 20 to 30 yards and began fishing again. It is now an hour past sunrise, you have not seen the first sign of a sow, and you begin to feel the need to make some additions to your stringer. So you replace the popper with a size 1/0 chartreuse-and-white Clouser Minnow, and soon you locate another school of fillet-makers.

In rapid order you string five, and, as expected, your fly is again clobbered on the next cast. This time, though, when you strip-strike the fish, it feels like you just drove the hook into a jetty! And immediately thereafter—instead of typically rising to the surface and sloshing its head as you strip it in—this fish streaks away against the pressure of your drag, leaving a series of mini-maelstroms in the surface of the placid Gulf. Jackfish!

I have no intention of expounding on the pros and cons of toying with the big jacks I see in the spring surf with a 9-weight outfit. If it is of the usual size—say, 20 to 30 pounds or more—you can count on burning at least a half-hour bringing it to hand, and in the process you will assuredly spook every speck around.

It's your call whether you want to spend that time trying to land it—and then wade through a couple of hundred yards of discomposed surf before you have any chance at all of catching another speck—or whether you decide to quickly break it off and go back to the business at hand. The point is that its initial presence probably caused the specks to scatter, and the longer you fool around with it, the farther way those fish will more.

So you decided to try to save your fly, and a considerable time later you slip it from the beast's jaw and allow him to swim away. Then you notice

Surf fishing at Grand Isle and other Louisiana barrier islands is a time-honored tradition and lends itself very well to fly fishermen.

what sounds like applause coming from somewhere behind you, and upon inspection you discover two Wildlife and Fisheries enforcement agents wading out to check your catch and your license.

No problem. Your eight fish are well over the 12-inch minimum-size restriction, and you produce your license—protected from a soggy mishap by one of those small, clear-plastic envelopes—from the band inside your hat. All is in order, and as they go their way you wade back to the beach, walk along it to the point where the water was undisturbed by the jack, and reenter it.

And suddenly you discover you are quite thirsty. That, too, is no problem with the small plastic flask of drinking water in your back pocket. Yes, it is a little warm, but it does the job—and beats the heck out of going without or returning to the motel for a drink.

As you wade across the first bar and back into the second trough, you notice something different a short distance away. There, the wavelets breaking easily against the bar make a sharp turn seaward and extend 70 to 80 feet offshore: a submerged point. And judging from the water's dark-green tint alongside the point, there is a deep pocket between it and the bar. So you wade alongside the bar until you reach casting range of the pocket, send the Clouser across its promising water, and immediately hook a nice speck.

The two anglers off the tip of the point notice this, cross the point as you are stringing your second quick fish, and wade waist-deep into the pocket—and you know your action there has just come to a screeching stop! You fish troughs and pockets from the edges, not from within them. You wish your competition knew that. . . .

Somewhat disgusted, but understanding the surf belongs to everyone, you wade along the top of the bar to the point, cross it, and continue along the bar. Ahead of you some birds are wheeling and diving just outside of where you figure the second bar should be, so you hurry along to a point directly shoreward of them, wade waist-deep into the second trough, and cast the big fly as far offshore as you are able. On the second strip it gets banged, and a thin bar of glistening silver immediately vaults skyward—and throws the hook. Ladyfish—and another grabs the fly, solidly this time, as you attempt to strip it in for another cast.

Unlike surf-prowling brawny jacks, I like ladyfish when I find them there, especially if I have already strung 10 or more specks. But playing with them is not conducive to stringing more specks—decent-sized ones, anyway. And besides that, they can quickly shred both fly and 30-pound mono shocker. So after you release the fish, you take the nippers that are hung on a lanyard around your neck and snip off the mangled fly and shocker. Then you replace both from the contents of your shirt pocket and wade slowly back to the first bar.

By now the tide has peaked; action will be slow to nonexistent for the next few hours. So you wade back along the top of the bar—always alert to ensure you don't pass up any fish, and re-join your buddies. They have not done nearly as well as you have, neither have they hooked a sow. Then you all retire to the motel for sandwiches and a short nap while waiting for the tide to begin to fall.

You awaken with a start and immediately wonder if you have slept too long. No, it's only three o'clock—just right. Now it's time to restrategize. You know that you might again find specks in the troughs along the beach, but better water on the falling tide will be in or near the mouths of any cuts leading from interior areas to the Gulf, and along the edges of the passes. But there is a strong tide today, so the passes will not be safe to wade. And there is only one such cut at Grand Isle; being a Saturday, it will probably be pretty crowded—just like the one separating nearby Elmer's Island from the Four-chon beaches. You know exactly where you would go if you were out at the Chandeleurs: the back-side flats. Now there's a thought. . . .

You realize there is no reason why the potential behind Grand Isle should not be worthwhile on the falling tide, but you also understand the chance for a sow from those waters is much less than it is from the surf. Still, you feel the back of the island is now the best bet, so you break down your rod, lay it on the seat of your truck, and drive along the highway to the clam-shell road leading toward the back of the island. Turning there you make your way past the last camp and park at the edge of the marsh.

Small schools of minnows are evident along the edges of the still-flooded grass as you wade a short distance out into the bay, then begin to parallel the shoreline. Occasionally you almost lose one of your slip-on tennis shoes in the bay's soft bottom, and you decide you really should spend the big bucks on a pair of those flats boots you see in the catalogues—sure don't want to lose a shoe while wade-fishing!

As expected, you find that there are specks behind the island, feeding on minnows and shrimp being drawn from the opposite surf-side marshes by the falling tide. By five o'clock your Clousers have accounted for eight more. They are smaller than those you caught earlier in the surf, but they are still fine fillet-makers. You now have seven to go to fill your daily quota; you could probably catch those here, but you know the last hours of daylight are best spent in the surf, no matter what the tide is doing. You arrive to find the first trough barely knee-deep; the top of the first bar is dry.

As you wade into the second trough you can feel the current washing the sand from beneath your feet; that should stir the fish up as much as it stirs the sand up, you think, but man, I bet it's really ripping through the passes now—dangerous stuff! You find the second trough not quite crotch-deep as you cross it, then ascend the second bar and make your way across it, stop-ping at the point where the water reaches your thighs. Ahead is the open ocean—the realm of great beasts, and you are now in their world. The thrill you feel is the stuff that makes a surf fisherman.

The light breeze that had built during midday has now gone; hereabouts, a breeze lays down. The Gulf is without a wrinkle save for those caused by a school of mullet a short distance away. You wade quietly along the edge of the bar toward them, and upon reaching casting range you send the fly—again, the big popper—on a search for any great something that might have driven them to the surface. And as it gurgles rhythmically across the placid sea, a huge yellowmouth speck explodes on it—and misses it. You stop your retrieve, allow the fly to rest for a few seconds, and give it a single slight twitch, and this time the speck has it squarely in her sights.

I hope you caught her—that she didn't tear free from the hook as she dashed toward the sunset. But if you didn't, you will remember those two strikes for a long, long time. They, and the 18 nice fish you now have iced down in your cooler, are the result of a little knowledge of surf fishing with flies in combination with any given spring day spent in the Louisiana surf. It doesn't get any better.

CHAPTER V

The Lafitte Area

The community of Jean Lafitte, or more commonly simply Lafitte, is a small settlement strung out along both sides of the Barataria Waterway just below the Intracoastal Canal south of New Orleans. Like those on Grand Isle, most of its residents are involved with some part of the petroleum industry or commercial fishing. There are, however, a number of marinas equipped for sport-fishing needs, and several notable guides work the surrounding marshes and bays for redfish, speck, and the occasional flounder. There's even a genuine fly-fishing guide hereabouts, and he goes with the territory just like cold beer goes with hot boiled crawfish.

There isn't a lot of variety out of Lafitte for a fly fisherman, but one opportunity—sight-fishing for redfish—can be conservatively rated as excellent throughout most of the year. Many of the better areas to the south and east can also be accessed from other marinas in the Delta, which is discussed in the next chapter.

Perhaps, and but for a couple of guides I know of down there—and a nice little "local color" restaurant—I might have. But Lafitte has been providing New Orleans anglers with such great fishing, especially for redfish, for so long that I felt I simply had to include it in this book. And as I mentioned in the tail end of the last chapter, it's not far from the big city.

Then there's the redoubtable Capt. Phil Robichaux who has enjoyed a long and profitable guiding career on the waters around Lafitte. He doesn't get to do much fly fishing too often, but he knows the ropes. And then there's

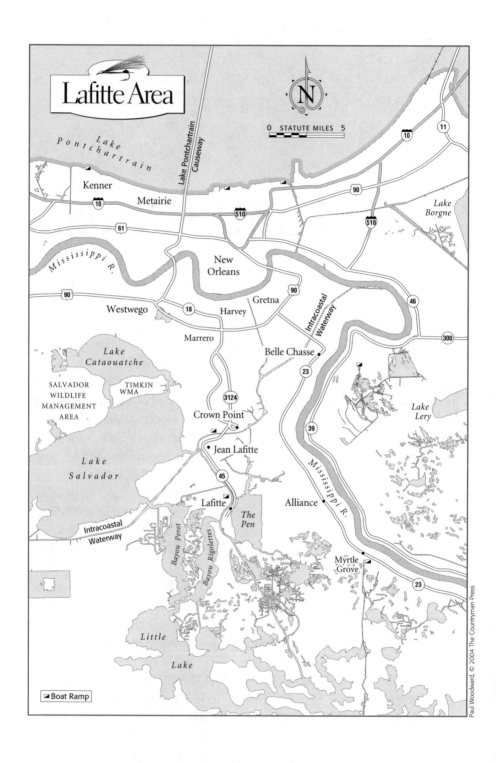

Lafitte Area

N

0 STATUTE MILES 5

Lake Pontchartrain

Lake Pontchartrain Causeway

Kenner

Metairie

10

61

Mississippi R.

90

Westwego

18

Harvey

Marrero

New
Orleans

Gretna

90

510

510

90

Lake
Borgne

Lake
Lery

46

300

Belle Chasse

Intracoastal Waterway

23

Lake
Cataouatche

SALVADOR
WILDLIFE
MANAGEMENT
AREA

TIMKIN
WMA

3124

Crown Point

Jean Lafitte

Lake
Salvador

45

39

Lafitte

The
Pen

Alliance

Mississippi R.

Intracoastal
Waterway

Bayou Perot

Bayou Rigolettes

Myrtle
Grove

23

Little

Lake

⬛ Boat Ramp

our beer-and-crawfish guy, Capt. Theophile (pronounced toe' feel) Bourgeois, who is a pretty creditable fly fisherman himself besides being a great guide.

You don't have to go far from Lafitte to find redfish. Lake Salvador, just to the west, can be full of them in summer and autumn, though if the Davis Pond Freshwater Diversion System ever begins its role of rebuilding the marsh in the Barataria Estuary, that fishery may be jeopardized. However, some of the best areas for sight-fishing are to its east and southeast; they should be somewhat sheltered from the main affects of the diversion. Generally, the marshes between The Pen and Alliance to the north, and Myrtle Grove to the south—both of the latter being on LA 23 well to the east of Lafitte—are hard to beat.

That marsh is also quite shallow, and since "it all looks the same," the wise thing to do here is hire a guide for your first 100 or so trips. That way you'll learn where you can go, where you can't go, and where the fish are.

The secret to successfully fishing these waters is in the way they are accessed. Almost all of the guides who work this area—fly fishing or otherwise—use mud boats: long, lean, flat-bottom aluminum craft that float on a heavy dew and are powered by straight-drive, air-cooled beasts known as Go-Devils. And they are that, requiring only liquid mud to go from here to over yonder and leaving virtually nowhere a redfish can hide from them. Once a concentration of fish is located, the guide, powers down, climbs up on the stern-mounted poling platform, and quietly push-poles you from fish to fish, many of which will be in water so shallow that their backs will be exposed— water I'd be reluctant to try to paddle my pirogue through! Anyway, it's a great opportunity, and that marsh is quite attractive, supporting several different-colored morning glories on the hummocks and lots of bird and animal life.

The wind is often less of a problem in this area than in others across the coast, a possible result of the area being farther from the Gulf. Whatever the reason, an 8-weight outfit is preferred by many who regularly fish here. As the water can be quite clear in places—and because it is so shallow—longer leaders produce better results than the 9-footers commonly used in other places; 12-footers tapered to a 16-pound tippet and with no shocker are favored. Use a minimum of stagings, since there is plenty of submergent grass in much of this area that can foul on leader knots and cause break-offs.

Another reason for the preference for an 8-weight outfit is that the flies commonly used here are smaller than those effective in other areas. Again,

Reds provide much of the fly-fishing action found around Lafitte, and there are plenty of them!

that is a result of the very shallow, clear water. Size 1 bend-backs, size 1/0 spoon flies, and size 1 poppers, all tied weedless, are preferred patterns. I still use a 9-weight here, but there's a lot of justification for the lighter outfit.

As mentioned earlier, the sight-fishing opportunity is available almost year-round. Add blind-casting to the equation—which is indeed a 9-weight drill—and only the coldest, windiest times of winter put an end to it.

Speck-fishing here is generally confined to the lakes, bays, and bayous, over shells and beneath gulls diving on prey that have been driven to the surface by the predators, and in the local oil-field canals, and its timing is consistent with other waters across the Louisiana Coast. Generally the fish are found in the canals and interior bays like Little Lake, Bay Round, Bayou Perot, and Bayou Rigolets early on, then begin to move outside as spring progresses. Some of the best speck action I've encountered in this area has come from the extreme northern edges of Barataria Bay near the Barataria Waterway.

You won't find many specks hereabouts that reach the size of just the "fair ones" in Calcasieu Lake, but there can be lots of them. Under the right conditions—relatively calm and with the fish feeding near the surface—poppers can be the best thing going. Indeed, most of the specks I've caught in this area have taken poppers. But then, I must admit that most of the specks I've caught in this area were taken during autumn, a time when the fish tend to throw caution to the wind as they feed heavily to store fat for the winter. They can get real dumb then—I love 'em like that! Notably, during autumn The Pen can be one of the best spots around!

Flounder, sheepshead, black drum, and even largemouth bass in places, are susceptible to blind-casting the deeper waters of the interior marshes, ponds, and smaller bays. Sheepshead and black drum will occasionally rap a spoon fly. I've seen that happen, though I have never experienced it firsthand as I refuse to tie an example of fly-fishing heresy to my tippet! To each his own, I guess—if you're not as ultraconservative as I am, it really is a very productive "fly."

While sheepshead, black drum, and bass will remain in water that is suitable for redfish throughout most of the year in this area, many ot these flounder will begin a late-summer migration toward Barataria Bay and then into the Gulf in late autumn, returning in late winter to early spring. Don't be surprised if you catch a few during summer and early-autumn trips, especially along the edges of the smaller bays—flounder do have a fondness for a size 1 chartreuse-and-white Clouser. But if you simply must catch a flounder on a fly, the lower Delta gives better odds.

Finally, ask Theophile about the herds of giant black drum that move into . . . well, in the oil-patch knowledge of things like that is referred to as "tight information": confidential stuff, so I won't break the trust. But it's one of the best inshore big-fish opportunities in Louisiana for a fly fisherman. So far, a 51-pounder is the largest taken on fly—and they get much bigger!

No matter where you fish, Lafitte is not a place to head out blindly in your own boat on your first trip there. Invest the dollars on a guide, ask him to show you a couple of decent spots that you won't have trouble finding yourself, and go from there. GPS units are nice, especially those that track your course, but don't rely entirely on them. Remember, as your guide sashays through meandering tidal cuts, across little bays, through seemingly impenetrable stands of spartina and over flats that seem way to shallow to traverse, he's been doing it for a long, long time. Use care while navigating these waters!

And with that, *pechez!*

Motels and Lodges

The New Orleans Westbank suburbs of Gretna, Harvey, Marrero, and West-wego offer overnight accommodations as well as some pretty darned good ("fine") restaurants. However, on-site overnighting—and some great Cajun-style groceries—are available in Lafitte. Personally, I'd get as much of the "local color" as I could!

Lafitte

- Bourgeois Charters (Theophile's place), 504-341-5614
- Lodge of Louisiana, 504-689-0000
- Victoria Inn, 504-689-4757

Westbank

- Econo Lodge, 504-366-4311
- Gas Lite Motel, 504-366-3233
- Holiday Inn, 504-366-2361
- Howard Johnson, 504-366-8531
- La Quinta Inn, 504-368-5600
- Oasis Motel, 504-366-3456
- Pelican Motel, 504-366-3507
- Pinnacle Motel, 504-366-3561
- Rodeway Inn, 504-424-4777
- Sentry Motel, 504-366-4551

Restaurants

(PC) indicates I've eaten at a particular establishment and plan to eat there again.

Lafitte

- Boutte's Restaurant (PC), 504-689-3889

Westbank

Once again, they'd have to cut down too many trees to make enough pages to list all the restaurants there are on the Westbank and in New Orleans it-self. The ones listed are again only seafood/steak or Cajun cuisine houses, along with one or two especially good Italian and Mexican food spots. Drive along any divided four-lane street (Lapalco Boulevard is representative and intersects Barataria Boulevard, which is also known as LA 3124 and the way to Lafitte) and you'll come across any number of chicken shacks, burger barns, and other types of fast-food outlets. Here, folks, you have a chance to dine—do it!

Gretna

- Bayou Po-boys, 197 Westbank Expressway, 504-367-0290
- C & L Cajun Seafood, 701 Westbank Expressway, 504-362-3322
- Cannon's Restaurant (PC), 197 Westbank Expressway, 504-364-1047
- Cucos (PC), 2766 Belle Chasse Highway, 504-393-7766
- G's Lil' Kajun Restaurant, 401 Realty Drive, 504-433-0500
- La Fiesta Restaurant (PC), 1412 Stumph Boulevard, 504-361-9142
- Tony Mandina's (PC), 1915 Pratt Street, 504-362-2010
- Red Maple (PC), 1036 Lafayette Street, 504-367-0935
- Visko's (PC), 516 Gretna Boulevard, 504-366-1516

Harvey

- Bertucci's Restaurant (PC), 3300 Fourth Street, 504-341-8193
- Boomtown Pier 4 Restaurant, 4132 Peters Road, 504-366-7711
- Chevy's Fresh Mex (PC), 1201 Manhattan Boulevard, 504-368-2100
- Copeland's (PC), 1700 Lapalco Boulevard, 504-364-1575
- Perino's Boiling Pot (PC), 3825 Westbank Expressway, 504-340-5560

Vieux Carré, New Orleans

If you feel you simply have to go into the city and sample the local delicacies, here are a few great spots that don't get the press—or have the prices—of some of the better-known New Orleans eateries. If you must have the names of some of those, get a local phone book!

- Acme Oyster & Seafood House (PC), 724 Iberville, 504-522-5973
- Andrew Jaeger's, 337 Rue Chartres, 504-524-6777
- The Bombay Club, 830 Rue Conti, 504-586-0972
- Brennan's (Okay, it's famous; so sue me!), 417 Royal Street, 504-525-9711
- Felix's (PC-YES!!!), 739 Iberville at 210 Bourbon Streets, 504-522-4440
- Mike Anderson's, 215 Bourbon Street, 504-524-3884.

Yeah, these places have some great groceries, but if I was me, I'd be spending my time—and eating my dinners—during a fishing trip in a lodge in Lafitte. The city is for afterward!

Now let's get back to the fishing part.

Sporting Goods Stores

Fly Shops

- Uptown Angler, 601 Julia Street, New Orleans, 504-529-3597

Others

With the exception of Professional Sport Shop, which carries a limited amount of fly tackle and does good repair work, the remaining listings are on the Westbank. There are other fishing tackle outlets in New Orleans proper and in its Eastbank suburbs, but if you are fishing the Lafitte area (And unless you are dining in the city), you have no business over there!

New Orleans

- Professional Sport Shop, 920 Julia Street, 504-522-3771

Gretna

- Academy Sporting Goods, 50 Westside N. Shopping Center, 504-363-8283

Harvey

- Gamefisher, 3509 Ames Avenue, 504-340-4700
- Wal-Mart, 2100 Alex Komman Boulevard, 504-394-0075
- Wal-Mart Supercenter, 1501 Manhattan Boulevard, 504-366-9155

Marinas

There is a public back-down ramp at the base of the bridge over the Intracoastal Canal at Crown Point.

- Cochiara Shipyard & Marina, 4477 Jean Lafitte Boulevard, 504-689-3701
- Joe's Landing, 1170 Anthony Lane, 504-689-4304
- Lafitte Harbor Marina, Hwy 45, 504-689-2013
- Lafitte Seaway Marina, 5057 Kenal Road, 504-689-3148

Guides

- Bourgeois Charters, 504-341-5614
- Robichaux Saltwater Guide Service, 504-348-3264

Other guides are available through the various marinas.

Four Flies for Redfish

While I was down at the marina the other day I met two elderly gentlemen from Tennessee. One of them recognized me from a picture in an article that had appeared in a national saltwater fly-fishing magazine, and the conversation soon turned to flies that are effective for redfish. One of the old boys then made a quick trip to his car, returning with a box-full of flies of all descriptions. "Would these work?" he asked hopefully.

"Well," I hedged, "they certainly are pretty flies. This one will for sure."

It was a chartreuse-and-white Clouser Minnow. The others—Deceivers, SeaDucers, Whistlers, and whatever, each and every one tied to perfection—might have worked under certain conditions. However, those situations can be successfully resolved by the use of one of four patterns that are unbeatable for everyday purposes as well. Fill your fly boxes with them, and you will find yourself catching redfish more and experimenting with "hopeful" patterns less.

The first is a popper. Of the 800-plus redfish I've taken on flies, fully three-quarters of them fell to this pattern. A popper is effective—and a whale of a lot of fun to fish with. It is most productive in water that is clear enough and shallow enough to gain the attention of a fish that is looking for its lunch on bottom, and it is best employed in a sight-fishing scenario.

With poppers, colors are usually not all that important: all yellow works well, as does green-over-white and green-over-chartreuse. Nevertheless, the best size and retrieve technique is important and is dependent on the water's depth and what the fish is doing at the time.

For instance, a fish tailing in water that is knee-deep or so is more likely to locate and strike a size 1 popper roughly 3 inches long and being retrieved with slowly paced and moderately audible pops than a size 4 some 2 inches long being retrieved by "sliding" it. On the other hand, a fish that is "crawling" (moving along in water so shallow that its back is exposed above the surface) will often spook from the ruckus created by a big popper but will strike the smaller one worked with a quieter retrieve. Then too, cruising fish respond well to the popper being worked in the fashion of a shrimp or small minnow skittering across the surface. In most cases, once a fish responds to your retrieve and begins to pursue the popper, do not alter its pace. A half-dozen of these flies in size 1 and size 4, half of each size in yellow and half in green over either white or chartreuse will suffice to fill your needs in most situations.

Occasionally, especially on slick-calm days in the shallowest water reds will be found, even sliding a small popper can be ineffective. After one or two fish either spook from it or show no interest in it, then it's time to show them a bend-back.

Bend-backs are at their best in shallow water that has thick beds of submergent grasses, though they can be successfully used in general applications. The fly rides with the hook's point up and shielded by the dressing, rendering it quite weed-resistant. It is light in weight, allowing it to be retrieved slowly with short strips without sinking too deeply, and it can be tied or purchased in a wide variety of materials and color combinations. Two considerations should be made with respect to the materials. In extremely clear water the fly should be tied rather sparsely, while full-bodied dressings are more effective in water that is dingy. In both cases flash material enhances the appeal of these flies—a little in the sparse versions, a lot in the fuller ones.

Color selection, as in all subsurface attractor patterns, should also be dependent on the water's clarity; lighter shades, like chartreuse or white, are usually best when it's clear, darker hues like green, purple, and black when it isn't. On dark days, no matter what the water's clarity is, darker patterns normally work best. Sizes 1 and 4 approximately the same lengths as the poppers are enough for most situations, and standard-length hooks are recommended over the long-shank versions because those tend to bend under the strain of a big fish. And that brings us to the one cautionary point about this pattern.

To create a bend-back, the hook's shank is bent outward at a point a short distance behind the eye; the dressing, being tied onto the inside of the hook above that bend, causes the fly to ride inverted. If the angle of the bend is too severe, the hook's point faces so far upward from the line of the fly's retrieve that setting it becomes quite difficult; the point will scrape instead of poke. To prevent a lot of missed strikes, tie or purchase your bend-backs with only the slightest angle in the hook-shank's bend—it doesn't take much for the fly to work like it is supposed to.

An innovative pattern that has proven to be immensely successful in many shallow-water areas is the spoon fly. This is just the ticket for those folks who have long held the Johnson Sprite spoon in highest esteem and have been trying to figure out a way to cast one with a fly rod.

No matter where you fly fish for Louisiana's reds,
these patterns should be all you will need.

My good friend, Capt. Bubby Rodriguez, introduced me to this pattern many years ago, and it is the one that he usually insists his clients use to begin their day. On a standard-length size 1/0 hook it is easily castable with an 8-weight outfit, it sinks very slowly, and its monofilament weed-guard makes it effective in some pretty grassy water. Long, slow strips make it dance and dart just like a spoon, and redfish absolutely love it. In clear water solid gold is usually the best choice; in darker water a combination of gold and black or solid black is often more reliable. It is a great "fly" for those who are not overly traditional.

Perhaps the best of all, though—the most adaptive, anyway—is the Clouser Minnow. It is effective in both shallow-water sight-fishing and deep-water blind-casting scenarios, and it can be created to appeal to redfish of all sizes. Indeed, each of my three largest reds—22–36 pounds—fell to Clousers. So have most of the "regular reds" I've caught on subsurface flies. Its only drawback is that it's not a fly for shallow, grassy water. With its inherent weighted eyes—which are tied to the outside of the hook's shank, therefore causing the point to ride up like a bend-back's—it sinks quickly, yet it's not prone to foul on the bottom; however, the eyes will pick up loose grass, so be forewarned. A size 1—also about 3 inches long—is a breeze to cast with an 8-weight. Chartreuse-over-white—a classic saltwater pattern—is best in clear water; dark-green-over-chartreuse or solid purple is usually a better choice in darker water and for probing the depths.

For sight-fishing in clear water up to around 2 feet deep, a size 4 about 2 inches long is just right when tied with lightly weighted eyes. I prefer to avoid using lead products whenever possible, opting here for x-small brass hourglass eyes. For blind-casting over shells, bars, and across tidal cuts of moderate depth, a size 1 with small brass eyes gets the job done, even with a floating line. For deeper applications a size 1 with medium brass eyes on a fast-sinking line will get down almost as fast as a quarter-ounce jig. Almost...

In areas where bull reds can be encountered, sizes 2/0 (4 inches) to 4/0 (5 inches) tied with medium brass eyes will get their attention. These should be heavily dressed and therefore require at least a 9-weight outfit for the size 2/0 and a 10- to 12-weight for the larger sizes. (At least they do for me.) Yes, blind-casting these monstrosities with heavy rods is work, but the ends can assuredly justify the means. So, Clousers in two-color combinations (light and dark) in sizes 4, 1, and "big" will cover the bases left open by the three other patterns.

And they are all you need to catch redfish—little and big, shallow and deep, over shells, in grass, and in open water, and by sight or by speculating. While using them within their best-suited parameters, you will catch reds. If you aren't, don't go looking for a "hopeful" in your fly box; look for another place to fish!

Have no doubts, Lafitte, Grand Isle, Houma, Cypremort Point, and Cal-casieu Lake all have some good to excellent fly-fishing opportunities. But our next destination—the Mississippi River Delta—offers what may be the best fishing for everything that swims along the Louisiana Coast. Of course, I might be a tad bit prejudiced, but these days you don't see me making too many saltwater fly-fishing trips anywhere else! And there are a couple of local-color restaurants down the river that just have to be tested. So now pour yourself a glass of your favorite beverage, fire up one of your best cigars, sit back in your easy chair, and read on—and just try to keep from imagining yourself in the upcoming destination!

CHAPTER VI

The Delta—Inshore

laquemines Parish, Louisiana, is the fourth and most recent delta created by the Mississippi River in recent geologic history. Presently almost all of its populated area has subsided below sea level and is protected from both the river and the Gulf by levees. With the exception of two batteries of siphons that allow river water to flow into small areas of the western marshes, the river no longer has any beneficial effect on that area. The spartina and widgeon grass, which create habitat for the juveniles of countless creatures, are dying because of the water's increasing salinity. As the grasses die, small ponds become big ponds, then erosion by wave action claims additional grass. And as the grass is washed away, there is nothing to hold the mud beneath it in place. Waves also wash that away; the water then becomes deeper, and nothing will ever grow there again.

At least, not without a tremendous freshwater diversion effort. And the handful of oyster fishermen who have leased much of the area from the state (for $2 per acre!) and get their oysters from public grounds (for free!) have sued the state and threaten to sue it further if such salvation for the rest of us is created! As a result many acres of valuable wetlands are being lost every year. And need I say that when I look across the back levee near my below-sea-level home in Buras, the sight of open water almost all the way to the Gulf leaves me feeling a tad bit insecure!

I can't blame the oyster fishermen for wanting to protect their livelihood; the diversions would assuredly ruin some leases. But I'd sure like the state to

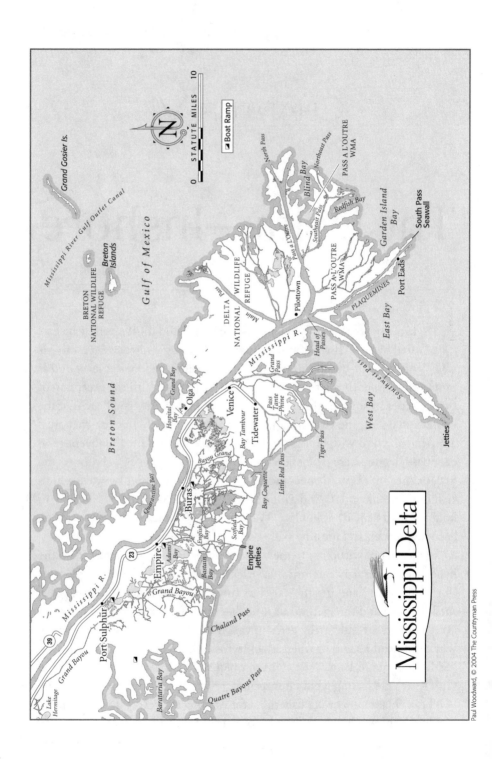

Mississippi Delta

Paul Woodward, © 2004 The Countryman Press

declare open season on the lawyers representing them and the Department of Wildlife & Fisheries personnel who continue to renew those leases. The limit: two per day, if you please. But enough about the oyster fishermen—and the fact that even a small hurricane passing up Barataria Bay would probably put an end to much of the lower Delta.

But until that happens, the inshore fishing should remain as it presently is: simply unbeatable. So with that, combined with the fact that so many opportunities exist in and around the Delta, it's best for the sake of clarification to divide those opportunities to "inshore" and "offshore," the line of demarcation being the point where the Gulf meets land's end.

Near Alliance, Myrtle Grove, Lake Hermitage, and Port Sulphur on the river's west bank, reds tail in thick patches of widgeon grass and crawl the edges of shallow ponds within still fairly large areas of spartina. To me, crawlers are every bit as exciting as tailers—maybe even more so. Here, sight-fishing is the rule throughout most of the year, but when the low tides of high winter drain the marsh, the reds stack up in the slightly deeper water of the nearby bayous, bays, and canals, and blind-casting can lead to numbers unheard of when fly fishing is involved. As elsewhere, sight-fishing is usually best done with weedless spoon flies, bend-backs, and small poppers; when blind-casting slightly deeper water size 1 or 1/0 Clouser-types are often a better choice. During the cold months they are *the* choice.

In this area the clearest water is frequently right against the back levee. It is also often the shallowest in the marsh, so like the Lafitte guides, most folks who fish this area use mud-boats powered by Go-Devils (a 24 hp Briggs & Stratton 4-cylinder straight driveshaft, suitable for pushing a narrow aluminum flatboat), alternating push-pole and rod with a buddy after a predetermined number of hooked fish or "shots."

Specks provide good to very good fly fishing action in such spots as Bay Round, Bay Raquette, Big and Little Chene Fleur, Bay Laurier (see page 162), and in the deeper ponds along the Lake Hermitage canal and the Jefferson Lake canal, usually on the falling tide. The bays are best worked with Clouser-types, while the ponds frequently give up great action on poppers. As might be expected by now, that surface action normally shines best during autumn—some of my best days with poppers have occurred well after Thanksgiving! It can be good in spring, too, but forget it all during summer and head outside to the mining area behind Port Sulphur, Bay Craig, and Barataria Bay. Clouser-types are the bread-and-butter flies during summer, though poppers and early-morning calm periods can make a great couple.

Between Port Sulphur and Buras most of the grass is gone. The primary structure here is oyster beds—shallow for reds, 3 to 4 feet deep for specks, and marked by long willow branches or lengths of white PVC pipe stuck into the bay bottoms and extending well above the water's surface. This area shines brightest during moderate winter weather, and it can produce very good action with both specks and reds through early spring and again in late fall. While there is some sight-fishing to be had during that time on low tides along the edges of what grass remains, the most productive technique is blind-casting. Here, the 9-weight and size 1 and 1/0 Clouser-type flies, usually in chartreuse over white or green over chartreuse, are used most often, but in late February and early March a big size 1/0 popper has accounted for a few almost-big specks! I've caught a lot of fish in this area, but forget it between the middle of May and Thanksgiving. Then the two inshore shrimp seasons, along with the plankton and algae blooms of summer, keep the water really turbid. Besides that, there are too many other opportunities around to be fishing in this area during that time.

Some of the best action actually begins a little earlier in the Pass a l'Outre Wildlife Management Area. In March and April big specks—and some pretty huge redfish—are fairly common along the roseau-lined seashore. (Roseau—ro' so—is tall cane that grows in thick brakes sort of like bamboo, but it can grow in up to four feet of water as well as on dry land.) Blind-casting Clouser-types on 9- or 10-weight outfits is the pattern, and down here, please do use a mono or fluorocarbon shocker!

In May some really big specks become fly fishable around the Delta. The Chandeleur Islands, the bar at the mouth of Blind Bay, and the South Pass seawall and mud lumps give up trophies every year during big-fish time. All those spots have been well-prospected with flies, and all have yielded some really good specks—and some redfish that were almost too big! Yeah, here goes that spoiled side of me again, but when one has about six honest weeks every year to catch a really big speck, and the bull reds—which are attainable for a much longer period—keep eating his fly, he does tend to get perturbed after a while. Maybe if I could finally tally a really big speck on a fly I could learn to appreciate those redfish more. Maybe . . .

While the islands and the Blind Bay bar can be worked effectively with floating lines, the South Pass seawall is simply made to order for a clear intermediate sinking-tip line. As everywhere else, big flies are best for tempting big specks, and here, too, they are best served with a 9- or 10-weight outfit on a leader with a 16-pound class tippet and a 40-pound fluorocarbon

*The Delta, though suffering badly from coastal erosion, still provides
excellent fly fishing for specks and reds throughout most of the year.*

shocker. One thing about using gear that heavy: Don't think you can wrestle
a big speck to the boat in a hurry with it! Big fish with tender lips cannot be
hurried! Keep firm pressure on them and keep any slack out of the line, but
don't rush 'em!

During the warm months good action with specks and reds—though
with few trophy-size fish—is possible along the West Delta seashore and the
seashore of the Pass a l'Outre WMA and the Delta National Wildlife
Refugee up to the mouth of Main Pass. Blind Bay occasionally offers a real
surprise in August when tarpon move into its relatively shallow waters to feed
on mullet—and specks! The rather dingy water there is not very good for
sight-fishing, but on reasonably calm days you can see rolling fish, dorsal fins,
and tails, and cast to them. So far none have been caught on fly; I hooked
one a while back, got one good bounce out of it, and lost it when the hook
fell out on slack line as it attacked the boat. If you are lucky enough to be
there when they are, you just might hook one. Like many other Louisiana
opportunities, this one is more likely to be experienced on a guided trip. I
would go with the intention of fly fishing for the specks and reds that are

found along and inside of the bar at this time, but I would have my 12-weight rigged and ready. The fish I lost stuck a size 3/0 Flashy Chartreuse Thing (see page 235).

Usually some time in August the river begins to clear, not long thereafter the redfish begin showing up in it and its passes, and sight-fishing for them along the shoreline sandbars of Grand Pass, Pass a l'Outre, South Pass, and Southeast Pass, to name a few, can become really great! By late September all the little cuts and passes in the WMA have cleared, and working sinking lines for nice-sized (and usually rather deep) specks—and working floating lines for (usually rather shallow) reds and flounder—is the best thing going.

At about this same time a variety of killifish known locally as "storm minnows" invades the passes of the lower Delta all the way up to Venice. These little delicacies get their name because of their tendency to appear as a storm's high tide falls, drawing them from the flooded marshes and into the passes, and everything that swims, flies, walks, and crawls eats them—often like there will be no tomorrow! When you encounter a gang of these creatures—and you probably will if you fish here during their time, your flies—surface or sinking—should be purple and between 3 and 3½ inches long.

Yeah, purple!

And during the calm periods between late-autumn's normally weak cold fronts, the waters from Alliance and Myrtle Grove south to Buras clear and become as fly fishable as any on the entire coast, providing consistently good to occasionally exceptional action with specks and reds—the kind you have to experience to believe! There is indeed no off-season in inshore Delta waters. The first fish I caught in the new millennium—four very nice reds—were taken sight-fishing in a short, shallow canal off Bayou Grand Liard on January 10; I then went on to a favorite oyster bed in Skipjack Bay and took 10 lovely specks! Nice way to start the next thousand years, huh?

Mississippi River Melange

If I was a betting man, I'd give some pretty good odds that fully 95 percent of the readers of this tome have never considered fly fishing in the downstream reaches of the Mississippi River. Any takers?

I would doubt it. Most folks would consider that to be blue catfish water, if anything, and even if those creatures would strike something like an oversized Spuddler with any regularity whatsoever, they'd have mortal hell finding it in all that muddy water.

Quite true, and that would be the response I'd expect from those who are not in the know. Yet normally by late summer, the mental picture those readers have of the Old Man becomes entirely inaccurate as the river transforms from a moving sea of liquid mud into the deep-green semblance of the purest emerald. Yes, it becomes quite clear, though at the expense of the Midwestern corn farmers. If I may explain . . .

Typically by mid-August the "up-country" (midwest Louisiana) dry season has set in (drought conditions up there are best for the river down here), and runoff from the river's major tributaries becomes minimal, resulting in the year's slowest current speeds, or "flow rates." Since fresh water has insufficient viscosity to suspend solids, that flow rate is what transported the part of Farmer Brown's Iowa corn patch that washed away with the late-spring rains down the river, making it quite muddy. Now, in the river's much slower current, that portion of his South Forty has fallen to bottom somewhere along the way, resulting in a marked increase in clarity.

Or something like that . . .

Well all that is simply wonderful, you say, except maybe for poor ole Farmer Brown's corn patch. But you are still not about to travel all the way to south Louisiana to fly fish for blue catfish!

I can understand that, but in not doing so you will miss out on what can be the most wide-open, no-brainer fly-fishing opportunity in the entire United States! For instance . . .

One late-summer morning, after a line of heavy squalls moved across the Delta, I drove down to Fort Jackson—a historic site some 60 miles below New Orleans on LA 23—to fish along the rocks that line the riverbank there. The maintenance folks were in the process of pumping the excess rainwater from the fort's moat, in effect creating a fine chum line in the river consisting of small minnow and grass shrimp that inhabited the moat. The water near the moat's discharge pipe was alive with white bass, small striped bass, and a few largemouths, and, while standing there on the rocks near the pipe and working a small popper with an 8-foot, 5-weight outfit, I caught 33 of them, most of which were small stripers.

While that incident was assuredly the result of good timing (the fish turned off once the pump was shut down), others like it have been common.

During late summer and much of autumn the Mississippi River and its passes frequently provide an unusual fly-fishing opportunity for several saltwater species.

White bass are indigenous to the Mississippi River, and they—as do all the river's sight-oriented predators—have a pretty tough time making a living during the months of high-flow rates and the associated turbidity. However, when the water clears they feed heavily, and they usually come in bunches.

They also simply love flies, though they occasionally prefer a size 4 green-and-white Clouser Minnow to poppers. They sure did on a certain early October afternoon when a friend and I caught 20 of them—along with about 60 members of several other species! I'll let you ponder that for a while before I expound on it. . . .

Besides the white bass, the river hosts a large population of striped bass, and the fact that they are naturally reproducing therein has been documented. They grow very slowly, however, apparently due to the difficulty of efficient feeding during the long-term period of winter and spring turbidity. These days, most of them will be in the 3- to 5-pound class, but they—like the white bass—often come in bunches.

The river's resident species—which include, besides the true bass, largemouths, crappie, and various sunfish—can be taken readily along the rocks and concrete riprap that reinforce the banks of the main-line channel. However, the small passes below Venice can provide even hotter action. Here, especially with the low tides caused by the season's first significant cool front—or as the tide again falls after the passing of a tropical system—the infamous "storm minnow" appears. This version of killifish is a topic of great interest to literally everything that swims (and fly fishes) in the lower Mississippi and its estuary, and the fact that when it comes it, too, comes in great bunches even enhances its appeal to the predators (and the fly fishermen).

In that case is it necessary to match the minnow?

Certainly not. I once tied some poppers and Clousers in a vague similarity, but by the time the "hatch" occurred, I had forgotten them. Green-and-white poppers and Clousers are consistently effective, apparently because there is also a tremendous number of shad in the river, and no self-respecting striper, white bass, largemouth, flounder, redfish, or speck—that can also appear in bunches—will ever pass up one of those! Nevertheless, when the storm minnows are appearing in gangs, purple is often a better choice.

Wait a minute, you think. Saltwater fish in the Mississippi River? Most assuredly! During this time of the year's slowest flow rates, salt water moves upstream along the bottoms of the passes and, eventually, well up the main-line channel, dispersing through the water column by upwellings and eddies. (In 1988 the river—our source of drinking water—became so salty that freshwater had to be barged down from New Orleans!) With the salt water comes a hoard of saltwater species: reds, flounder, and sheepshead, initially, then specks and ladyfish, among others. Those, along with the largemouths and true bass, which have a greater toleration for the increased salinity than the river's other residents, create a fly-fishing melange that is second to none.

Just how good does it get? You may not believe it even while you are experiencing it! Take that early-October afternoon I mentioned earlier. Besides those 20 very respectable white bass, we caught 35 redfish in the 4- to 6-pound class, 20 specks to 17 inches, a handful of ladyfish, and a pair of 3-pound stripers!

Sure, that's close to top-end, but it does happen—and on that day it happened in Tante Phine Pass just a short distance downstream of the Venice Marina. The point is, you don't have to be intimately familiar with this area to catch fish. Just look for the signs: diving birds, flying minnows, and working fish—and for the fish themselves. Reds are often plainly visible atop sandbars along shorelines—even those of the river itself—offering an excellent sight-fishing opportunity.

So you think all this sounds too good to be without some hitch? Well, I guess another Great Midwestern Flood of 1993 could occur just prior to your trip. But even with that, you would have plenty of forewarning for replanning. Here, there is a foolproof way to determine if the river is fishable. In the weather section of many newspapers the river's stage at New Orleans is posted daily. When that falls to 3 feet or less (less is better) and appears from upstream readings to be stable or still falling (Cairo, Illinois, is a good reference point), it is right. Next, call the Venice Marina for an update. Their hotline provides daily information on the recent action, the weather, and the water conditions. And as far as the weather goes, the trees along the passes create very nice windbreaks; somewhere you will find a protected shoreline where you can fish in all but a young gale.

If there is a cloud somewhere in all the sunny fly-fishing opportunities that the river and its small passes offer, it is the boat traffic—ships in the main-line channel and oil-field support vessels and shrimp trawlers in the passes. Tante Phine and Red Passes are the least used by those types, but there, too, your solitude will occasionally be shattered by the passing of a trawler. But I'll tell you this: When the storm minnows gang up and the reds, specks, white bass, stripers, etc., etc., etc., are doing their best to eat every last one and as quickly as possible—and in the process are merrily chewing the bucktail off my Clousers—I couldn't care less! I don't think you will, either!

CHAPTER VII

The Delta—Offshore

As it is everywhere else along the Louisiana Coast, the Mississippi River Delta offers fly fishermen few offshore opportunities during winter. However, there is one that is outstanding: chunking for tuna on the Midnight Lump.

The technique and the Lump have been covered thoroughly in other parts of this book. The opportunity begins in early season, though normally few days are calm enough then, especially in January, for fly fishing in the ocean while at anchor.

Better conditions and possibly better action arise in February and March. April and May tend to lie to you, promising light southerlies, which often kick up to 15 knots or more by midmorning. Still, this is my preferred time for dueling with the archbeasts with a fly rod, since by then most of the triple-digit yellowfin have left the area, leaving the much less brutal fish in the 20- to 40-pound class to provide the entertainment.

May is usually the first, and often the best, month for sight-fishing for tripletail. The upper half of West Delta is a great area for these fish. It is defined roughly by parallel lines running south from the mouths of Four Bayous Pass (aka Quatre Bayous Pass) and Southwest Pass and north of a line connecting those around 6 miles south of Southwest Pass, and there is normally at least one good rip within it that tends to hold these fish. Of course, tripletail can show up anywhere at this time; that part of West Delta is simply my normal hunting grounds, and I have found no need to look for others. Nevertheless, no matter where you are, always keep an eye out for a random piece of flotsam—and don't ignore it!

During May cobia can occasionally be found with tripletail along both nearshore rips and the blue-water rip, though better action with them usually comes a little later. However, May is a great time for pursuing dolphin along the blue-water rip. Bulls are present, but expect most of the action to be with chickens and school-sized fish; the big boys and girls become much more plentiful as summer waxes. In past years a strong blue-water rip has often moved to within 12 miles of the mouth of Southwest Pass during the first week of June, and besides holding billfish, it was typically loaded with cobia, bull dolphin, and other rip-dwellers. The folks at the marinas in Venice keep up with the status of the blue-water rip and are happy to pass along information on its whereabouts.

By the summer solstice all the area's offshore fly-fishing targets are active, though some offer much more consistent action than others. Jacks can be encountered from now through September and beyond; look for them in open-water blitzes and behind offshore trawlers in West Delta, and along the east jetty of Southwest Pass. Sudden eruptions of the lesser types can occur virtually anywhere in this same area during that time frame, but if you encounter one while in search of bigger game—especially if the perpetrators are discovered to be little tunny, you would be wise to ignore it. There are too many other bigger and more desirable creatures around for you to waste good time on a lesser type!

(I'd bet that comment probably chapped the butts of a bunch of Northeast fly fishermen who target those fish! Nevertheless, I'd also bet they haven't seen anything like the summer fly-fishing potential that West Delta offers anywhere else along our entire coastline. Well, perhaps the Florida Keys. Perhaps.)

While it is not the best around, some very good action with bull reds and medium-sized king mackerel takes place along Southwest Pass's east jetty during August. Expect to also take a few of the lesser types while fishing for them, probably some respectable specks, and possibly some creatures not mentioned elsewhere in this book—another potential wilderness for me to explore. Grey snappers, gag groupers, and small—and not so small—cobia are occasionally taken here in summer by conventional fishermen. It could happen to you! Bring plenty of flies in anticipation of wrecking a lot of them, and work them deep, but always keep an eye out for schools of bull reds patrolling the surface!

These fertile waters support a host of prey species and a variety of pelagic predators that can be taken on flies.

August and September are the Delta's prime months for tarpon. While the opportunity offered by the hallowed trolling grounds of the West Delta, Southwest Pass, South Pass, and Northeast Pass is not very viable for fly fishermen, occasionally fish move into the relatively shallow waters of Blind Bay. There, they are a viable target.

Catching them there, though, will require being there when they are— no guarantees for that—and having wind and sea conditions such that you can see them. Yes, it's iffy, but even with only one known tarpon hooked in this area on a fly, Blind Bay could still offer Louisiana's best chance for a fly-caught tarpon. We'll see.

West Delta's cobia season peaks in September, then rapidly winds down with the coming of the cool fronts. However, some of the best action and largest fish come just before the fish leave for the year. I got my largest off a rip not 4 miles from the mouth of Tiger Pass on October 2. Not long after that they either begin heading south or they go deep. Same apparently goes with the tripletail.

But about that time the little (and not so little) yellowfin tuna begin to show up, along with blackfins, around the deep-water platforms. I know of no one who has fly fished them successfully in that setting yet, but I'd

The Southwest Pass's east jetty could be the quintessential redfish spot on the entire Louisiana Coast. (It's not too shabby for king mackerel, too!)

imagine live-bait chumming would work; they need to be concentrated in a relatively small area to be really fly fishable—which is the reason chunking works so well on the Lump. Incidentally, a good source of live-bait chum that can be acquired on site is small (5- to 6-inch) blue runners, and I can't think of a better end for those aggravating little "lesser types" than serving as tuna appetizers! Amass a mess of them with Sabiki rigs on a spinning outfit, then dispense them two or three at a time until the tuna show up. Then you shouldn't need to be told what to do! This is also the time for chasing offshore trawl-boats in water depths appropriate for tuna. I have fly fished for them successfully in that manner, and brother, that's a real boot!

Dolphin remain available along the blue-water rip and around the mooring buoys of platforms and semi-submersible drilling rigs well into November, and I have also successfully fly fished for them! Fact is, those holding to the mooring buoys are almost a no-brainer, though they don't seem to reach the size attained by the ones found in summer along the blue-water rip.

Expect rainbow runners and other types to also be found around rigs standing in blue water, in summer as well as in autumn. If I can ever get at a rainbow runner without having to fight a boatload of anti-fly-fishing personnel and equipment at the same time, I will catch it! I promise! I want to do that almost as bad as I want to catch a 'hoo on a fly, and that's saying something! But that's my problem. . . .

November and early December is also the time of the bull red and king mackerel madness along Southwest Pass's east jetty. This is an opportunity every fly fisherman should experience, as it is an offshore adventure that takes place mere minutes from sheltered water. And the potential for catching one's biggest redfish and one's biggest king—provided the lesser types aren't particularly thick in the area that day—cannot be beat! There are some awfully big reds and kings in these waters at this time; the main difficulty with catching them is the profusion of fish of both species in the 20- to 30-pound class! Getting your fly in the face of a brute before one of those baby beasts eats it can be a real problem!

Isn't that just awful!

The Chandeleur Islands aren't really "offshore," but they deserve a mention here, as during mid-autumn they can become aesthetically overwhelming. On those calm, crisp afternoons when—thigh-deep in the surf—you find a friendly emerald sea before you, a cloudless azure sky above you, the dusky dunes behind you, and not another soul within 100 yards of you, you'll see. The fishing is also worth experiencing, though most of the action will probably involve reds—regular reds and bulls. Sight-fishing for them is best during the time of brightest sunlight—9 A.M. through 2 P.M.; blind-casting the troughs and pockets could lead to some surprisingly nice specks, lots of reds, and perhaps some flounders and other types. And usually there's nothing out there then but you or your buddies, a few birds, and the fish. The Chandeleurs are truly an autumn wonderland.

Around year's end chunking for tuna begins in earnest on the Midnight Lump, and if you don't get beat to the bone catching a bunch of little tunny first, you just might hook a blackfin or a yellowfin small enough to whip before it whips you! So far, the state-record fly-caught yellowfin is around 76 pounds, but fish close to 200 are caught conventionally every winter. When you go fly fishing on the Lump, you take your chances. Bring at least two outfits!

The Delta's outstanding offshore opportunities may arouse suspicion in some readers: Fishing down there just can't be that good! Well, it can be; I've experienced it—and I've been told that by others who have fished with me. But I must say that I live right in the middle of it and can take almost immediate advantage of the opportunities when they arise; most folks won't be that fortunate.

Living as closely to those opportunities as I do, I can also pick my days. And I must confess that as I have gotten older I have become a lot more selective in choosing the days I will fish. A lot of folks from outside the area cannot afford that luxury, having to fish when they can rather than when they want to. So need I say that my successes with some of Louisiana's available opportunities have resulted from my selecting almost ideal times to try them.

Still, all that aside, those opportunities have been proven to exist. Many of Louisiana's saltwater fly-fishing opportunities that are covered in this section of the book—both inshore and offshore—were developed at least in part by yours truly and a few close friends. There are assuredly other opportunities that have slipped my mind, and I have little doubt that if the Good Lord allows me the time—and if my boat-sponsor keeps providing me with the means—I will discover others; there are some things I've been wanting to try for years—just haven't gotten around to them yet. Then too, there are a lot more folks waving fly rods around coastal Louisiana now than there were only a decade or so ago, so some of them are likely to discover others. And bless Pete, there are finally some really good guides around who know enough about fly fishing to be a help rather than a hindrance. We've come a long way, baby!

We've also stopped measuring our catches by the ice-chest full! Indeed, some of us even practice catch-and-release, occasionally even when we don't have to! We've learned a lot in the past decade: not all the cobia leave for the winter, tarpon stick around—deep—a lot longer than was once thought, reds grow much quicker—and live much longer—than we ever imagined, the removal of the gill nets has made a huge difference in the size of the specks that we commonly catch, released fish do live to be caught again—and to spawn again, and fly rods are no longer looked upon as "sissy gear."

Like I said, we've come a long way, and the fishing for some species is much better now than it once was because of it. Of course, none of it was ever bad—not in my lifetime, anyway! If you are a capable fly fisherman and come here to see for yourself, and if you have anywhere near decent fly-fishing conditions, at day's end you may have some trouble believing what you just experienced. A lot of fly-fishing folks I know have had that problem.

Bon chance!

Motels and Cabins (and a houseboat!)
Most folks who fish the Delta down to the Port Sulphur area overnight and dine in the city. The (New Orleans) Westbank listings in the section about Lafitte are also suitable for this area.

Belle Chasse
- Larosa Motel, 7667 LA 23, 504-394-9544
- Riverside Motel, 8280 LA 23, 504-391-0133

Empire
- Chateau Royale, 32835 LA 11, 985-657-9471
- Empire Inn, 32022 LA 23, 985-657-9853
- Hideaway Lodge, 31975 LA 23, 985-657-6100
- Morel's Chateau, 32368 LA 23, 985-657-8532

Buras
- Cajun Fishing Adventures, 35427 LA 23, 985-657-8717
- Joshua's Marina, 309 Buras Boat Harbor Road, 985-657-7632

Venice
- Cypress Cove, 226 Cypress Cove Road, 985-534-9289
- Fishing, Inc., Venice Marina, 985-534-9183 (the houseboat)
- Lighthouse Lodge, 42256 LA 23, 985-534-2522
- Little Fish, 40265 LA 23, 985-534-7008
- Venice Inn, 42660 LA 23, 985-534-7424
- Venice Marina, 237 Sports Marina Road, 985-534-9357

Campgrounds, Cabins, and RV Parks

Myrtle Grove
- KOA Campground, 17537 LA 23, 985-656-2181

Lake Hermitage
- Bayou Log Cabins, Lake Hermitage, 985-656-2569

Buras
- Angel's Hideaway, LA 11, 985-657-7018

Venice
- Cypress Cove, 226 Cypress Cove Road, 985-534-9357
- Nell's Cabins & RV Park, LA 23 in Boothville, 985-534-2570
- Venice Marina, 237 Sports Marina Road, 985-534-9357

Bed & Breakfast

- Woodland Plantation, LA 23 in West Pointe a La Hache, 985-656-9990

Restaurants

Belle Chasse

Belle Chasse, like other Westbank suburbs, has its share of fast-food places. So, being out of the official Cajun belt, only seafood and specialty spots are included here.

- Adams Catfish House, 8523 LA 23, 504-392-0541
- Angelo's, 2019 Concord Road, 504-392-9882
- Hoagie Hutt, 7670 LA 23, 504-393-1125
- Salvo's Seafood, 7742 LA 23, 504-393-7303 (anything boiled, and shrimp po-boys are highly recommended)
- Sullivan's, 9052 LA 23, 504-433-0444

Port Sulphur

- Cajun Kitchen, 105 Camelia Drive, 985-564-3113
- Buddy's Seafood, 29158 LA 23, 985-564-2675 (very good po-boys)

Empire

- Pam's Place, 32239 LA 23, 985-657-5910
- Tom's Place, LA 11 just below the drawbridge, 985-657-7766 (simply the best oysters around!)

Buras

- Camp Seafood, 109 Rodi Lane, 985-657-5124 (great food and atmosphere)
- China Sea, 36498 LA 11, 985-657-7557 (great shrimp kung-bo!)
- Joshua's Marina, 309 Buras Boat Harbor Road, 985-657-7632

Venice

- Barbara's Place, 42921 LA 23, 985-534-2017 (roast beef po-boy!)
- Cypress Cove, 226 Cypress Cove Road, 985-534-9289
- Fishing, Inc., Venice Marina, 985-534-9183 (Miss Sandy feeds her overnight customers, and how!)
- Little Fish, 40265 LA 23, 985-534-7008
- Venice Inn Restaurant, 42660 LA 23, 985-534-7703

Sporting Goods Stores

The fly shops and sporting goods outlets mentioned in the section about Lafitte are also appropriate here. The only fishing tackle you will find down in the Delta will be at Fill-A-Sack convenience stores and hardware stores—where there typically isn't much, and at the marinas. Again, bring everything you think you'll need and then some!

Marinas

Myrtle Grove
- Myrtle Grove Marina, 161 Marina Road, 985-656-9980

Lake Hermitage
- Lake Hermitage Marina, 126 Marina Lane, 985-656-2020

West Pointe a la Hache
(There is a public back-down ramp on the side of the canal here.)
- Happy Jack Marina, 289 Martin Lane, 985-564-8668

Port Sulphur
- Hi-Ridge Marina, 113 Hi Ridge Road, 985-564-2232

Empire
- Delta Marina, 317 Rosemarie Drive, 985-657-9726

Buras
- Joshua's Marina, 309 Buras Boat Harbor Road, 985-657-7362
- Riverside Marina, 35311 LA 11, 985-657-8184

Venice
- Baptiste Collette Launch, 42511 LA 23, 985-534-2628
- Cypress Cove, 226 Cypress Cove Road, 985-534-9289
- Venice Marina, 2037 Sports Marina Road, 985-534-9357 (hotline: 985-534-7701)

All the above marinas are accessible from LA 23. Should you choose to try the more remote eastern marshes and such infamous spots as Black Bay (Where I once worked and fished almost every day, catching some really humongous specks, even on flies!), then cross the river on the Belle Chasse Ferry and head south on LA 39. At the fork take the left, and on the backside of Pointe a la Hache you will come across Beshel's Landing (985-333-4469).

I doubt if many folks over there have ever seen a fly rod, so don't be surprised at the reactions you might get. But don't let that deter you; some of the best inshore fishing in the Delta is out of Pointe a la Hache.

Guides

There are now more recreational fishing guides working the Delta than there once were gill-netters. Like the situation at present on Calcasieu Lake, some come, some go, and I've no idea as to who comes or goes among those I don't know. The ones listed below have been guiding for enough time to have established a good reputation. Many of them have guide "services" that employ other guides. Book your trip early, as these guys stay busy!

I—Inshore; C—Coastal; O—Offshore;
F—The guy knows more than just the basics of fly fishing.

Myrtle Grove Area

- Capt. Mark Brockhoeft (I, F), 1-800-966-4868
- Capt. Barrett Brown (I, F), 504-908-3474
- Capt. Kirby LaCour (I, F), 504-464-1697

These three guys are real, honest-to-God fly-fishing guides!

Port Sulphur to Venice

- Capt. Kevin Aderhold (I, C, F), 985-564-2947
- Capt. Brandon Ballay (O, F), 985-534-9246
- Capt. Brent Ballay (I, C, O, F), 985-534-9246
- Capt. Barry Colligan (I), 985-657-8410
- Capt. Bryan Dickinson (I), 985-657-9214
- Capt. Chris Dinwiddie (I, C, O, F), 504-722-8103
- Capt. Mike Frenette (O, F), 985-341-4245
- Capt. Jay Friedman (I), 985-657-8958
- Capt. Ryan Lambert (I, C), 985-657-8717
- Capt. Damon McKnight (O), 504-643-1720
- Capt. Peace Marvel (O, F), 985-534-2278
- Capt. James Peters (O, F), 504-834-7097
- Capt. Anthony Randazzo (I, C), 504-656-9940

- Capts. Nash Roberts III & IV (I), 504-837-0703
- Capt. Brent Roy (I, C), 225-907-8420
- Capt. Bobby Warren (I, C, F), 504-368-7084
- Capt. Allen Welch (I, C), 601-799-0110
- Capt. Dick Welch (I, C), 504-643-4855

Eastern Marshes

- Capt. Dan Lambert, 504-682-5135
- Capt. Charlie Thomason, 504-278-3474

So many great opportunities, so little time . . .

Depechez!

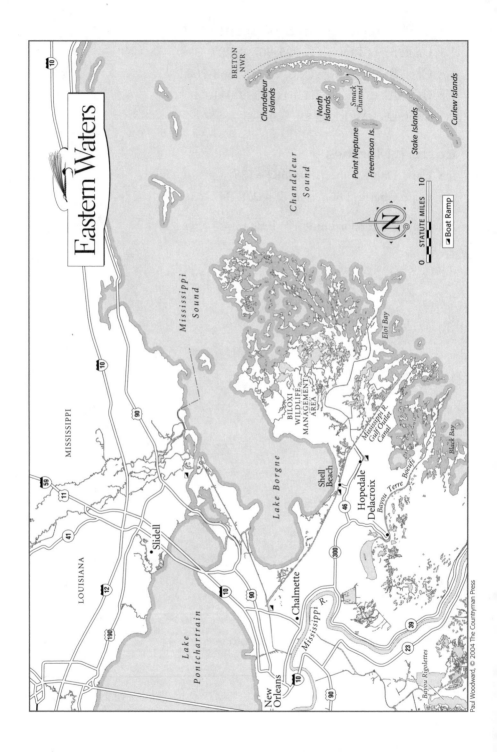

Eastern Waters

LOUISIANA

MISSISSIPPI

Lake Pontchartrain

Lake Borgne

Mississippi Sound

Chandeleur Sound

BRETON NWR

Chandeleur Islands

North Islands

Smack Channel

Point Neptune

Freemason Is.

Stake Islands

Curlew Islands

Slidell

New Orleans

Chalmette

Mississippi R.

Shell Beach

Hopedale

Delacroix

BILOXI WILDLIFE MANAGEMENT AREA

Mississippi R. Gulf Outlet

Bayou Terre Boeufs

Eloi Bay

Black Bay

Bayou Rigolettes

N

STATUTE MILES

0   10

■ Boat Ramp

Paul Woodward, © 2004 The Countryman Press

CHAPTER VIII

Eastern Waters

The easternmost part of Louisiana's coastline can be divided into two parts: the marsh and the Pontchartrain Basin. Fishing either is almost entirely inshore and involves primarily speck and redfish. The bays and ponds within the marsh, which surrounds Delacroix Island and lies south and east of Shell Beach and Yscloskey, and north and east of Hopedale, are popular and productive. They hold the same species during the same seasons as other areas of marsh across the coast and are fly fished in similar fashions. For sight-fishing for redfish seek out shallow ponds choked with wigeongrass; speck are often found around the oyster beds that are abundant in the numerous small bays in this area.

Eloi Bay and Black Bay lie between that marsh and Breton Sound and are infamous for their speck. I recall a day back in 1986, while I was working in Black Bay, when my oil-well remedial operation allowed me a few hours to slip away to a nearby island and "test bottom" (fish). That day I did it for the first time with a fly rod. (A little pre-planning was involved, as I almost never carried a fly rod to work with me!) Standing in the shoreline waters there, in steel-toed work boots, company coveralls, and plastic hard hat, I caught 29 lovely specks, 11 of them on poppers!

I haven't been back to fish there in a while—busy in other places—but I'm told Black Bay is still full of specks during spring, summer, and much of fall. It is handily reached from Delacroix Island via Bayou Terre aux Boeufs. Eloi Bay is best accessed via the Mississippi River Gulf Outlet from Hopedale. (The Mr. Go is a dredged channel from the Gulf to New Orleans for major shipping traffic.) In both places work the grass islands and any diving birds you might come across; Clouser-types and poppers—both in size 1/0—should do the trick. Expect your best chances with the biggest fish in May and June. There'll be lots of smaller fish during summer, and some good ones again in autumn.

The string of islands in far eastern waters called the Chandeleurs can be handily reached from this area, the most popular route being the Mr. Go, which crosses the southeastern marshes and Breton Sound, passing between Breton and Grand Gosier Islands, before terminating well offshore in the Main Pass area. Of note is the fact that the buoys marking the offshore reaches of the channel can hold a lot of cobia during summer days with little current, and they are quite fly fishable. And as it is with cobia all across the Louisiana Coast, this opportunity is also sight-fishing. Just be ready to chase a fish around the buoy's cable after it's hooked or you're destined to shred your fly line!

When taking the Mr. Go to the islands, a fairly large oil field will become evident a few miles off to port. This is petroleum company Kerr-McGee's Breton Sound Block 21 field, and it holds some real good specks—and more than a few reds—during spring. Some brute specks were taken here a few years back by Venice's Capt. Mike Frenette guiding Trey Combs and Ray Beadle of West Coast renown. Sea Habit Deceivers worked deep with fast-sinking lines around the individual wells was the productive pattern. I saw the fish; four of them cracked the 6-pound mark! Mercy!

In summer this field offers another opportunity. The compressor station (or the "Central Facility") is well lit and can provide some outstanding night-fishing—as can any other well-lit platform in the bays across the state! The bright light draws plankton, which in turn draws shrimp and minnows, and those draw the predators. On calm nights poppers often generate the wildest action; in any case, cast the fly into the darkness across the bright water, then work it into and across that area. Strikes often come along the edge of the dark and bright water. Night-fishing like this for specks is a tradition of sorts—conventionally, anyway—and it's a really good way to beat summer's heat. And it's made to order for fly fishing!

The marshes and small bays in the Biloxi Wildlife Management Area can provide excellent fly fishing for specks and reds. Reaching this area does require a relatively long run from the marinas in Hopedale, Shell Beach, and Yscloskey, but the competition is often negligible. It is also a very pretty

Louisiana's coastal waters east of the Mississippi River offer a variety of fly-fishing opportunities for several species in diverse settings.

place—and a favorite area for my friend Capt. Gary Taylor. Gary fishes out of the Rigolets (rig' o lees) near Slidell, and besides fishing the WMA, he has a setup that makes accessing the northern Chandeleur Islands a piece of cake!

Lake Borgne—a part of the Pontchartrain Basin—is another popular and productive spot and is only a short hop from Campo's Marina in Shell Beach. Its south shoreline is a great place to fish for the lake's abundant specks when summer's prevailing southerlies have other hot spots roiled and choppy. And don't be surprised if a bull red or a big, bad crevalle jack crashes your party. Because of that possibility, this is also 9- or 10-weight country.

If you've got your sights set on a really big speck and you'd prefer to fish near New Orleans rather than head over to Calcasieu Lake, spool up a high-density sinking line and try working big Clouser-types deep around the abutments of the bridges crossing the eastern end of Lake Pontchartrain. A speck weighing only a hair under 12 pounds was caught here in January a few years back, and fish in the 5- to 7-pound class are taken regularly by in-the-know locals while fishing conventionally. I know of one 5-pounder taken from the lake on a fly, but few folks presently practice that exercise in those waters. Again, I suggest a 9- or 10-weight outfit, not for jacks—which assuredly do move into the lake during summer—but for striped bass that are rumored to provide a fair winter fishery for a group of very tight-lipped locals. The bridges—US 11, I-10, and a railroad trestle—are easily accessed from the marinas in Slidell and the Rigolets. Utilizing a guide for your first trip or two to this hotspot is highly recommended! This fishery is best in late winter and spring; periods of light current—either direction—and of course light winds are preferred.

Wade-fishing along the lake's north shore near Lacombe is a fair opportunity to catch school-sized specks and "regular" reds. Lots of fly fishermen from both the New Orleans area and the northshore communities enjoy this fishery during summer and early fall. The submergent grass-beds found here, along with the cessation of clamshell dredging in the lake several years ago, have resulted in water that is quite clear—a rare commodity in much of southeastern Louisiana. Generally the fish are relatively small, but it's a great opportunity for someone without a boat or the desire to hire a guide—or for someone who hasn't the time for a full day's trip.

While this area might not seem as appealing as some of the others across the coast, there are some fine fly-fishing opportunities here. Capt. Gary Taylor can show some of them to you, and he knows the fly-fishing part of them very well. One of these days he and I are going to figure out the striper part of Pontchartrain's potential—or perhaps he will before we put our heads together. In any case, don't neglect Louisiana's eastern waters; they can provide you with some great action.

Get yourself some of it—*maintenant!*

Motels

Chalmette

Chalmette is easily reached from New Orleans's Westbank by taking General de Gaulle Drive to Holiday Drive; turn toward the river there and continue to General MacArthur Drive, then turn right, then left as soon as you see a road leading to the river, then right again on the river road, and follow that to the ferry landing. Chalmette is the jumping off spot for the marinas in Delacroix Island, Hopedale, and Shell Beach.

Chalmette

- Quality Inn, 5353 Paris Road, 504-277-5353

Slidell

This town should be your base of operations should you choose to fish with Gary or one of the hot Lake Pontchartrain guides.

- Best Western, 120 Taos Street, 985-646-1382
- City Motel, 2101 2nd Street, 985-649-1156
- Comfort Inn, 2010 Old Spanish Trail, 985-641-4147
- Crescent Hospitality, 124 Goldenwood Drive, 985-781-1194
- Days Inn, 1645 Gause Boulevard, 985-641-3450
- Guest Lodge Motel, 58512 Tyler, 985-649-2040
- Hampton Inn, 56460 Frank Pichon Road, 985-726-9777
- Holiday Inn, 372 Voters Road, 985-639-0890
- King's Square Apts., 400 Voters Road, 985-649-5555
- La Quinta Inn, 794 E. I-10 Service Road, 985-643-9770
- Motel 6, 136 Taos Street, 985-649-7925
- Shoney's Inn & Suites, 1516 Gause Boulevard, 985-726-5100
- Sleep Inn, 142 Oak Court, 985-641-2143
- Super 8 Motel, 1662 Gause Boulevard, 985-641-8800
- Value Travel Inn, 58506 Yaupon Drive, 985-649-5400

Restaurants

Chalmette

Besides the inevitable burger barns, chicken shacks, and pizzerias commonly found in any U.S. city, there are lots of mom-and-pop spots in Chalmette that are too many to list, much less to have been sampled. I've dined at only one spot here (noted with "PC"); the following listing falls only into the predetermined (and totally arbitrary) categories of seafood and local-interest goodies.

- The Bean Pot, 809 E. Judge Perez Drive, 504-271-5457
- Bert's Broiler, 3358 Paris Road, 504-279-1316
- Brother's Po-boys, 1603 E. Judge Perez Drive, 504-279-8672
- Bubba John's Seafood (PC), 9212 W. Judge Perez Drive, 504-279-1589
- Café Leblanc, 1010 E. Judge Perez Drive, 504-271-6882
- Char Lou Café, 203 W. Judge Perez Drive, 504-271-7573
- Louisiana Seafood & Steakhouse, 1310 E. Judge Perez Drive, 504-271-3300

- Tony's Po-boy Restaurant, 434 E. Judge Perez Drive, 504-271-5211
- Tony Russell's Fine Italian, 3201 E. Judge Perez Drive, 504-271-7877

Contrary to what my listings may imply, Judge Perez Drive is not the only drag in town!

Slidell

- Bavarian Chalet German/American Restaurant, 2142 1st Street, 985-645-0400
- Boiling Point, 2998 Pontchartrain Drive, 985-641-5551
- Char Lou's II, 2528 Front Street, 985-781-7575
- Chris's Seafood Restaurant, 3333 Pontchartrain Drive, 985-646-0500
- Copeland's, 1337 Gause Boulevard, 985-643-0001
- Fisherman's Reef, 2107 Gause Boulevard, 985-641-2326
- Leblanc's Creole Kitchen, 797 Robert Boulevard, 985-781-8100
- Le Petite Chateau, 153 Robert Street, 985-645-3600
- Phil's Marina Café, 1194 Harbor Drive, 985-641-0464
- The Po-boy Factory, 632 Robert Boulevard, 985-641-4784
- The Port Hole, 4406 Pontchartrain Drive, 985-643-1419
- Salvaggio's Restaurant, 4416 Pontchartrain Drive, 985-641-8360
- Thonn's Seafood, 3273 Pontchartrain Drive, 985-641-3333
- Vincent's Old Towne Creole Kitchen, 220 Erlanger Street, 985-639-3977

Sporting Goods Stores

Need I repeat myself again about what you need to bring with you?
Everything!

Chalmette

- Army Surplus & Outdoor Store, 3525 Paris Road, 504-271-8919

Slidell

- Busy B Bait & Tackle, 376 Sun Valley Drive, 985-641-5976
- Gus's Tackle & Nets, 726 Old Spanish Trail, 985-643-2848
- Mike's Sporting Goods, 530 Brownswitch Road, 985-641-5524
- Oshman's Sporting Goods, 150 Northshore Boulevard, 985-781-5578
- Slidell Army Surplus & Outdoor Store, 778 E. I-10 Service Road, 985-641-1092

- The Slidell Sportsman, 3305 Pontchartrain Drive, 985-641-9797
- Smith Brothers Sporting Goods, 1600 W. Lindberg Drive, 985-646-2266
- T & M Bait & Tackle, 52250 US 90, 985-781-4400

Marinas

Chalmette

The following provides access to Bayou Bienvenue and the surrounding area. While at times fishing here can be quite good, it is often in deep water. Unless you know a local who knows something special, use Chalmette only as a base of operations and head southeast down LA 46.

- Quality Inn's Gulf Outlet Marina, 5353 Paris Road, 504-277-8229

Delacroix Island

- Serigne's Boat Launch, 5934 Delacroix Highway, 504-684-3502

Hopedale

- Breton Sound Marina, 7600 Hopedale Highway, 504-676-1252
- Hopedale Marina, 4618 Hopedale Highway, 504-676-1244

Shell Beach

- Campo's Marina, 1301 Yscloskey Highway 504-676-3679

Slidell

- Bayou Liberty Marina, 58047 LA 433, 504-641-1529
- Bonfouca Marina, 33370 Rivet Drive, 504-847-7893
- Harbor View Marina, 118 Harbor View Court, 504-649-3320
- Marina Chamale Cove, 75 Chamale Cove W., 504-641-2404
- Oak Harbor Marina, 1640 Harbor Drive, 504-641-1044
- Rigolets Bait & Seafood, 52250 US 90, 504-641-8088
- Rigolets Sportsman's Marina, 52246 US 90, 504-847-0005

Highway Guides

Chalmette area

- Bayou Charters, 504-278-3474
- Capt. Brian's Bayou Adventures, 504-488-5581
- Escape Fishing Charters, 504-643-5905

Redfish and specks may be the predominant fish found around the Chandeleur Islands, but the waters here offer the fly fishermen a whole lot more.

- Louisiana Fishing, 877-271-2059
- Marshland Adventures, 504-682-4396
- Rather Be Fishing, 985-863-7563
- S.S. Charters, 504-887-7120
- Titeline Charters, 504-908-4874

Slidell

- Capt. Dee Geoghegan, 504-254-9799
- Capt. Kenny Kreiger, 985-643-2944
- Capt. Gary Taylor, 985-641-8532

Gary is the bona fide fly-fishing guide. Kenny just started but has been fishing the Pontchartrain Basin for many years, and he has the prestigious credit of having taken the second largest speck ever caught by a recreational fisherman in Louisiana. Dee's just a real good guide who knows the lake and how to catch its big specks—conventionally! Let him know what you intend to do, then compare notes. Fly fishing deep in currents isn't easy, but the rewards could be priceless!

Louisiana's fly-fishing opportunities for most of the species discussed can be second to none, but there are assuredly more. Having the Chandeleurs to yourself and a best buddy on a handmade late-winter day will—not "can," will!—create a memory that you will take to your grave. When you finally locate the rip and find it is tight, its color change is well defined, and it's loaded with flotsam, you'll feel a rush that may send your pulse-rate into the danger zone. If you don't get a severe case of buck fever at the first sight of the big brown beast that just appeared from beneath that patch of grass, consider playing a little more poker—and for higher stakes, too! The raucous racket a flock of gulls make when they're diving on big white shrimp being driven to the surface by Calcasieu Lake's mega-specks can become the finest symphony you've ever heard. When those king mackerel skyrocketing just outside Southwest Pass's east jetty are close enough to cause you to duck, you'll suddenly realize for the first time in your fly-fishing life that you've never been more certain of an immediate hookup. All that—and over there by that little patch of wigeongrass a redfish's tail breaks the mirror image of the sunrise and sends a thrill through you just like it has every other time for more than three decades.

Great fishing in great settings and great meals and groceries, too—what more could a guy ask for?

Just a few more years to enjoy it.

Join me?

Appendix A

Boats, Bugs, and Other Concerns

It is highly advisable that, with the exception of surf fishing, every saltwater opportunity that Louisiana offers should be initially experienced on a guided trip. That way, should you later decide you would like to indulge in one or another of those opportunities a little more thoroughly, you will have some idea of what type of boat is appropriate and what type isn't.

Boats

You won't find a boat that's suitable for every opportunity. However, a 20-foot bass-boat will suffice nicely for inshore waters as well as for the surrounding gulf jetties on fly-fishable days. You won't be able to get into the really skinny stuff with it like you would with a flats-boat or a mud-boat, and you won't (shouldn't!) be able to run the nearshore rips when sea conditions are less than ideal, but a bass-boat will cover a lot of everything in between.

Unless you have absolutely no interest in fishing for beasts and are certain that, if conditions suddenly become perfect for an offshore run, you still won't go, stay away from flats-boats. On the other hand, if you really get your bell rung from push-poling a buddy from redfish to redfish across shallow, widgeon grass-choked interior ponds, then knock your lights out. The problem with this type of boat, as well as with bass-boats, is its limited fuel capacity. It's unlikely you will ever run short on even an extended inside trip, but when the wind lays, the seas calm, and the Gulf beckons, you just might. (That happened on a trip in a friend's flats-boat once, and need I say it was quite embarrassing as well as not a little precarious!) Fifty gallons is a good starting point; 80 is better.

Somewhere in that range is normal for a typical bay-boat. This is the type that allowed me to do a great part of my "pioneering" with pelagic beasties, as well as to keep my freezer stocked with speck and flounder fillets. It has also led to some great sight-fishing for reds when the fish were found along shallow shorelines next to slightly deeper water. Over the years I found mine to be reasonably fuel-efficient, fast enough, great as a fishing platform, and on the rare times when the gulf got a little uncomfortable for them, I shouldn't have been out there trying to fly fish anyway!

Though bay-boats may all look basically alike, there are some significant differences. Since 1994 I have run three and have gotten pretty particular about my preferences. Understand, those have been established because of the boat's use in many situations, inshore and offshore, but they are worth considering.

First of all, the boat should be in the 21- to 22-foot range. Any shorter and they are typically crowded and lacking in storage space; any longer and they become simply too much for shallow-water fly fishing, yet still not enough to be a true offshore boat.

The boat should float, loaded, in around a foot of water. It should have 16–18 degrees of "dead-rise" (the angle at which the bottom slopes up horizontally at the stern)—not enough to become "deep vee" but enough to soften the bumps you'll hit offshore. I stoically avoided a tunnel hull, having never experienced how one of those responded to a 2-foot swell topped with a foot of chop (and not especially wanting to). And I grew to prefer a high-sided model over my initial low-sided boat. The latter was lighter and more efficient in interior waters, but that extra height—little as it really was—became very welcome when the ocean was a-motion!

I don't know enough about outboard motors to offer much on them. Four-strokes are divine—except for their initial cost. Whatever your finances allow, make sure your boat has sufficient power—in other words, err on the side of more. That way you will have some horses in your hip pocket when you have to run from a squall!

Should you get soundly smitten by the beasties and decide inshore creatures are simply too tame to entertain you properly, deep-vee center-console boats are a great choice. Those in the 26-foot class powered by a pair of 200-hp outboards are fast enough to get you out there and back without burning up a lot of fishing time, and they are seaworthy enough to get you home fairly comfortably after fly-fishable conditions have deteriorated. And that second motor is very, very comforting when you are way out yonder and the other one starts acting up! Believe me! Here are some thoughts you should consider on offshore fly-fishing boats.

They should have a raised casting platform in the bow. Handrails there should be recessed into the deck, not elevated above it. That will allow you to hold the rod low when the retrieve is being made; otherwise you must hold it high—above the elevated handrail, creating a big bow of line between the rod's tip and the water. Not good! Anchor-line guides should be well forward, pop-up cleats are highly desirable, and pulpits are not as beneficial to fly fishing as they might seem!

If you're considering a boat at least 26 feet long, and you or anyone you might invite on a trip in it know what's going on, a T-Top is a wonderful thing. Conversely, if you desire a smaller boat, and you and your friends tend to become a little, uh, "focused" on an opportunity when one arises, a T-Top will assuredly lead to broken rods. No recommendations here—your call.

You can save some dollars by eliminating any rocket launchers and flush rod-holders, though that will probably have to be done by special order. I do recommend trim tabs on an offshore boat of any size, and a boat with the motor-mount beyond the stern offers a nice get-on-and-get-off spot for wade-fishermen, should you decide on a change of pace.

Accessories other than those that are required by the U.S. Coast Guard should be personal preferences. Nevertheless, I would recommend a GPS unit with the feature that allows you to retrace your route. In any case, get some kind of GPS unit, learn how to use it, and drop waypoints liberally! Bringing along a VHF radio and a cell phone is highly advisable!

Licenses

You will need a license. If you hire a guide he usually is able to furnish you with one. If you fish on your own you can gamble that the marinas or local convenience stores haven't all sold out, or you can order one through the Department of Wildlife & Fisheries' Web site at www.wlf.state.la.us. Call them if you have questions at 225-765-2800. You must have a basic license as well as a saltwater license; several options to match the length of your stay are available.

Insects

I would imagine if most folks would give some thought to the biggest nuisance they'd find along the northern Gulf Coast, it would have to be mosquitoes. To be sure, those little nasties can be problematic at times, but they quickly give way to any decent DEET-enhanced insecticide. Gnats won't!

These little demons are the scourge of much of this area. I've been told they are not really gnats but midges. Well, I couldn't care less what they are other than a royal pain! They are grayish-black, around 1⁄16-inch long, and are apparently made up entirely of a single tooth! (That's what it feels like when they bite you, anyway!) I don't know of anyone who has died from their bites, though I and others like me have been really close to coming unglued when they have gotten thick. And when conditions do get right, they can come in swarms! Fortunately for all warm-blooded creatures hereabouts in the region, those conditions don't arise all that often.

Gnats are basically cool-weather creatures, appearing over inland waters during calm periods and most often from December into April. In this case a fly fisherman should never curse a little breeze, as it is complete salvation! So is Avon's Skin-So-Soft Bath Oil! (I don't have a clue as to who discovered this unlikely deterrent, but humanity owes him a debt of sincerest gratitude!) However, if the sun is bright it will also cook you into the semblance of a boiled crawfish! Until recently we have simply to choose the lesser of the two evils to be tolerated.

One early-April morning not long ago on a speck-fishing trip, the light southeasterly breeze that had been forecast for the entire day went flat calm. Guess what happened then! And owing to the late "season" combined with the forecasted breeze, none of us had considered bringing along some gnat repellant. Fortunately the sun was bright, and one of the crew broke out a tube of Coppertone Sport Sunblock in SPF 15, applied it, and was instantaneously relieved of his persistent painful problem. Needless to say, the others aboard immediately requisitioned the tube of balm, and that was the end of the gnats—and no one got sunburned!

Finally, every well-equipped bay-boat should come with a flyswatter. Sand flies, deer flies, horseflies, and greenheads may not be as abundant as gnats, but a persistent one can bite you several times, and in your errant attempts to swat the agile little devils you can actually bruise yourself! These bites don't leave the lasting impressions of those compliments of gnats and mosquitoes, but initially they are painful—and downright aggravating after your ankle has been hit for the third time in as many minutes! However, the flies do tend to land between attacks, apparently to plan their next move—that's when you pop 'em with the flyswatter.

But you have to be fast!

Tackle Care

Care of tackle is a lot more important when fishing in saltwater than in freshwater. After a day's trip it is always best to completely back off the reel's drag, remove it from the rod, then soak it in a sink for a few minutes, ensuring that no soap has gotten into the water. Slosh it around a time or two, then shake out the excess water and place it on a table to allow it to dry. You may spray the rod down with freshwater to clean it, but never spray the reel!

Drinking Water

While the drinking water across coastal Louisiana no longer poses any dangers to your existence, it differs in hardness and some of it can taste pretty bad. Fact is, during late summer and early autumn the Mississippi River— our source of drinking water in the lower Delta—has gotten so salty that potable water had to be barged down from New Orleans. (And that didn't taste much better!) Point is, local drinking water shouldn't put your life in danger, but it may upset your tummy. Drink bottled water if you think that could happen.

Emergency Medical Information

There are full-blown medical centers in Lake Charles, Lafayette, Houma, Galliano—up the road a ways from Grand Isle, the Westbank suburb of Harvey, New Orleans proper, and Slidell, and there is an emergency medical center in the Delta in Port Sulphur. However, the launch-sites each of those cities serve are at least a half-hour's drive from them. Add the travel time on the water to that, and you can see that even a minor mishap could pose growing problems. That's real good incentive for being careful—and for fishing barbless!

Alligators

In recent years alligators have become quite common in some areas of coastal Louisiana, and they will definitely strike poppers. Therefore there's absolutely no reason why you need to find that out for yourself. Besides, molesting them—like casting a popper at them—is against the law. Taking my word for this—which I learned from, uh, I forget—might save you a big fine as well as a popper!

Storms

From June well into November the northern Gulf Coast is subject to being hit by tropical weather systems, and in case you've never experienced one of those, it can really screw up the fly fishing for a while! These days there is plenty of forewarning, and the predictions of a storm's anticipated track are occasionally in the ballpark. If one of these little nasties shows any indication of making landfall along the Louisiana Coast within half a week or so, stay home or go home! The local folks will have more than enough to do without having guests in their hair—I know!

You can always come back.

Checklists

Wade-fishing trip

_____ 9- or 10-weight outfit

_____ "flats boots" or tennis shoes (chest waders during the cool months)

_____ proper seasonal attire

_____ polarized sunglasses

_____ hat

_____ one box of flies

_____ spools of butt section, class tippet, and shocker material

_____ cord stringer without float (optional)

_____ stainless-steel knife and pliers worn on belt sheath

_____ fishing licenses (keep in a small Ziplock bag inside your hat)

_____ small hip flask of water

_____ sunscreen applied before you hit the water

Guided trip—inshore

_____ 8- to 10-weight outfit

_____ proper seasonal attire

_____ slicker suit

_____ polarized sunglasses

_____ hat

_____ sunscreen

_____ insect repellant

_____ lots of flies and leader material

_____ extra spool of sinking line

_____ lunch and drinks, if not provided by guide

_____ fishing licenses (both basic and nonresident "trip" licenses)

_____ camera

Guided trip—offshore

_____ 10- and 12- or 14-weight outfits

_____ anti-seasickness patches

_____ proper seasonal attire

_____ slicker suit (optional, depending on type of boat)

_____ back brace of some sort

_____ glove and wrist brace for rod hand

_____ tube of Ben-Gay and bottle of Aleve

_____ polarized sunglasses

_____ hat

_____ sunscreen

_____ lots of flies of all types and sizes

_____ leader material and wire

_____ stainless-steel pliers and knife

_____ lunch and drinks, if not provided by guide

_____ extra water

_____ camera

Trip in your own boat

_____ outfits appropriate for target species

_____ all accessories required by Coast Guard, including flares

_____ lots of flies of all types

_____ leader material and wire

_____ polarized sunglasses

_____ proper seasonal attire

_____ slicker suit

_____ hat

_____ sunscreen

_____ insect repellant

_____ charts and GPS unit with extra batteries

_____ cell phone

_____ flashlight and extra batteries

_____ lunch, drinks, and extra water

_____ extra outboard motor oil and small funnel

_____ extra wheel, nut, and washer

_____ extra rope and boat-bumpers

_____ a lot of common sense and courtesy!

Appendix B

Flies and Such

One *Ugly* Fly!

For over ten years now I have fished almost exclusively with flies on my frequent trips to the Chandeleur Islands. Most often I have had at least good action on those occasions—on some days it was great action.

One Ugly *Fly!—Purple is a rare color in most saltwater fly boxes, but it has a definite place for use on Louisiana's coastal waters.*

Tying One *Ugly* Fly

Place a size 1/0 stainless-steel hook with a standard-length shank and a slightly "dropped" point (like an Orvis Pre-Sharpened Saltwater Hook) in the vise with the point up. Grasp the shank just behind the eye with a pair of needle-nose pliers so that the pliers cover about ¼-inch of the shank. Bend the shank down slightly, creating an angle in it of about 15 degrees and ensuring that the bend is in the same plane as that of the hook's bend.

It doesn't take much effort, and if you bend it too far, do not try to correct the error. In other words, never try to rebend a bent bend-back hook!

Reposition the hook in the vise with its point down. Start the thread (purple, or as close to it as possible) in the shank's bend and wrap a thread-base back to the beginning of the hook's bend. Tie in a strand of large purple crystal chenille and apply a drop of superglue to the tie-in point. Advance the thread to where the bobbin hangs in front of the hook's point.

Compactly wrap the chenille forward to the point where the thread is hanging. Overwrap the chenille tightly with one turn of thread, then advance the thread to the start of the shank's bend. Compactly wrap the chenille to that point, tie it off with five or six turns of thread, and trim it. Apply a drop of superglue to the tie-off point, then create a base of thread to the hook's eye, then back to the forward end of the chenille. At that point, tie in small brass hourglass eyes, and finish those wraps with

Besides accounting for a lot of "regular redfish" out there, I have had the fortune of tallying several bulls. The islands have also given up a very satisfying number of specks to my flies—fish averaging much larger than those I normally encounter in inshore waters. Also, the largest specks I have taken on flies—a pair of 25-inchers—came from the Chandeleurs, and I'd imagine if I ever catch a bigger one, its capture will take place in a similar setting.

While I've caught both specks and reds at the islands on green-and-white Deceivers, and, on a few occasions, had great fun with green-and-white poppers, most of the fish were taken on chartreuse-and-white Clouser Minnows. Size 2/0s accounted for most of the bull reds and the two big specks, size 1/0s another drop of superglue. There should be roughly ³⁄₁₆-inch of the bent part of the shank between the brass eyes and the eye of the hook.

Invert the hook in the vise (point up). Tie in a clump of purple buck-tail about the diameter of a pencil and some 3 inches long to the shank between the brass eyes and the eye of the hook. Now tie 8–10 strands of purple Krystal Flash to each side of the fly, ensuring they extend to the end of the bucktail. Finally, tie a half-dozen peacock herls to the top of the fly. Smooth out the fly's head with thread-wraps, whip-finish, and coat the head with either head cement or clear Sally Hanson Hard as Nails fingernail polish. For added appeal, place a dot of black enamel paint on the faces of the brass eyes with the head of a small nail. The fly is easily cast with a 9-weight outfit.

Materials

- Hook: Size 1/0 Orvis Pre-Sharpened Saltwater Hook
- Thread: Purple Danville Flymaster Plus
- Purple bucktail
- Peacock herls
- Purple crystal chenille
- Purple Krystal Flash
- Small brass hourglass eyes
- Superglue
- Black Testors Enamel and a small nail to doll up the eyes

for probably 90 percent of all the others. To be sure, there have been a few times—usually in slightly roiled water—when a size 1/0 dark-green-over-chartreuse Clouser produced the most strikes, but not often. Invariably, when I have first gone overboard on a trip out there, a chartreuse-and-white Clouser has been tied to my shocker.

And so it was recently on my first spring trip to the islands. Initially the pickings were pretty slim. We soon scattered, and while exploring I eventu-ally came across a friend on the sound side of the island. He'd had no better fortune than I had, but that was soon to change.

I found the fish—nice specks—in a wide trough. My friend Brandon

Ballay quickly joined me, as did the rest of the crew shortly thereafter, and the action was hot and heavy for about an hour—at least it was for Brandon. He used a purple soft-plastic on a light jig-head to take his limit; I—standing maybe 15 yards to his right—caught only a fraction of that number on my trusty chartreuse-and-white Clouser. Apparently I had a serious need for something purple in my fly box!

Now would be a good time to explain why I have a preference for certain colors for my saltwater flies. With only a little imagination the chartreuse-and-white Clouser Minnow resembles a big white shrimp, and the green-and-white poppers could easily be taken for small menhaden. On the other hand, the dark-green-over-chartreuse Clouser (which does very well in deep or off-color water) was created to match the colors of a soft plastic lure that is a favorite of mine. Purple is a favored color of many of my guide-buddies, so once again it seemed expeditious for me to tie a fly that matched a productive conventional lure.

It was created by combining some of the attributes of a bend-back and a Clouser Minnow. By using a slightly bent hook-shank I could fashion a body—something a pure Clouser lacks. The bent shank, in combination with brass hourglass eyes tied to the outside of the shank at the point where it is bent, caused the fly to ride point-up—a desired feature. And a large purple bucktail wing enhanced with purple Krystal Flash and finished with a half-dozen peacock herls on top resulted in a "near-nuff" semblance to Brandon's purple soft-plastic minnow. I tied four of them in size 1/0.

A week later we sallied forth again to the islands. Again I found the fish, though they were in another trough across a sandbar from the one where they'd been on the previous trip, and I had strung five beauties—all on the purple fly—before my friends joined me.

The action lasted throughout the top half of the rising tide. For a while I hooked up on virtually every cast I made, and they were good fish—several pushed 4 pounds. During the melee Brandon's brother Brent waded over to me—he fly fishes with me on occasion—and asked if he could borrow my rod for a few casts. As I handed it to him, he noticed the fly, scrutinized it for a moment, then muttered "Man, that is one *ugly* fly!" Then he proceeded to quickly catch six fine specks with it, one of them the largest of the day and the biggest he'd ever taken on a fly!

Without boasting (Yeah, sure!), I caught a total of 34 very nice specks while the best my conventional-fishing buddies could do was 25! The fly was a resounding success!

And it works very nicely on specks, reds, and flounders found inshore, especially during fall. However, it is not a fly for all occasions; most often my "prettier" flies still take their fair share of these fish, and I've learned that in most cases if those flies are not being taken, then I need to change spots, not flies.

Nevertheless, on future trips to the islands you can safely bet there will always be a good supply of those purple creations in my fly box. I don't know if I will begin prospecting with them—old habits are hard to break, and my historic successes with the chartreuse-and-white Clouser Minnow cannot be ignored. But let one of a trip's crewmembers start catching fish on a purple soft-plastic, and I'll be doing some mighty fast fly-swapping!

It may look ugly to us, but, at times, the fish apparently think it looks lovely. Try it the next time your "old faithfuls" are leaving much to be desired.

The Flashy Chartreuse Thing

I don't experiment too often when I'm tying flies. As a writer for a number of fishing magazines, I usually try to concentrate on the theme of "where to go and how to catch them," and I feel I *must* catch 'em when I go in order to verify data. I have several patterns in my fly box that I rely on for that purpose, and from which I seldom stray.

The Flashy Chartreuse Thing (FCT)—In different sizes, the FCT is an excellent pattern for Louisiana's tripletail, cobia, tarpon, and bull dolphin.

Tying the Flashy Chartreuse Thing (for general offshore use and fish to 25–30 pounds or so)

Wrap a thread base along the shank of a size 2/0 Mustad 77660SS from the eye back to the beginning of the bend. At that point tie in a generous clump of chartreuse marabou about 2 inches long. Next, tie a yellow saddle hackle on each side of the hook convex side out. Use the upper end of the feather, which should be trimmed to just over 2 inches long. Discarding the feather's point and rounding the cut for the tail will make the feathers less likely to wrap themselves around the hook while casting. Tie a similarly sized and shaped chartreuse saddle hackle over each yellow hackle, and continue the thread to the hook's eye. Overwrap back from the eye about ⅜ inch, apply a line of superglue along the wraps, and allow to dry.

Tie a pencil-sized clump of chartreuse bucktail to the inside of the shank, ensuring it extends just past the tip of the feather "tail." Then tie a clump of green bucktail—same size and length—to the outside of the shank. Add a dozen pieces of chartreuse Krystal Flash to each side of the fly—they should extend to the ends of the bucktail, and finish with a half-dozen peacock herls on top. Finally, build a head about ⅜ inch long with the thread, whip-finish, apply a couple of drops of superglue or penetrating head cement, and allow to dry.

Remove the fly from the vise and lay it on your desk. Beside it place two 7MM roving-pupil doll eyes, tweezers, and superglue. Apply a drop of the glue to the fly immediately behind the thread-wrapped "head," then quickly take the tweezers and place a doll eye in that position. Be sure it is not askew, let the superglue dry; then attach the eye on the other

I am also a devoted advocate of the use of spoons, jigs, downriggers, surface plastics, and mullet heads—in their places. That helps to pay a few more of my bills, since I also pass along hopefully helpful conventional information that I feel must be validated by the "catching part."

Across much of the Gulf Coast one of the most productive conventional lures I have ever used is a molded soft-plastic minnow with a flattened tail that wiggles as it's being retrieved. It comes in two shapes (a deep-bodied "shad" and a thinner "minnow"), ranges in lengths of barely an inch to more than half a foot, and is made in every color imaginable. There's not a fish that side of the fly in the same manner. Finally, coat the bucktail between the eyes (above and below them), and the head, with a coat of clear Sally Hanson Hard-As-Nails fingernail polish. The finished fly should be around 3 inches in total length when tied on the designated hook; it is easily castable with a 9-weight outfit, though I prefer a 10-weight because of the big cobia it entices.

Materials

- Hook: Size 2/0 Mustad 77660SS (an extra-heavy, radically short-shanked stainless model with a *very* sharp point—all you could ask for in an offshore setting)
- Thread: Chartreuse Danville Flymaster Plus
- Tail: Large chartreuse marabou; yellow and chartreuse saddle hackles
- Body: Green-and-chartreuse bucktail
- Chartreuse Krystal Flash
- Peacock herls
- 7mm roving-pupil doll eyes
- Superglue
- Tweezers

(Note: This fly is best tied in winter with a Jimmy Buffet CD in the player and a rum and tonic with a twist of lime beside the vise. Tie plenty of them then, because you certainly don't want to be tying replacements during summer when you should be fishing!)

swims that will not try to eat it—even mullet! (I once caught a 3-pounder while jigging a small one for winter crappie!) My personal color preference for everyday saltwater use is clear chartreuse with glitter and a black back—and what particular minnow it matches, I haven't a clue! Still, I rely on it if I "must catch fish" with conventional gear. And much more often than not, I gather my data with it alone.

One day at the vise I had a thought. Now, if that chartreuse-with-glitter soft-plastic worked so well, a fly that matched it should be effective, too. Because of my limited engineering capabilities, I decided to forego attempting to create a tail that wiggled, using a wad of marabou in that position to get almost the same effect. Other than that, the result was a reasonable facsimile. I tied three—in size 1 for no particular reason—put them in a saltwater fly box, and promptly forgot them.

I remembered them one day some time later when the sink-tip line I was saddled with, along with some other flies that were apparently much too heavily weighted, combined to send those flies much deeper than I had intended. Tripletail was my target that day; they were typically holding beneath flotsam and quickly lost interest in the fast-sinking flies. The new flies, however, sank much slower, giving the fish ample time to chase down and strike that semblance of the soft-plastic on which we have taken so many of these often quite finicky fish. With these new flies, I caught more than enough for supper—and for "data"—and I should note that those were the first of the species I ever took on fly, though I'd had several decent shots at them in the past using other flies.

So it worked, but size 1 is a bit small for many of the beasties you can pursue in saltwater—like the larger versions of the "tails" and cobia that are frequently found beneath the same surface structure and usually appreciate more of a mouthful. Size 2/0 seemed more appropriate, so I tied up a bunch of those—and a few in 4/0, just for the hell of it.

All of the originals were destroyed long ago, and I couldn't be happier because of it. Besides the tripletail, the fly—my Flashy Chartreuse Thing has accounted for numerous and quite respectable cobia and king mackerel, my largest bull dolphin, and Louisiana's fly-caught tarpon #3! And I have no doubt the smaller versions would perform very well inshore on specks and redfish—the "proving grounds" for the effectiveness of the chartreuse-with-glitter soft-plastic.

Those fish may not have refused such time-honored patterns as a green-and-white Deceiver or an orange-and-yellow SeaDucer. But, in the past, other fish have, and those are good flies. Still, I don't give the flies many chances anymore. I have confidence the FCT will produce, allowing me to gain the necessary "where to go and how to catch 'em" data when it's needed.

The Monster Clouser

Slaying saltwater dragons—or counting coup with them—is becoming fashionable in widening circles along the Louisiana Coast. Lately I have seen some very nice, intricately tied flies that were intended to draw the beasts

*The Monster Clouser is a proven pattern for king mackerel
and bull reds found along jetties.*

into battle. Most hopeful dragonslayers view them as "the way," and are therefore faced with two options: Buy them or create their own along those same lines. The former can become cost-prohibitive; some patterns wear the price tags of big-game trolling lures. The latter requires considerable time at the vise and an assortment of rather esoteric materials.

If your dragon of choice is one that may only seek battle once or twice a day on a high-priced trip to the blue-water rip, then the cost of your flies will be insignificant; use the most appealing, even though those will probably be the most expensive or time-consuming to create. On the other hand, many offshore beasts can attack in waves, time after time on the same day, like cobia, or bull dolphin—or, worse yet, king mackerel. If you start pitching those flies at them, then you will need a week's vacation and a bank loan to tie a new supply yourself.

Here at home in the lower Mississippi River Delta, the realm of the dragon is just beyond that hill (the back levee that protects us from the Gulf), so I meet them frequently. When I do I'm armed with two batteries of weapons. The first are prerigged tarpon-style flies. It takes about an hour apiece to tie the fly, combine a class and shock tippet, and tie on the fly. Those are intended for tarpon encounters, run-ins with exceptionally large cobia, and for the blue-water rip. I have no intention whatsoever of casting one into an area of the Gulf where some Bobby Bad-ass Beastie, like a jack or king mackerel, might mangle it.

Tying the Monster Clouser

Using red thread, wrap the shank of the hook from the eye toward the bend for ½ inch, and tie the eyes onto the top of the shank at that point, securing them tightly with figure-eight wraps. Now tie the white bucktail also to the top of the shank and both ahead of and behind the eyes, creating a ⅛-inch-wide set of "gills" just behind the eyes. Whip-finish and trim the red thread.

Rotate the vise or invert the hook within it. The following will be tied to the inside of the hook's shank and only in front of the eyes.

Using the chartreuse thread, tie in 12 to 16 strands of white Krystal Flash, chartreuse bucktail, 12 to 16 strands of chartreuse Krystal Flash, green bucktail, and a half-dozen peacock herls. Whip-finish and apply a drop of superglue or head cement to the head. If you feel the need, dab a little black Testors Enamel onto the eyes with the head of a small nail.

The fly should be between 5 and 5½ inches long and with the chartreuse bucktail, and some, but not all, of the flash material extending just beyond the white-and-green bucktail. An 11- or 12-weight outfit will probably be needed to cast it—you will definitely need an 11- or 12-weight outfit to come out on top in the affrays it will instigate!

Materials
- Hook: Size 4/0 Orvis Pre-Sharpened Saltwater Hook
- Thread: Red-and-chartreuse Danville flat-waxed nylon
- White and chartreuse Krystal Flash
- White, chartreuse, and green bucktail
- Peacock herls
- Medium brass hourglass eyes
- Superglue
- Black Testors Enamel and a small nail (if you want to doll up the eyes)

The other is my Flashy Chartreuse Thing, which also requires some time to create. I had four in my offshore box, left over from a bull dolphin expedition a while back, when a friend and I decided to make an autumn foray after some king mackerel that had been located alongside a local jetty.

I was pretty sure the FCTs would prove effective on those toothy beasts, but the mental image of them rent asunder after a duel was pretty disheartening. What else could I come up with that would be big, flashy, fairly easy to cast, and would sink reasonably fast—and still be quick and easy to tie so that I wouldn't develop a personal relationship with each one? Why, a Clouser Minnow (of sorts).

I sure hope Bob Clouser doesn't ever find out about all this; he might sue me for sticking his name on that fly: the Monster Clouser. But they sure worked—all three of them—which I was able to tie before our raid into the dragons' lair. On that trip, I had thought that three were enough. . . .

They weren't, as the beasts were quite persistent that morning, and as I expected, each fly died after a single contest—as did the four FCTs I also had with me. Well, would you have quit after you and a buddy had gone through only three flies and the beasts were still quite willing to give battle? Anyway, I always make sure to have a slew of 'em in my box now!

One particular note on tying these flies. I fish with Clouser Minnows in smaller types for a variety of inshore saltwater species. When I tie those, I try to make them as durable as possible in order to hold up to repeated strikes. That "toughness" comes in part from supergluing the eyes and each different clump of bucktail into place and allowing each the time to dry. However, one bite from an offshore beast will render all that effort a waste of time. On the Monster Clouser, add a drop of superglue to the finished head to prevent the thread from unwrapping, and that's it.

Pete's Perch-Float Popper

Living in the extreme southeastern Louisiana boondocks has its perks. Sure, the region is an inviting target for wandering tropical systems, Big Macs and Whoppers are nonexistent, and the nearest Wal-Mart is a good hour's drive away. But a marina is only five minutes from my house in Buras, and from that point some outstanding saltwater fly-fishing opportunities begin within scant yards.

Trouble is—or so it was back when it all began—if you chose to fish with poppers and didn't "roll" your own, your entire supply could be rendered into

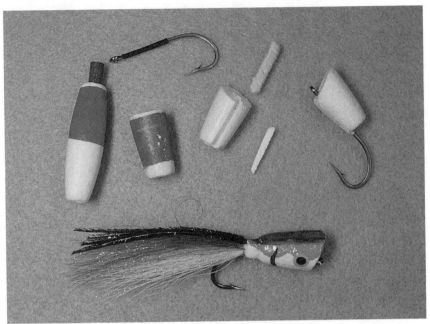

A popper is an excellent choice for shallow-water reds and specks.

"File-13" material on a single trip. Besides being rather expensive and some-what fragile, they were the only option available (they were created as fresh-water "bass bugs"), and they required a 120-mile round-trip to town for replenishing. That was usually made with numerous and impassioned prayers that the local bass boys hadn't recently bought up the entire selection. Occa-sionally, I discovered that had happened.

Finally it happened once too often, and I decided to start creating my own. Initially, the bodies were created from wine-bottle corks, and though they were, uh, "inconsistent" (the least derogatory description I can think of), they worked just fine. For several years I was able to fish more and drive less to town to replenish my supply of poppers. Then I caught a pretty good red, entered it for consideration as a state-record fly-caught fish, and received by return mail a note from the curator stating, in effect, that he doubted whether even a redfish could be dumb enough to strike a "lure" that ugly!

Well, the record committee finally accepted it, but they sure hurt my feelings along the way! But that aside, someone had begun making cylin-drical perch-floats by then; I saw their potential and began using them for popper bodies—no more whittling and sanding, much more consistent ap-pearances, and lots of fish.

Tying the Perch-Float Popper

The initial step in creating the perch-float popper is to tightly wrap the shank of the hook from the eye back about ⅝ inch with a midstrength nylon thread. Tie it off and trim it closely.

The body is made by first cutting a float in two at its midpoint with a razor, then cutting a shallow-angled bevel across that end for the face. This can all be done in one step, but I prefer doing it in two because that helps prevent beveling the face too deeply into the body, resulting in a shorter, less-efficient contact area for the hook. The "long side" of the float is now the popper's back, the short side is its belly.

Lay the body on its back and make two parallel longitudinal cuts along its belly. The resulting "slot" should be just wide enough to accept the thread-wrapped hook; if it is too wide, the hook can become off-center. Retain the piece of body that you removed to create the slot, and trim it to allow for the space to be occupied by the hook's shank.

Next, take a pipe cleaner (the soft and absorbent kind, not the bristly type) and cut it to the length of the float-stem hole that runs through the body. The pipe cleaner serves as the contact point for the hook, providing a bond that is much stronger than something along the lines of a wooden dowel. At this point, lay the pieces out on your desk from left to right in this manner: body, pipe-cleaner contact point, thread-wrapped hook, and trimmed piece of slot material.

As quickly as you can, barely insert the piece of pipe cleaner into the stem-hole, apply a couple of drops of superglue to it, and push it completely into the body. Next, lay a line of superglue along the hook's thread-wrappings and insert it into the slot, insuring it is properly centered and aligned with the body's back and belly. Then add a drop of superglue into the slot and replace the trimmed piece of slot-material. A note of caution: Too much superglue at that point may cause a destructive reaction with the float-material. Allow it all to set for a half-hour or so, and trim any protruding slot-material with a razor.

You can create the remainder of the popper with your choice of tail-material and favorite colors. Total length should be about 3 inches; gain that by trimming the ends of the material to be tied onto the hook, not the tail ends. I prefer green over chartreuse or chartreuse over white for specks and green over yellow for reds. I like bucktail instead of the synthetic materials here, but I also like plenty of Krystal Flash in the fly, and I usually finish it off with a half-dozen peacock herls for a back.

The body is painted with Testors Gloss Enamel (model airplane paint) applied with the pipe cleaners—no cleanup hassle that way; just pitch 'em when you're done. And if you simply take the white half of the perch float and tie in a clump of white bucktail and white flash material, you don't have to fool with paint at all! That's the most durable version of the perch-float popper—the one you should use in a blitz instead of a "pretty" one. Try them both; they will catch fish—and lots of them!

Materials

- Thread: Cotton or polyester sewing thread (any color)
- White 3/0 Danville Flat Waxed Nylon
- Hook: Size 1 Mustad 34007 or Orvis Pre-Sharpened Saltwater Hook
- Flash: White and chartreuse Krystal Flash
- Tail: Green, white, and chartreuse bucktail. Peacock Herl.
- Paint: Green, white, and yellow Testors Gloss Enamel (Mix very small amounts of green into the yellow to get the hue of chartreuse you want.)
- Perch floats
- Pipe cleaners (and wire cutters)
- Superglue
- Razor blade

Since then they have accounted for redfish, speck, flounder (!), ladyfish, stripers, a couple of alligator gar, and several freshwater species. They hold up nicely, too (except when trying to catch a gar with one). One such fly took 10 reds in the 4- to 6-pound class before it was wrecked; another got 13 specks and only required repainting.

That's the greatest attribute of the Perch-Float Popper: its ability to withstand the rapid-fire strikes of a wide-open blitz (when time spent replacing a fly is time spent not catching fish). Of course, the effort necessary to make it tough dictates you should not pitch it at a bluefish—or an alligator gar. Two factors lead to the durability of this popper's body: the strength of the highly compressed plastic of the float and the way the hook is anchored within it.

The floats I use for everyday poppers are 1⅜ inches long and ⁷⁄₁₆ inch at their widest (they come five to a sack for around 90 cents at your nearest Wal-Mart). When cut in two, each half is almost a perfect fit for a size 1 Mustad 34007 or an Orvis Pre-Sharpened Saltwater Hook, the latter being the type I now use almost exclusively for inshore applications. The floats are manufactured by the Comal Tackle Co., P.O. Box 606, Buda, Texas 78610. I mention that so you won't buy the cork floats another manufacturer offers that are similarly packaged and look much the same but don't hold up nearly as well.

Index

H/I

J

Q/R